KARATSU WARE

KARATSU WARE

A Tradition of Diversity

Johanna Becker, O.S.B.

KODANSHA INTERNATIONAL
Tokyo, New York and San Francisco

Publication of this book was assisted by a grant from
The Japan Foundation.

Distributed in the United States by Kodansha International/USA
Ltd., through Harper & Row, Publishers, Inc., 10 East 53rd Street,
New York, New York 10022.

Published by Kodansha International Ltd., 12-21 Otowa 2-chome,
Bunkyo-ku, Tokyo 112 and Kodansha International/USA Ltd., with
offices at 10 East 53rd Street, New York, New York 10022 and The
Hearst Building, 5 Third Street, Suite 400, San Francisco, California
94103.

LCC 85-45308
ISBN 0-87011-749-1
ISBN 4-7700-1249-7 (in Japan)

Library of Congress Cataloging-in-Publication Data
Becker, Johanna, O.S.B.
    Karatsu ware: a tradition of diversity.
    Bibliography: p.
    Includes index.
    1. Karatsu pottery.   2. Pottery, Japanese—Japan—
Saga-ken.   I. Title.
NK4168.S24B43 1986   738.3'7   85-45308
ISBN 0-87011-749-1 (U.S.)

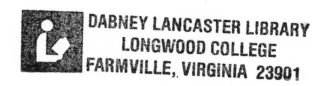

CONTENTS

Preface   7

CHAPTER I
History   11

CHAPTER II
Examples, Influence, Problems   37

Plates   53

CHAPTER III
Kilns and Techniques   145

CHAPTER IV
The Karatsu Style   161

Notes to the Plates   177

Karatsu Kilns and Kiln Groups   191

Glossary   200

Bibliography   212

Index   217

To my parents

Arthur J. Becker
and
Irene E. Becker

Certainly your goodness and love
will be with me as long as I live.
Ps. 23:6

Preface

Insight beyond reason and logic—*satori*—is that the only key to understanding the Japanese ceramic called Karatsu? Pondering the apparent contradictions of its history, use, and appearance seemed like meditating on a *kōan* to me. Enlightment is not guaranteed the Zen devotee, and I, the follower of quite another monastic tradition, had no assurance the time spent with this *kōan*, Karatsu, would make it understandable. Even now—after years of looking at, handling, researching, analyzing Old Karatsu; after making pottery at the ancient kiln, Ochawangama, using old clays, traditional glazes, firing the wood-burning climbing kiln; after sifting through mounds of shards—unanswered question still remain, secrets the *kōan* has not illuminated. My pondering and search are not ended with this book. Nevertheless, what insights and knowledge this engagement has yielded are shared here in the hope that others—potters, historians, lovers of art and Japan, collectors, students, scholars, the curious—will share some measure of the delight I have found in Karatsu.

Karatsu is not just the subject of the book, but its core, the source from which all else flows. The standard for terminology and technology, for history, analysis, interpretation is based in Kyushu, Karatsu territory. Accordingly, kiln names, for which there is no standard writing or pronunciation, are those used by the Kyushu potters who continue making Karatsu today; glazes, techniques and tools are named and described according to the usage of past and present makers of Karatsu. The tea ceremony has imposed a complicated system of names on teabowls; for the sake of clarity, many of these are not used in the text, but are defined only in the Glossary. In classifying the types of Karatsu pots, how they look became secondary to *how* and *of what* they are made—the materials and techniques that cause them to look as they do. As an art historian I realize this approach is not customary; as a potter I know it is the key to understanding what has been a confusing and ill-defined ware.

The ceramics shown here are not just illustrations of the text, but are intended to be "read" as carefully and pondered as seriously as any printed page. Only a few non-Karatsu pieces are included for comparison, items that are not frequently illustrated. Ceramics that appear in numerous other publications, such as Mino wares and *punch'ŏng*, are omitted. The pots illustrated cover a wide range of both typical and rare examples of Karatsu, famous and little known pieces, old and contemporary products, and show a variety of shapes and techniques.

I was engaged both as an art historian and potter, studying Asian art history at the University of Michigan and making stoneware at the Ann Arbor Potters' Guild, when I was first introduced to Karatsu by Professor Kamer Aga-Oglu. The potter in me was attracted by the skilled, natural freedom of Karatsu; the art historian was challenged because such an important ware was vaguely identified as a "diverse group of household wares sometimes adapted to tea ceremony use." Dr. Richard Edwards encouraged my interest in Karatsu, and Dr. Calvin French guided me through Japanese art history, particularly the exciting seventeenth century. Eventually Karatsu became my research thesis topic. I saw original Karatsu in museums of the United States and Canada through generous grants from the Horace H. Rackham School of Graduate Studies, which also subsidized phases of my later work in Japan. Dr. John Alexander Pope, then director of the Smithsonian Institute's Freer Gallery of Art, had examined the kiln sites of Kyushu where Karatsu was produced. His enthusiasm as an advisor and perceptions as a critic, his availability and personal interest in Karatsu enriched this study immensely. Dr. Oliver Impey of the Ashmolean Museum, Oxford, also interested in the Kyushu kilns, but for their early porcelain products, generously shared information and photographs. My quest for the origin of the light and dark glaze characteristic of Korean Karatsu led me to trade routes along the South China Sea. Dr. Barbara Harrisson, now director of the Gemeentelijk Museum het Princessehof, Leeuwarden, took me along the North Borneo coast, where many a vessel carrying ceramics had left residues of shards for centuries. The search through her extensive shard collection in Brunei yielded no prototypes of Korean Karatsu, nor have other investigations. The puzzle remains unsolved. All of these, and many unnamed others, assisted with their knowledge and expertise as I began exploring Karatsu; many have continued their involvement with this work for several years; all have my sincere gratitude.

Karatsu was made and used in Japan. It never became an export ceramic as Japanese porcelains did, and until recently did not appeal to Western collectors' taste, so the largest number and majority of famous pieces remain in Japan. Koyama Fujio, then Japan's noted ceramic historian and connoisseur, invited me to work with the collection of Karatsu at the Idemitsu Museum of Arts, Tokyo. The extensive Karatsu collection, shards from old kiln sites, library resources, all were fully accessible to me. From my first day at that handsome museum across from the Imperial Palace until the conclusion of this work, Etō Takashi, Curatorial Manager of the Idemitsu Museum of Arts, made the holdings, facilities, and services of the museum available and shared his own considerable knowledge as well. There Professor Mikami Tsugio brought back discoveries from his kiln site digs in Korea and Kyushu, all Karatsu related. Dr. Sugimura Toh provided valuable criticism and guidance. Discussions with Nishida Hiroko of the Nezu Art Museum were always informative and lively. Igaki Haruo of Kyobashi Arts, connoisseur and long-time researcher of Karatsu, not only shared his most recently discovered pieces of Karatsu, but also answered difficult questions, assisted in my introduction to the Nakazato family of potters, and called my attention to any new publications and exhibitions of Karatsu. Amano Tazu initiated me into tea ceremony rituals and the practical and aesthetic function of tea ceramics. Translations of complex passages of seventeenth century Kyushu history were refined by Professor Konishi Masatoshi. The time and interest all of these people have given so graciously have been indispensible to this project, and I am deeply grateful to each one.

Although I had long anticipated going into northwestern Kyushu, Karatsu territory, I had no preconception of Karatsu city and life at Ochawangama, the traditional kiln. I knew going there was essential. Examining pieces in collections, reading about Karatsu, interviewing—all were important, but reaching back to the people and place of its origin was vital. The approach to Karatsu city from Fukuoka goes through that historic shore, Matsubara, where in the fourteenth century the Japanese stopped the advances of the Mongols. Beyond that pine forest by the sea, the road bends and suddenly, across the water, Karatsu Castle appears, topping a small promotory. The city pushes back from the shore until stopped by rolling mountains, which form a backdrop for the kiln, studio, and family dwellings of the Nakazatos, the thirteenth-generation Karatsu potters. The trace their lineage back to the Korean potters entering Japan as a result of Toyotomi Hideyoshi's Korean campaigns. When I first arrived, there had just been a generational change in leadership. Nakazato Tarōuemon XII, later known as Muan and designated a "Living National Treasure," had resigned in favor of his son Tadao, now Nakazato Tarōuemon XIII. Together with his brothers Shigetoshi and Takashi he was making and firing Karatsu resembling the wares of four centuries earlier. With warmth and openness, I was accepted not as an observer but as a participant in the life and activities at Ochawangama. Between the Nakazato hospitality and the graciousness of Den O'Coach, my *ryokan* host, time spent in Karatsu became a blend of intense work, informative exchanges, and pleasant living. Over a series of visits I came to know the studio and its rhythms, was allowed to learn and practice the ancient techniques—throwing off the hump, using the *hera*, forming pots with the *tataki* technique—and to participate in firing Ochawangama, stoking it with wood throughout the night. The earlier, domed eighteenth century kiln stood idle and overgrown; we fired the "new" kiln dating from the first quarter of this century and built with a vaulted ceiling like the earliest Karatsu kilns. Tarōuemon XIII generously shared family records, shards unearthed from old kilns, and his own theories of the origins and nature of early Karatsu. He welcomed me to his family home, where the tasty foods prepared by his wife and daughters, Keiko and Yumiko, complimented the liveliness of their wholehearted welcome. Takashi, the youngest brother, became my studio mentor, guide to old kiln sites, and informant. He shared experiments made with old shards, tests of the firing range of traditional clays, records of firings, and debated which processes gave effects seen on Old Karatsu. Robert Okasaki, American potter and husband of Nakazato Keiko, was particularly persevering in sorting through photographs and overseeing the exacting details of securing images and dates from the Nakazato collection.

The doyen of Kyushu ceramics, Professor Nagatake Takeshi, was filled with enthusiasm and knowledge. He guided me through Kyushu ceramic collections, being certain that nothing of importance went unnoticed—the small, select collections; porcelain production centers that once made Karatsu; distinguished public collections. His writings, advice, and keen perceptions have been of immeasurable help; his personal warmth and generosity are unforgettable. He provided me with two "enlightening" moments in my pursuit of the Karatsu *kōan*. Through Professor Nagatake, Tanakamaru Zenpachi invited us to his home to see his most famous reserved pieces. His collection of rare quality ceramics is partially housed in the Tamaya gallery in Fukuoka (the Tanakamaru Collection), but pieces of special character or charm remain in his private home collection. After a luncheon interspersed with ceramic viewing, Mrs. Tanakamaru, a tea devotee, served ceremonial tea. To my astonishment and delight, unexpectedly, she presented me with tea in the renowned Ayame teabowl, one of the most famous and admired Karatsu pieces! And, when I was making inquiries about a well-known handscroll showing Kyushu ceramic techniques and tools, the *Yakimono taigai*, at the Saga Prefectural Museum, Professor Nagatake intervened and I was brought the original handscroll to unroll and inspect directly.

Most ceramics illustrated here without notation of a collection are in the Nakazato family collection and are reproduced through their courtesy. The Nakazato collection photographs, those of Karatsu city and Ochawangama, and ceramics of the Tanakamaru collection are the work of Minematsu Chūji of Fukuoka. Kumura Michiharu, Presidential Secretary of the Tanakamaru Collection, accomodated me by securing photographs both of the collection he supervises and the private Tanakamaru collection. Mr. Nittō of the Tōki-shi Mino Ceramic Research Center, gave me useful insights into the relationship of Karatsu and Mino wares. On several occasions, my former student Hayashi-Inoue Kazuko of Fukuoka was a gracious and resourceful assistant. Each of these have played an important role in my search for the meaning of Karatsu. I am indebted to and and most grateful to every one.

The more I knew about Karatsu, the more I realized the necessity of going to Korea, where the potters and techniques originated. Choi Sunu, then curator of ceramics and later director of the Seoul National Museum, opened the storage collection to my search for pieces that resembled Karatsu. He had his own excavated shard collection, Korean examples with Karatsu similarities, which we examined as he presented his theories about the relationship of the two wares. Interviews, museum studies, searches into the countryside, visits to contemporary potters were made intelligible and enjoyable because a long-time friend and native of Inchon, S. Stephana Chong, accompanied me through Korea.

For the three years I lived in Japan and during shorter visits, the Tokyo house of studies of the Benedictine Sisters of Japan was my home. There, in the shadow of Tokyo Tower, both Japanese and American sisters listened to and advised me as my search grew from first questions to final photographs. The prewar Japanese-Western style house has been razed to be built anew. It lasted just long enough for this work to be completed. My gratitude and keen memories of the companionship and support received there cannot be taken down nor rebuilt—it will remain. My monastic community, the Sisters of the Order of Saint Benedict, St. Joseph, Minnesota, and the College of Saint Benedict, where I teach, encouraged this study from the start with grants of time and research opportunities. Not content with granting me a sabbatical, the college supported me with faculty grants from the Bremer Foundation and Charles E. Merrill Trust. The trip to Korea was underwritten by a Tri-College East Asian Studies Grant. Numerous other groups made facets of this project possible—The Arthur J. Schmitt Foundation of Chicago; The Mary Livingston Griggs and Mary Griggs Burke Foundation; The American Association of University Women granted a fellowship with special concessions to maximize its benefits. From Japan, the Metropolitan Center for Far Eastern Studies has supported final work on this book and the Japan Foundation has generously assisted with its publication. The publishers, Kodansha International, have been encouraging and patient as this work progressed. Special appreciation is due their staff for the role in completion of this work. I am sincerely grateful to all who have assisted this project, thank them earnestly, and hope this publication will bring them satisfaction.

My parents, Arthur J. and Irene E. Becker, to whom this work is dedicated, have given me constant encouragement and assistance and cared enough to come to Japan twice to see the country of Karatsu's origin for themselves.

Final thanks must go to those unknown men and women, the potters who made Old Karatsu and who through thirteen generations kept its traditions alive. I have tried to discover some details of their lives and situations and have been able to do that only partially. The beautiful, nonchalant products they produced communicate their skills and sensitivity, keeping their spirit vital today. I thank them for having provided a *kōan* so worthy of contemplation.

Denver, Colorado
December 17, 1985

Note: Japanese names throughout are written in the Japanese manner, family name first.

CHAPTER I

History

Pottery, the art of earth, fire, water and air, is inevitably bound to the land of its origin. Karatsu ceramics originated in Kyushu, Japan's southernmost island. Here, amid rolling hills, low mountains, woods and streams—terrain rich with clay, water, and fuel—conditions were ideal for pottery-making to flourish. The mild climate allowed kiln firings throughout the year without marked seasonal interruptions. Kyushu lies close to China and Korea on the mainland; the old port city, Karatsu, is just some 115 miles across the Genkai Sea and Tsushima Straits from Korea (map, page 12). Consequently, it was not ceramics from the main Japanese island of Honshu, but those of Korea, that influenced Karatsu wares.

Kyushu, "nine provinces,"[1] had the ancient name Tsukushi, "where the land ends"—where Japan ends, but also where it opened to the outer world: to Korea, China, and ports of the South China Sea. Hizen (modern Saga Prefecture and Higashi-Sonoki-gun of Nagasaki Prefecture), the northwestern province of this kite-shaped island, is an area of natural harbors, navigable rivers, and rolling timbered mountains richly endowed with deposits of sandy clay. In the late sixteenth and seventeenth centuries hundreds of Japanese and Koreans built kilns in the Kishidake and Matsuura mountain ranges, between the ports of Karatsu and Imari. Imari city, nearer the Matsuura range, is less than twenty miles southwest of Karatsu. This part of Hizen was called Matsuura, after the powerful lords who ruled the territory. Under them was the Hata clan, lords of Kishidake, where the first Karatsu pottery was made.

Karatsu city, at the mouth of the navigable Matsuura River, faces Korea across the Genkai Sea; to the northeast is the Japan Sea and the western coast of Honshu, and the Kammon Straits lead into the Inland Sea and the home provinces (map, page 13). The oldest Karatsu ware kilns surrounded the city from at least the early seventeenth century. At the beginning of the eighteenth century, the official Karatsu kiln, Ochawangama, was located there. The city continues to be an active site of production.

Now a city of about seventy thousand, Karatsu appears on a map of kiln sites like a comet spewing a trail of pottery kiln sites in its wake (map, page 13). About ten miles northwest is the castle town of Nagoya, which had its own potters, and six miles to the west is the ancient Kojirōkaja kiln, possibly dating to the early Sue pottery days.

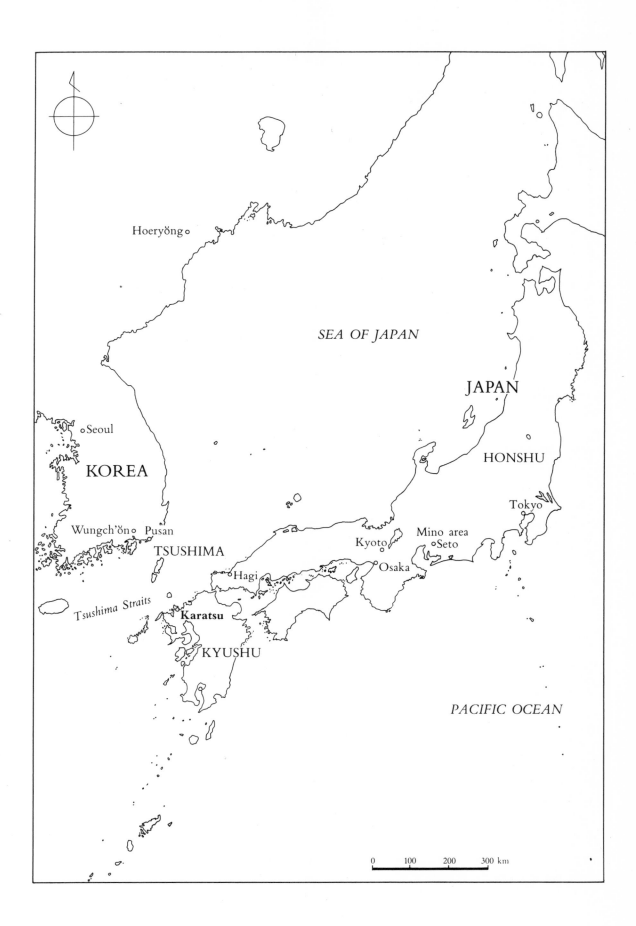

Hoeryŏng o

SEA OF JAPAN

JAPAN

o Seoul

KOREA

HONSHU

Tokyo

Wungch'ŏn o   o Pusan

Mino area
Kyoto o   o Seto

TSUSHIMA

Osaka

Hagi

Tsushima Straits

Karatsu

KYUSHU

PACIFIC OCEAN

0   100   200   300 km

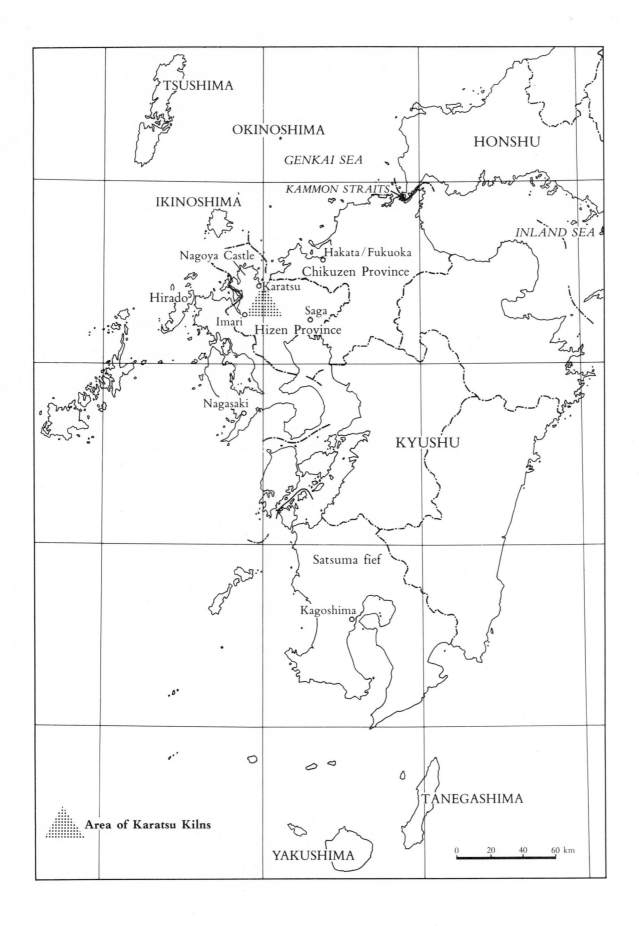

TSUSHIMA

OKINOSHIMA

GENKAI SEA

HONSHU

KAMMON STRAITS

IKINOSHIMA

INLAND SEA

Nagoya Castle

Hakata/Fukuoka

Chikuzen Province

Karatsu

Hirado

Saga

Imari

Hizen Province

Nagasaki

KYUSHU

Satsuma fief

Kagoshima

TANEGASHIMA

Area of Karatsu Kilns

0   20   40   60 km

YAKUSHIMA

Fanning out to the south and west are, first, the Kishidake group of kilns, then Matsuura, Takeo, and Taku—all groups of Karatsu kilns. All except the Kishidake group developed during or subsequent to the Momoyama period immigration of Korean potters, whose names and histories are directly related to Karatsu ceramics.

Legends, tradition, old records, and historic remains are all evidence of the deep-rooted linkage between Kyushu and Korea prior to the late sixteenth-century arrival of the Korean potters who stimulated the production of Karatsu.

The *Kojiki* (712) and *Nihon shoki* (720), Japan's earliest records of history and legend, underscore the importance of Kyushu. This is not surprising, since the early Yamato sovereigns who ordered these books' writing probably were Kyushu men.[2] In the *Kojiki*, the sun goddess, Amaterasu-Ōmikami, sends her grandson, Ninigi-no-mikoto, to Kyushu, promising an empire for him and his descendants. Although he later moves to the Yamato region in central Honshu and founds the Japanese state there, his grandson, Jimmu Tennō (c. 660 B.C.), is said to have promoted the making of pottery in Kyushu.[3] Similarities between the mound tombs, excavated artifacts, and ceramics from Kyushu and the Yamato plain suggest a historic reality behind these legends. Furthermore, the tomb shapes and pottery forms relate to those of a similar date in Korea.

The *Nihon shoki* tells of Empress Jingū (c. A.D. 201), who led a campaign to Korea to avenge the killing of her husband, Emperor Chūai, at the hands of Korean rebels in Kyushu. Returning, she stopped at Matsuura, where she left three captive Korean princes, one from each of the Korean kingdoms. "They started producing pottery in those villages which now bear their names [Tarōkaja, Kojirōkaja, and Tōbeikaja of Matsuura], and their products are called *ko-Karatsu*."[4] Although this relationship to Karatsu ceramics is denied by the fifth-generation Karatsu chronicler, Kiheiji, the fact is that there was a wave of Korean immigrants—scholars and artists—who came to Japan in the late third and fourth centuries.

In the early historic periods of Japan, Kyushu served as the cultural corridor between the Yamato plain, where the emperors lived, and Korea. When students and priests departed for Korea and China to bring back the wisdom of Buddhism, they departed from the Matsuura region.

From excavations, it is known that the area of Karatsu city was settled as early as neolithic times and seems to have been inhabited continuously since then. From the age of mythology to the seventeenth century, there were political and trade agreements with Korea, waves of immigrant Koreans coming to Japan, and, at an early time, Japanese settlements in Korea.

Karatsu Castle, now a museum, houses numerous artifacts dug from land and sea beds showing constant continental contact from prehistoric times on. There are, for example, artifacts from the mainland dating from the Qin dynasty (221–207 B.C.). From the fourth through the sixth centuries, the Japanese maintained a "colony," Mimana (Korean: Kaya), in South Korea, and entire Korean villages resettled in Kyushu. A hoard of Nara period (710–784) treasures was uncovered on the sacred Shintō island of Okinoshima, located in a direct line between Kyushu and Korea.

Trade, both legal and illegal, helped make Kyushu the most cosmopolitan of Japan's islands. A record dated July 874 (16 Jōgan) speaks of a Chinese ship docking at "Jikirinoura in Kami Matsuura . . . later . . . known as Karatsu. . . . Among the imported materials were quantities of pottery and many continental potters came as well.''[5] Prior to the Momoyama period (1573–1615), references to Jikirinoura call it a fishing town. Nevertheless, excavations of Southern Song dynasty (1127–1279) celadons and white ware from China, as well as items from countries "as far as Greece and Rome," indicate that further up the Matsuura River, in Nakibisu no Mori, international trade and pirate ships docked. In the 1930s, hundreds of Song shards were excavated at Onizuka (also known as Yamamoto) in this region.[6]

By the Muromachi period (1392–1573), the Kyushu lords had annual legitimate trade contacts with Korea. The Korean *Yijo silrok* ("Annals of the Yi Dynasty") speaks of Korean porcelain and craftsmen entering Japan.[7] In addition, there was the influx of people, wares, and information through the activities of *wakō* (Japanese pirates).

The busy Kyushu ports were bases for the *wakō*, traders and cultural catalysts on the seas, looters, kidnappers, and pillagers on land.[8] From the thirteenth through the sixteenth century they attacked the coasts at home and abroad.[9] The *wakō* were beyond control and by 1563 had a regular smuggling trade with the Portuguese at Canton. Chinese merchants at the same time were bringing cargo to Kyushu ports despite Ming restrictions. They established themselves as trading merchants in Hakata, Hirado, and southwestern Satsuma.

Consequently, when the first Karatsu ware was being made (1550–60), there were intense, widespread influences in Kyushu of wares and peoples from as far as Southeast Asia, Indonesia, the Philippines, South China, and Korea. By mid-sixteenth century, Kyushu, separated from the imperial and military centers on Honshu, was in contact more than any part of Japan with international goods, both Asian and Western.

From the earliest times, ceramics were produced in Kyushu. Numerous inland and offshore sites have yielded shards of Japan's first pottery, the neolithic Jōmon ware.

In his *History of Korea*, Han Woo-keun says that the neolithic combware of Korea is clearly related to Siberian combware and also no doubt to combware unearthed in western Japan. He makes the interesting observation that the ancient pottery types correspond to relationships of language and follow the Altaic route; this of course had to be a migration route. The seemingly unique Japanese language has now been fairly convincingly shown by linguists to be in great part Altaic in origin. As one would expect, some of the earliest settlers (in Japan) were of the same stock as the Koreans.[10]

In the Yayoi period (250 B.C.–A.D. 250) the Korean linkages are striking, with an obvious dominance of Korean pottery methods and shapes. The Yayoi innovations included the potter's wheel (not the much later Korean kick wheel). This early wheel was hand-turned, allowing the pots to achieve an elegance of shape and an exactness not seen in Jōmon pieces. At this time also a paddling process was introduced, the predecessor of the *tataki* technique of Karatsu potters.

An expeditionary force from the Yamato court to Korea in the late Tumulus period (A.D. 250–552) is given credit for an influx of Korean ceramic techniques and styles, resulting in the Japanese Sue (Iwaibe) wares, though this ware must have had multiple origins over a period of time. This ware was marked by a hard, often vitreous gray body and a new repertoire of shapes. It spread throughout Japan, and in some instances the techniques continued into the sixteenth century. Some say that Sue production ended in the tenth century, when numerous kilns closed. Indeed, there was a change in quality and forms at that time, but we now know that, despite this change, the Sue genre continued in scattered areas.

The sloping cave kiln (*anagama*) introduced then was carved into a hillside for twenty feet or so, with openings at each end. The lower opening served as a fire box; the upper, the flue. Temperatures in the stoneware range could be achieved in this revolutionary kiln. Air intake was restricted by closing part of the lower opening, resulting in a reduction firing with a dense carbonized atmosphere. Although Sue ware did not vitrify into true stoneware, the high temperature (probably as high as Seger cone 6; 1200° C/2190° F) and reduction firing of the unglazed pottery produced both the characteristic gray color and, by closing the pores with penetrating carbon, a dense, moisture-impervious body. Most Sue ware was unglazed, except for the natural glaze caused by ash falling on pieces during firing. A better wheel was introduced. Vessels were made by coiling and were paddled. This resulted in a thin, dense, strong wall, often with fine textured paddle marks. Some Sue shapes and body qualities resemble Korean Silla ware so closely that even experts find it hard to distinguish them. Sue technique became the basis for Japanese ceramics in Kyushu for centuries. To this ceramic heritage the Karatsu potters brought a new tradition at a time of great political, social, and economic ferment.

In the late sixteenth century, Oda Nobunaga (1534–82) and Toyotomi Hideyoshi (1536–98) were the active agents of a catalytic age of cultural deepening and change, the Azuchi-Momoyama period. After them, Tokugawa Ieyasu (1542–1616) established structures that insured the stability of a new political unity, fostering the tremendous outburst of creativity during the Edo period (1615–1868).

A marked growth of cultural activity in the outer provinces had occurred in the latter part of the preceding Muromachi period (1333–1573) as the result of increased patronage from wealthy daimyo and traders. "With the growth of their military power most of the successful warlords developed an interest in learning, and invited to their castles distinguished scholars, learned clerics, and poets and painters of high repute."[11] In addition, the Ōnin War (1467), in which Kyoto was destroyed, ushered in a century of civil wars and strife, driving scholars and artists from the capital to the provinces, where rich and powerful daimyo offered protection and patronage. The Ashikaga shoguns had a predilection for the art and culture of Southern Song China. Military leaders found a natural affinity with the strict disciplines of Zen Buddhism and later, the tea cult. *Budō*, the way of the warrior, and *chadō*, the way of tea, flourished. The *shuin-sen*, authorized ships, brought volumes of luxury goods from numerous countries to satisfy the increasing opulence of the warlords' tastes.

It was this war-weary, culturally attuned world that the minor daimyo Oda Nobunaga began to consolidate in the early 1560s. He united the provinces and ended the military-political power of the Buddhist temples. When he was assassinated in 1582, only the provinces of Kyushu and western Honshu remained unconquered.

Five years earlier, Nobunaga had sent his general, Hideyoshi, to lead a campaign against the powerful Mōri clan in western Honshu. Hideyoshi left this assignment to avenge the treacherous death of Nobunaga, then assumed leadership himself. The following era was colored by the personality of this man who brought it into being—one accustomed to success in conquest, who conceived and carried out grand schemes, loved ostentation, demanded intense loyalty, who was at once generous and exacting, tender and ruthless—a military and political genius. Born a peasant without a family name, he took several, finally settling on Toyotomi, a house destined to exist less than thirty years.

The influence of such a man leaves a trace wherever it passes. Five years after he assumed power, in 1587, he personally led 130,000 troops against the mighty Shimazu clan of southern Kyushu after other campaigns had failed. Conquering, he did not destroy the house of Shimazu, but rather lessened its power and appointed his loyal retainer, Lord Konishi of southern Higo Province as lieutenant-general of Kyushu. Hizen Province, the Karatsu region, was divided, the southern Saga section going to Lord Nabeshima and the rest staying in the hands of the Matsuura clan.

Hideyoshi was such an avid tea devotee that he took his master with him on his campaigns. He acknowledged this excessive interest when he wrote to his adopted heir, Hidetsugu, "You should follow my example, except in three things—addiction to tea, a love of falconry, and a craze for women."[12] After subduing the Shimazu, he remained for a while in Hakata (Fukuoka), where he and his celebrated tea master, Sen no Rikyū (1522–91), mingled with tea enthusiasts and fanned their craze for tea utensils. Nor was this just a passing encounter; Kamiya Sōtan, a rich merchant and tea devotee of Hakata, recorded in his diary, the *Sōtan nikki*, that later in the year he attended a great tea gathering at Osaka Castle together with Rikyū and others from Sakai.[13]

Kyushu was subdued in the early part of 1587. During that year, Hideyoshi suppressed the pirates on the Inland Sea and turned his attention to Korea and China. By 1590, when Korean envoys came to Japan, Hideyoshi was looking for new worlds to conquer. He apparently was interested in Korea only as a passage to China, where he unrealistically thought of erecting his capital. An astute leader within his own realm, his vision of the world beyond Japan was naive and possibly glazed by his own heady successes at home. On the other hand, the Korean court regarded the Japanese with disdain, considering them uncultured and, particularly because of the *wakō*, unruly and troublesome. Each country held a false image of the other. The Korean delegation returned home rightfully certain that war was inevitable.

In 1592 (Bunroku 1), Katō Kiyomasa, a prominent leader in the ensuing Korean campaign, conducted a survey in northwest Kyushu for the reconstruction and completion by Ishida Mitsunari of a castle called Nagoya. It was on a small peninsula about ten miles northwest of Karatsu city (map, page 13). A lord entitled Nagoya Hizen no Kami had ruled there in the twelfth century.[14] On April 25, 1592, the ambitious Hideyoshi came there to establish his headquarters and direct the mainland campaign. Nagoya Castle, with its murals by Kanō Mitsunobu and Kanō Naizen, suddenly became a center of political and cultural activity. With the exception of a brief return to Osaka at the time of his mother's death, Hideyoshi stayed there together with an estimated 100,000 troops. Furuta Oribe, who had replaced Rikyū as Hideyoshi's tea master, arrived a month before his lord and remained until August, 1593.

Korea was hardly prepared for hostilities and did nothing effective to correct the situation. Having long enjoyed a peaceful civil rule, the soldiers were unpracticed in war. The court lived in sumptuous ease, in a world apart from the poverty and confusion of much of the country. The Japanese had adopted gunpowder, which the Koreans did not have. The only arena in which the Koreans were capable of meeting the Japanese with any degree of success was on the sea. In short, the Japanese were at a point in history of creative unification and powerful leadership, and life for the peasants and merchants was constantly improving. Korea, however, was in a state of decline, the supply of leaders inadequate, the army depleted, and the condition of the common people impoverished and disordered. It was not surprising that within twenty days of their landing in Pusan, the Japanese successfully entered the capital city of Seoul.

Apparently the Korean king had not taken Hideyoshi's demand for passage to China seriously, and the navy was still debating tactics when the Japanese landed. The defending Korean troops were outnumbered and disorganized, and Ming China delayed sending the requested assistance. The Korean court fled to the border, leaving an oppressed populace to loot the cities even before the arrival of the Japanese. When Ming troops finally appeared, they were far too few and unprepared for the aggressive and practiced Japanese. The Japanese navy arrived late and was outmaneuvered by the agile two-directional armored "turtle ships" under Korea's competent Admiral Yi Sun-sin, who inflicted Japan's only defeat prior to modern times. With supply lines cut off, the Japanese withdrew to the south in May, 1593, while peace talks ensued. The following year Hideyoshi, who had directed the campaign from Nagoya Castle, returned to Osaka and by 1596 began to reengage his troops. In March of the second year of Keichō (1597), the Japanese returned. In September, 1598, Hideyoshi died. The following month, the troops withdrew from Korea. Although there was no real victory, the Japanese assaults had effectively devastated the land and resources of Korea and demoralized a populace already suffering want. Moreover, the drain on the economy and defense of China was sufficient to weaken the waning house of Ming.

Although Hideyoshi had been in command, the actual campaign was carried out by contingents under regional lords. Five of the first seven contingents were led by twenty-two lords from Kyushu. These men ruled their own domains with practically absolute power, according to their own "house laws," exercising control over the private affairs and mobility of their vassals. They were men accustomed to power, intrigue, and rivalries. The keen skills of the Japanese soldiers accounted only in part for the rapid success in Korea. Internal rivalries and personal ambitions among the participating Kyushu daimyo, who even prior to the campaigns were divided into antagonistic Buddhist and Christian camps, made them compete for conquest abroad.

Many daimyo returned to their territories with Korean potters and craftsmen, in some instances offering protection only, in others establishing private factories attached to castles, giving salaries and rank to the immigrant artisans. The Korean campaigns came to be called the "Potters' Wars." "The powerful lords in different districts vied with each other in obtaining the best of craftsmen to bring about a race in ceramic production. It was only natural under such conditions that the industry should make rapid progress."[15] Tea ceramics had become the most prized treasures in Japan, coveted not only by lords and nobility, but also by the increasingly affluent cultured merchants.

Imported tea wares from China and Korea were still prized, but a new taste for domestic pottery was flourishing, having received Rikyū's stamp of approval. The ceramic industries of China and Korea had been highly developed for many centuries, but Japan had lagged behind. At first, Chinese porcelains were preferred as tea vessels; later, with the stress on subdued taste in the *wabi* school of Rikyū, simple Korean food vessels took precedence. The irregular, coarse Ido teabowls (Plate 209) were especially prized. A more ideal moment for a new influx of Korean potters into the world of Japanese ceramics could hardly be found. "The Korean potters who were brought back to Japan as captives became the founders of the most important traditions of pottery making during the following centuries."[16]

In Western histories the potters are called captives or prisoners, but it appears that some came willingly, if not by actual choice. Potters held a very low social position in Korea, and they lived in poverty even prior to the war. Then the country was devastated by the Japanese. Some of the large kilns were closed, and royal patronage withdrawn. Unquestionably there were forced migrations and ruthless treatment by the Japanese, but immigration as a whole took place in many ways. In addition, there was the centuries-old precedent of Korean potters coming to Kyushu. The immigration included entire families, several households often going to a single location. Some immigrant craftsmen, according to records, had been collaborators with the Japanese troops and left Korea for their own safety. Still others were renegades from the Korean army.

The Kyushu they came to was under some of Japan's most wealthy, powerful, independent lords. The island was flourishing with international and domestic trade, the port cities influenced by the outer world as never before. The first Japanese contact with the Western world had happened at Tanegashima island off Kyushu's southern coast about fifty years earlier, and the boats of the Portuguese and Spanish had commenced trade at Nagasaki. At the same time, Kyushu was responding to changes within Japan. The previous era, with its increased mobility across class lines and territorial borders—a condition that had permitted Hideyoshi's own rise in status and power—ended when he reorganized the country. His sword hunt stripped arms from all but official warriors and degraded the peasant-soldiers, while a land registration policy did away with the holdings of lesser lords. Thus, edicts under the red seal of Hideyoshi created a growing number of masterless samurai, *rōnin*, some of whom ended up becoming potters.[17]

In northwestern Kyushu there were new political developments as well. Hizen had been under the Ryūzōji clan until the second year of Hideyoshi's rule. Then, in 1584, they fell at the hands of the powerful Shimazu of Satsuma and were replaced by their former vassals, the Nabeshima.[18] Part of this domain, the Kishidake region, had been under the Hata family as far back as the seventh century, when Hata Hisashige came there from Kyoto. Around their castle on Kishidake mountain was a chain of kilns— the first to produce Karatsu ware. Hideyoshi deposed the ruling Hata lord in 1594 (Bunroku 2); the castle was razed by its own members, the kilns abandoned, and the potters dispersed throughout the country.[19] Kishidake Castle had fallen once before to Tsuruta Eichizen no Kami in 1560 (Eiroku 2), but by 1569 the Hatas had repossessed it. The actual reason for Hideyoshi's action is lost in traditional stories of intrigue, jealousy, and personal slights by Hata Mikawa no Kami Chikashi. With him, seventeen generations of Hata rule in Kishidake ended just as the Kyushu lords began returning from Korea. Lord Hata committed *seppuku*; his wife, Hidenomae, went into exile together with some of the clan's dispossessed samurai (*rōnin*). Other *rōnin* became vassals of the new regional lord, Terasawa; some remained on the land, losing their samurai rank, and still others became potters.

The fief's potters dispersed, many going south and opening kilns in the Matsuura range region, some to Mikōchi (Mikawachi) south of Arita, and still others to the Mino region of Honshu, where their superior knowledge of kiln construction and firing techniques made them most welcome. While this is all according to undocumented tradition, the development of the Matsuura kilns and introduction of the Karatsu style climbing kiln at Mino did occur at this time and lend credence to the essence of the stories. Some Karatsu kilns are specifically cited as being founded by these Kishidake potters—Kojirōkaja or Yamase at the time of the first take-over of the castle, and Hazenotani and Ōkawabaru when it was finally destroyed.[20]

Kishidake region's new lord, Terasawa Hirotaka (aka Shima no Kami and Shishūkō) built a new castle, Maizuru-jō ("Dancing Crane Castle"), some eight miles north of Kishidake mountain at Karatsu (Plates 229–31). Terasawa was not only a tea devotee but a tea master as well. When Sen no Rikyū had been in Kyushu in the 1580s, the new lord had been his student. In a letter to Matsuura Shizunobu dated 1594 (Bunroku 2), Terasawa mentions a jar from the Philippines he wished to show Hideyoshi.

Under his rule, the official kiln (*han yō* or *goyōgama*) of the fief was established at Shiinomine in Imari city. His second son succeeded him after thirty-nine years and gave an even greater support to pottery making. He welcomed back the dispersed Kishidake potters who had opened kilns elsewhere, had the early kiln at Bōzumachi in Karatsu city mended, and attracted many Koreans who had opened kilns in Matsuura.[21] The second Lord Terasawa's oppressive policies in other matters, however, led to the Shimabara peasant revolt in 1637, and ten years later the family rule ended. Although the Terasawa rule lasted a brief fifty years, it turned the fishing village and port of Karatsu into a castle town, which it remained until the Meiji era (1868–1912). The prime period of Old Karatsu (*ko-Karatsu*) production occurred during the late Hata and Terasawa rules.

When the Terasawa lost control, the fief was under the direct jurisdiction of the shogunate for two years. From then on, the governing of the fief shifted from one family to another, each with relatively short ruling periods—the Ōkubo for less than thirty years (1649–77); the Matsudaira, relatives of the Tokugawa and renowned in tea circles, for a brief dozen years (1678–90); the Doi (1691–1762); the Mizuno (1763–1816); and the Ogasawara (1817–72).[22] From the fall of the Hata, who had been in Kishidake for over four hundred years, to the abolition of the feudal clans, no rule extended to seventy-five years. The average was about forty years, about a generation and a half. Such political instability affected the lives and production of the potters.

The hundreds of Korean immigrants faded for the most part into the mass of nameless artisans, fitting into the stratified social system of the times:

> Tokugawa Japan was divided into four main social classes known as *shi-nō-kō-shō*; the samurai (*shi*) from which came the scholars, the soldiers, and policemen and the bureaucrats; the farmers or *nōmin* engaged in agriculture and related activities; the artisans or *kōjin* dealing in metal and wood work [and pottery]; and the trader or *shōnin* was the peddler, banker, shopkeeper, and wholesaler. Above these four classes was the court nobility or *kuge*.[23]

The feudal system resembled its European counterpart. The daimyo provided the potters with housing, food, and the tools of their trade; in return, they worked for and within the borders of the fief. Although the hereditary four-class system already existed, Hideyoshi had begun tightening it as early as the second year of his rule by decreeing that "a samurai may not become a townsman, that a farmer may not leave his land and work for hire, and that no landowner may give protection to vagrants and men who do not cultivate the soil."[24]

> Those settled in a castle town usually worked for the daimyo with little salary, in return for the privilege of an assured market for their goods. . . . There artisans formed guilds to protect their interests—one guild for one trade. . . . Their system of apprenticeship was severe, but efficient.[25]

Trade guilds of one sort or another had close to a thousand years' history in Japan. Their significance for the potters was the continuity of a hereditary membership and status within the group, which passed from father to son.[26] The Kyushu potters lived and worked under these conditions of professional solidarity, hereditary status, and paternalistic but restricting protection. Their rank in society, level of livelihood, and degree of mobility varied considerably, depending on the ruling lord.

The degree to which Japanese society assimilated these immigrant Koreans varied. In Japanese texts, the generation first arriving is called "naturalized Koreans." This could mean just the adoption of Japanized pronunciation of Korean names, or the conferring of new names plus relative freedom in developing new kiln sites and engaging in trade, or even strict confinement to living and working areas behind guarded walls. One thing is obvious—those Koreans brought to northern Kyushu, settling close to Karatsu city, were less controlled in both their mobility and the disposition of their products than those further south in Nabeshima territory. Judging from the records, the potters of north Kyushu, especially north Hizen, were more assimilated than those to the south or east and those associated with private kilns. In Shimazu territory, the southernmost part of Kyushu, the Koreans were kept quite isolated, so much so that today in some villages certain language usages, dress, and customs remain Korean.[27]

Korea did not entirely forget its children and periodically appealed to them to return. In 1618, after diplomatic relations had been reestablished with Japan, a call went out:

> Korea has suffered much, and twenty years have now passed. Many who went to Japan have suffered hunger and poverty. We pity them. Upon returning to Korea, those who were guilty of crimes will be forgiven, those owing military service will be released, and outcasts will be received to live freely in the security of their homeland. Let this land be their paradise. . . . The time is right for those in Japan to return. If they can do so they will be given the above privileges. Let this communique be announced abroad without fear of government reprisals.[28]

How did the potters respond to such an inviting appeal? We have no information. But more recently there have been similar invitations to the potters of Satsuma. At the close of the nineteenth century, at least one family returned to Korea,[29] and in the early 1920s the pottery family of Kawanami Kōzō of Kuromuta, Takeo, returned. At that time, potters as well as farmers, basket-weavers, lacquerers, candy-makers, and textile-designers were invited back.[30] Without doubt, many of the Koreans, despite being "naturalized Japanese," were set apart either by choice or legislation. "They had to be kept out of touch with Japanese and avoid misunderstandings.'' Separate Korean settlements were part of the castle towns (Plates 232, 233). Karatsu, Saga city, Hirado, and Nagoya each had a *tōjinmachi* (''Chinaman's town'').[31] From one point of view, this was a benevolent protection. The Nabeshima clan office has a 1637 record that speaks of ''controlling the number of Japanese pottery workers in order to protect the Korean potters and also to prevent the cutting down of trees [for fuel].''[32] When, as late as 1876, Ernest Satow visited Satsuma pottery villages, he found a sense of dignity and status among the people plus remnants of Korean customs in dress, hairstyles, religion, and language. They had seldom intermarried with Japanese except for members of the samurai class. He remarked:

> I gathered, in fact, from the conversation of the villagers, that they considered themselves much superior to the aboriginal natives of the country to which their ancestors had been transplanted.[33]

All the immigrant potters at first produced wares in the Karatsu style, but it was those not attached exclusively to a lord's official kiln who continued making the ceramic wares we call Karatsu today.

> Aside from the pottery made in the official kilns, many Korean potters, who came to Japan after the expedition, built a number of small private kilns in various localities of Kyushu, especially in the province of Hizen. . . . The products of these kilns were mostly simple pottery designed for daily use, and are collectively called Karatsu ware.[34]

Both Japanese and Korean potters worked the kilns at Shirosakiyama attached to the castle-fortress at Nagoya. At Hideyoshi's order, they constructed kilns and produced tea ceremony utensils. To underscore the unity between *budō* (the way of the warrior) and *chadō* (the way of tea), he even had a tea house from Osaka castle moved there. In response to the preferences of some of his warriors for Korean pottery, Hideyoshi, as some old records show, sought captured Korean potters for his kiln:

> An ancient document kept by a certain potter of Hirado says that Hideyoshi ordered Matsuura Shigenobu to look for an excellent potter. They say he found one called Jū Jikan from Wungch'on of [South] Korea and sent him to Nagoya castle where he had to produce pottery. . . . There were many besides who fired tea ceremony utensils at Nagoya castle wishing to glorify their ancestors by pottery making.[35]

In addition to the Koreans who produced for the *chajin* at Nagoya, we know the name of at least one Japanese potter working there—Ienaga Hikosaburō Masachika.[36] He was the third son of a roof-tile maker, Ina Masanori, belonging to an old family originally from the Mino area. They had settled in Kawarayashiki, Takagise, of Saga and remained there for ten generations beyond Masachika's time. One document refers to them, together with another potter, Naosaki Chōemon, firing everyday household pottery as well as roof tiles.

When Nagoya Castle was first being renovated for Hideyoshi's occupancy, Ogawa Sōemon made the roof tiles. In 1591, he was appointed ''chief construction contractor,'' and Masachika was called there to take over. According to a document of December 26, 1592 (Tenshō 20), bearing the red seal of Hideyoshi, Masachika was ordered to fire tea utensils and was given the title of chief potter (*Iki no Kami*).[37] Later, Masachika accompanied Lord Nabeshima Naoshige to Korea in search of potters. In 1596 he came back with the Korean, Hankyū, who carried out Hideyoshi's orders to construct a new kiln in Shirosakiyama for the firing of tea ceramics.

The kiln was flooded with orders from the lords going to and returning from Korea. ''The fame of Masachika was so great that when everyone else went to the Korean war from Nagoya, he was left there to produce wares for the generals of Hideyoshi's army.''[38] Hideyoshi was supplied with wares he used as gifts for the great lords—Tokugawa Ieyasu, Maeda Toshiie, Mōri Terumoto, and many others as well. To Masachika went the fame, the title of distinction, and the salary, although the wares were most likely made by Hankyū, who today is recognized as the most important potter at Shirosakiyama.[39]

The fame of Masachika placed him in demand, and in 1601 he went to the Chikugo area, just south of Saga, to construct kilns at the invitation of Lord Nabeshima Naoshige, urged on by a Tanaka Yoshimasa. Hideyoshi had died, and the stay in Chikugo was cut short by Tokugawa Ieyasu, who wanted Masachika back in Nagoya to make his (Ieyasu's) own tea ceremony wares. Whether by Masachika or Hankyū, the ceramics of the Nagoya Castle kiln undoubtedly had an influence throughout Hizen—the potter was most renowned, had the highest patronage, and had worked in Saga and Chikugo as well as at Nagoya. Today the wares made at Shirosakiyama remain unidentified; those extant, if any, are probably intermingled with numerous other Old Karatsu pieces. The kiln site is unknown, and only a few stony ramparts remain of Nagoya Castle.

While all these events were taking place at Nagoya, the nameless potters around Kishidake Castle had been making their wares until the 1594 destruction of the kilns. Meanwhile, additional potters, whose names and traditions have survived, came from Korea. They fall into three groups: those brought over by lords in order to establish their own official kilns, whose wares resembled the Karatsu style at first but eventually developed distinctive characteristics of their own; those who first made both everyday and quality stonewares but who, after the discovery of kaolin around 1616, made both stoneware and porcelain, and finally converted completely to porcelain production; and those who began stoneware kilns, continued making stoneware exclusively, and eventually became the potters for the official Karatsu kiln.

Regarding the first group, Roy Andrew Miller comments:

> One of the exceptions which somewhat complicates the nomenclature of Karatsu wares occurs in the case of kilns operated, usually on a small scale, by important landed families in the Kyushu area. In most cases these kilns have well recorded histories, data usually being available even down to such details as the names of the Korean immigrant artisans who began the work. In general the output of these particular Karatsu wares was limited to tea utensils and other items for the immediate use of the local patrons, but in some instances the tradition thus begun has survived even into modern times.
>
> It is customary among Japanese collectors to label such wares with the

name of the particular local kiln in which they are thought to have been produced, thus obscuring the fact that they are simply further examples of the same Karatsu ware.[40]

Accordingly, potters such as Chon Hae, Pal San, Imamura Sannojō, Ko Kwan, Ri Sampei, Kim Hae, Kim Hwa, Yi Kyong and Yi Pyo-kwang must have made wares in the Karatsu style when they first arrived from Korea, even though their names belong now with the particular wares they established (table, page 24).

Lord Nabeshima, Kyushu's second most powerful lord and tenth in rank in all Japan, is credited with bringing the largest number of Korean potters, "how many hundreds we cannot say,"[41] into his domain, the Saga part of Hizen. Unlike most of the daimyo, he was not a tea devotee but was interested primarily in fostering ceramics for trade. In this he was more than rewarded, since among his Korean potters was Ri Sampei (Kanegae Sambei), who is traditionally credited with sparking the explosive development of the Japanese porcelain industry and trade by discovering kaolin in Nabeshima's realm in 1616.

LORDS, IMMIGRANT KOREAN POTTERS, AND WARES OF OFFICIAL KILNS

Kyushu Lords	Korean Potters	Ceramic Ware	Kyushu Site
Gotō Ienobu	Sōden	Karatsu	Takeo (Uchida or Kuromuta)
Hosokawa Tadaoki	Chon Hae (Sonkai)	Agano Yatsushiro	Kamanokuchi Yatsushiro
Kuroda Nagamasa	Pal San (Hassen)	Takatori	Kurate (Fukuoka Pref.)
Matsuura Sadanobu	Imamura Sannojō (son of Ko Kwan)	Hirado	Mikōchi (Mikawachi)
Matsuura Shigenobu	Ko Kwan	Nakano	Hirado Island
Nabeshima Naoshige	Ri Sampei and 120 others	Karatsu, porcelain	Taku Tengudani near Arita
Shimazu Yoshihiro	Kim Hae, Kim Hwa, and 23 families	Satsuma	Chōsa Village, Kagoshima
W. Honshu Lord			
Mōri Terumoto	Yi Kyong, Yi Pyo-kwang	Hagi	Hagi area

Potters operating official kilns are named in feudal records. Their products, at first similar to Karatsu, became known as separate wares. Some were for the exclusive use of the lord, but "nonreserved" pieces were also made at most kilns.

See Miller, *Japanese Ceramics*, 60–61; Mizumachi and Nabeshima, *Karatsu*, 1; Koyama, *Japanese* . . . , 31–34.

Ri Sampei must have been about twenty-one years old when, early in the seventeenth century, he arrived in Japan and opened his first kiln, Tōjinkobagama, in Nishi no Hara, Taku.[42] Because of his political alliance with the Japanese during the war, Sampei was unable to live within the Korean settlement (Saga's Tōjinmachi) and was given separate accommodations for himself and 120 followers in Taku. An 1806 record describes the ceramics produced there: simple, deformed, and distorted teabowls and small plates with a plain glaze, all of stoneware. Moving to Yamanoguchi (later called Kōraidani), he made underglaze iron-decorated wares including dishes and *kutsu-gata chawan* (teabowls of a squat, warped shape; Plates 116–18) decorated with violets and creepers, as well as plain wares. He finally went to Fujinkawachi (Fujinokōchi), where the "fragments were much the same." There he taught Japanese potters various techniques, and his pupils produced deep bowls with spiral *hakeme* (brushed slip), jars with combed incising, mortars (*suribachi*), and spouted dishes (*katakuchi*). All these shapes and decorations are typical of early Karatsu domestic wares. As in the case of many of these Korean potters, he is described as dissatisfied because he could not find "good clay"—i.e., kaolin—which for centuries the Koreans had been using to make fine porcelain. Although it is now recognized that kaolin deposits were found by other potters as well, probably somewhat in advance of the 1616 date associated with Ri Sampei, he is given the credit for its discovery and the subsequent shift in ceramic production. When he did locate it, he took an "entourage of nine hundred" to the great kaolin mountain, Izumiyama, set up a kiln at Tengudani near Arita, and began making porcelain;[43] the following year, 1617, he reported the move to Nabeshima.[44] With eight others, also named Kanegae, not necessarily related but from the same part of Korea, he began the porcelain business. A shogunate document assured protection and a salary (Ri received that of three men, *sannin buchi*), warned them not to cut wood from the government preserves and to observe the laws for traveling, maintaining proper decorum "because you are protected officials under the government's officers."[45] When Ri Sampei died in 1655,[46] the demand for these new wares was already causing the majority of the kilns to convert to porcelain, at first partially but eventually completely.[47] Some Karatsu kilns were abandoned for new porcelain kiln sites.

A somewhat legendary figure, Sōkan (Kawasaki Seizō), also worked in Saga. Having served Nabeshima as a spy and guide, he was taken to the castle in Saga and given the generous salary of ten persons (*jūnin buchi*).[48] By April of 1600 he was living at Tōjinmachi, Saga, and two years later was in charge of a kiln producing both tea ceremony and everyday pottery. It is not clear whether he ever made pottery himself or just managed the kiln, but he is credited with aiding Nabeshima in finding eight potters in Korea who returned with him "for eternity." One tradition says he looked for clay like that of Korea (kaolin) and found it in Arita.

Of the hundreds of Koreans Lord Nabeshima brought to Japan, Ri Sampei and Sōkan became the most renowned; both had been collaborators with the Japanese during the "Potters Wars."

> In the Saga region where most Koreans are said to have come we find no original Korean names and do not know why. . . .
> [One explanation is] that those who came took refuge in Japan because they

helped the Japanese army, and perhaps the lord in consideration of their situation gave them Japanese names upon arrival.[49]

Different circumstances surround the life of Sōden (Fukaumi Shintarō; the characters for "Fukaumi," when given Sino-Japanese pronunciation, "Shinkai," refer to Korea). Sōden was attracted by the virtues of the Japanese Buddhist priest, Bessō, who had accompanied Lord Ienobu of Takeo to Korea. At the age of thirty-six, Sōden came to Japan to be in the lord's service, bringing his family and a group of potters along. At first, he stayed at Kofuku-ji temple in Takeo where the Buddhist name Sōden was given him. Like the other Koreans, he searched for better clay and moved eventually to either Kuromuta or Uchida in Takeuchi, both of which claim him. Apparently he made only tea ceramics, including a teabowl he presented to Lord Ienobu and an incense burner for Bessō. Sōden lived until 1619, a few years after kaolin was discovered. Hyakubasen, his widow, and son Heizaemon tried working in porcelain but found the Takeo clays "were too impure and melted," so, with the lord's permission, they moved with "over nine hundred persons" to the Arita area.[50] Although this would have meant a boon for Nabeshima in tax revenues, by 1636 the drain on wood supplies became so great that the potters were dispersed and resettled. Hyakubasen became renowned for the exodus she led, and finally she settled in Hiekoba. She died a year after Ri Sampei, 1656, at the age of ninety-six. A stele in the Hōon-ji temple compound recounts her life story,[51] and a sanctuary stone, the Hiekoba Kannon Iwa, carries the two names Kanegae (Ri Sampei) and Fukaumi (Sōden).

The Korean potters who abandoned making Karatsu-style stoneware once they found kaolin were located in the southern part of Hizen Province. They worked among themselves with other Korean potters, having few, if any, Japanese potters with them. Indeed, their very separation as Koreans gave them special protection and privileges. In the northern part of Hizen, however, the situation was quite different. We know there were Koreans and Japanese, such as Hankyū and Masachika, working together at Shirosakiyama. This does not seem to be at all unusual.

Other than Masachika, only a few of the Japanese potters' names have come down to us, and these were all *rōnin*, samurai without lords. They produced stoneware only. Among them is Igarashi Jizaemon, a *rōnin* of the Terasawa of Karatsu, who was appointed the official potter for Lord Kuroda Tadayuki in 1628 with a salary sufficient for thirty persons.[52] The Komatsu family became *rōnin* about 1590 as the result of Hideyoshi's land reform and within ten years became potters.[53] By 1617 they were in the pottery village of Shiinomine, where they remained until the kiln was officially closed about a century later. They were last heard of in 1769 in Tatsugawa village, and by that time had abandoned potting.

The most legendary of the *rōnin* potters is Mori Zen'emon, who was probably attached originally to Kishidake Castle.[54] His name is consistently linked with the introduction of the Karatsu-style climbing kiln to the Mino region, where, despite a long history of pottery making, a form of tunnel kiln (*anagama*) was still in use. According to one source,[55] Zen'emon went into Mino territory "because of his relationship to the priest Ikkan Oshō who lived in a temple there" and was astonished at the "wasted fire" he saw gushing out of the kilns. He suggested that some Mino potters come to

Karatsu and learn more efficient kiln construction. Katō Kagenobu, the Oribe-style potter credited with being the first to use a *noborigama* at Motoyashiki kiln, went to Kyushu. "Mori Zen'emon took him to Karatsu [possibly Shiinomine or Oyamaji], and subsequently Kagenobu redesigned the traditional kilns of Mino."[56] While there are many versions of these events, including some suggestion that the Mino potters resorted to stealth, it is Mori Zen'emon and Katō Kagenobu who are mentioned consistently. The fact is that the early climbing kilns of Mino do resemble those of Kishidake, and it is quite possible that a *rōnin* potter such as Mori was involved.

Among the Korean potters settled in northern Hizen were those who within twenty years would become the first official Karatsu potters (table, page 24). Coming to Japan in about 1596 when Terasawa Hirotaka was made the first lord of Karatsu, they opened a kiln, Tashirotsutsue-*gama* in Kameya, Higashi Tashiro, Ōkawachimachi, Imari city within a year.[57] Of these potters, the Nakazato family has the longest and most complete history. Together with the Ōshima and Fukumoto families they trace their origins to the late Momoyama period when, as immigrant potters, they began a tradition lasting to the present day. They survived the Shiinomine kiln scandal, which, early in the eighteenth century, forced many pottery families to abandon their craft (see page 32). Prior to that time, the Fukumoto family of potters who had worked with them seem to have discontinued making pottery, though the Ōshima family continued into the Taishō era (1912–26). Today the thirteenth-generation Nakazato Tarōuemon continues the production of Karatsu at Ochawangama in Karatsu city.[58]

Sometime between the end of 1593 and 1595, early in the interim between the two Korean campaigns, Koma no Ōna, "The Old Woman of Korea," widow of the Korean potter Nakazato Mouemon, came with her family to Kyushu together with the family of Ōshima Hikoemon.[59] They settled in the territory awarded to Lord Terasawa Hirotaka. Fukumoto Yasaku must have arrived at about the same time. Terasawa, in the first year of lordship over Karatsu, had the naturalized Korean potter Yasaku, Yasaku's son Tōemon, and grandson Tazaemon begin an official kiln in Karabori, Nishinohama, Karatsu city. This beginning of the Karatsu clan kiln carried a salary sufficient for two men. In rapid succession, the site was moved to Karafusa, Sashi village, adjacent to Karatsu city, and then to Hieda Saraya. Within a year after the first establishment, Yasaku was joined in the opening of Tashiro kiln in Imari city by Nakazato Matashichi, Koma no Ōna's son, and Ōshima Hikoemon. This was in the Matsuura region, south of Kishidake. After working there for about seven years, in 1604 they all moved to Mominokidani, Ōkawabaru, Minami Hata, Imari city, and by 1615 closed that site to establish themselves at Shiinomine in the same region. So within the first twenty years of official Karatsu kilns, six different sites had been used. Shiinomine remained open for almost a century, becoming one of the largest and most renowned Karatsu production centers.

There were, apparently, different types of official kilns. Some were diversified and produced wares the lord wanted for his own use and for gifts, predominantly tea utensils. But special chambers of larger kilns—usually the central ones where the temperature was most even and controlled—were also used for the exclusive production of pieces for the lord. Then there were kilns used for the lord exclusively. This last type, such as the kilns of Takatori, Agano, etc., apparently never produced Karatsu ware except in the kilns' earliest phases and later developed styles distinct from Karatsu.

Fukumoto　福本　　　　　　　　　　from *Nakazatoke kyūki*　中里家旧記
- I. Yasaku　弥作
- II. Tōemon　藤右衛門
- III. Tazaemon　太左衛門
- IV. Bunshichi　分七　　(farmer)

Ōshima　大島　　　　　　　　　　from *Ōshima kyūki*　大島旧記
- I. Hikoemon　彦右衛門
- II. Hikoemon　彦右衛門　　d. 1701 (Genroku 14)
- III. Hikohachi　彦八　　d. 1703 (Genroku 16)
- IV. Yajihei　弥治兵衛　　d. 1750 (Kan'en 3)
- V. Yakichi　弥吉　　d. 1759 (Hōreki 9)
- VI. Ikkaku　一角　　d. 1801 (Kyōwa 1)
- VII. Gennosuke　源之助　　d. 1828 (Bunsei 11)
- VIII. Kichiemon　吉右衛門　　d. 1871 (Meiji 4)
- IX. Yoshisaburō　吉三郎　　d. 1875 (Meiji 8)
- X. Mannosuke (last potter)　満之助　　d. 1882 (Meiji 15)
- XI. Inosuke　猪之助　　d. 1920 (Taishō 9)
- XII. Mannosuke　満之助　　(carpenter in Karatsu city)

Nakazato　中里　　　　　　　　　　from *Nakazatoke kyūki*　中里家旧記
- I. Matashichi　又七　　d. 1663 (Kan'ei 10)
- II. Tarōuemon　太郎右衛門　　d. 1670 (Kambun 10)
- III. Jin'emon　甚右衛門　　d. 1703 (Genroku 16)
- IV. Tarōuemon　太郎右衛門　　d. 1744 (Enkyō 1)
- V. Kiheiji　喜平次　　d. 1757 (Hōreki 7)
- VI. Tarōuemon　太郎右衛門　　d. 1786 (Temmei 6)
- VII. Tōji　陶治　　d. 1811 (Bunka 8)
- VIII. Tarōuemon　太郎右衛門　　d. 1817 (Bunka 14)
- IX. Shōhei　荘平　　d. 1825 (Bunsei 8)
- X. Tōtarō　藤太郎　　d. 1892 (Meiji 14)
- XI. Tenyū　天祐　　d. 1924 (Taishō 13)
- XII. Tarōuemon　太郎右衛門　　d. 1985 (Shōwa 60)
- XIII. Tarōuemon　太郎右衛門

adapted from Mizumachi, *Karatsu*, pp. 324–25.

Kiln remains show the considerable range in focus and products of Karatsu. The earlier ones, including the Kishidake kilns, produced wares for the lord and others as well, both everyday and tea ceramics. Supplying household utensils for sale and shipment to other parts of Japan always was one of the functions of a Karatsu kiln. As for the status of the potters, Fukumoto Yasaku was an official potter for the lord from the start. Whether Matashichi and Hikoemon shared this title when they first joined him is not certain, but by the time they founded the Shiinomine kiln (1615) all three enjoyed the title.

Shiinomine opened at a time when many potters were being lured to porcelain production; nevertheless, or quite possibly even because of this, the kiln flourished and a potters' town sprang up around the kiln site. The *rōnin* potter Komatsu Gennojō was among those joining the Shiinomine colony. Others as well were moving to new sites. Koma no Ōna and one of her younger sons, Nakazato Mouemon, went to the porcelain manufacturing center of Mikōchi in 1622. At the invitation of Imamura Sannojō, the son of Ko Kwan, three Shiinomine potters, Fukumoto Yajiemon, Maeda Tokuzaemon, and Yamonouchi Hyōe, went in 1637 to open the official kiln of Hirado, the porcelain kiln Nagahayama at Mikōchi.

As for the three families of official Karatsu potters, the Fukumoto continued only into the fourth generation, by which time they became "poor potters and turned to farming."[60] After the period of Terasawa rule, their name no longer appeared with the remaining official potters, the Nakazato and Ōshima.

In general, the life of the potters during this period combined intense production and mobility. They had relatively good salaries, extensive kiln sites, and their wares were in demand. It was not uncommon for them to have other part-time work such as farming, gate keeping, etc. While some had a social rank comparable to a samurai, for the most part their status in society was low. When in 1673 Lord Terasawa announced a policy for attendance at the great hall, he instructed "inferiors to sit on the *engawa* [porch]" while "potters and whale fishermen are to be seated on the edge of the *engawa* behind the village men."[61]

With the end of Terasawa rule, 1647 (Shōhō 4), the classic age of Karatsu passed. The development of porcelain and overglaze enamel wares, with the consequent alteration in markets and taste, was more responsible for the change than the shift in ruling families. The Terasawa reign coincided with the production of the finest Old Karatsu (*ko-Karatsu*) wares. Potters up to the present have sought to capture or reproduce their quality and spontaneity.

Within the life-span of the first Koreans brought in by Hideyoshi's warriors, Karatsu kilns multiplied phenomenally, spreading westward across the Matsuura range, into Takeo in the east, and fanning out across southern Hizen (map, page 194). Over two hundred Karatsu kilns are said to have filled this small area; *Sekai tōji zenshū*[62] and Mizumachi's *Karatsu*[63] list over one hundred by name (list, pages 198ff). Those few potters whose meager records remain constitute but a fraction of the Japanese and Koreans active in those early days. Though information about them is only fragmentary, it is enough to let us trace later Karatsu developments.

During the years the Karatsu area was directly under the shogunate (1647–49), a most unusual and enterprising figure came to the area. Umemura Wahei, a "person from Edo," arrived with the lord Mizutani Ise no Kami, the shogunal representative. He first went to a small village in Fukuoka Prefecture, where he drew paintings on fans and made dolls, developing a circle of followers. Later he moved to Saga Prefecture and began making pottery, having trained first in Hirado and Mikōchi. The *Nakazato kiroku* makes it quite clear that Wahei never mastered the potter's wheel and could only make hand-built pottery. In fact, it appears that Wahei was not so much a ceramic artist as a skilled entrepreneur. He brought some Hirado potters to Karatsu and applied to the new lord, Ōkubo, for a business permit. He opened a kiln at Hirayama village, was given a considerable salary (thirty persons) plus expenses for firing—completely endowed by the lord. Eventually he closed the Hirayama kiln and moved to Ōkawabaru.

Meanwhile, under the rule of the Ōkubo daimyo, production at Shiinomine accelerated. Even though the Terasawa tea devotees had been active kiln patrons, the Ōkubo increased demands for teabowls even more. It was at this time that the type of Karatsu known as *kenjō* ("Presentation") Karatsu (Plates 152, 180) began to be produced, marking a decided change in taste towards a more slick and refined product. Even the materials and methods of manufacture altered. According to Nakazato Kiheiji's writings, the fine type of clay used for the *kenjō* pieces had not been dug during the Terasawa rule. The clay's preparation differed in that it was levigated, finely ground, and slaked. Earlier clays had been used in a relatively natural state with minimal preparation. Kiheiji speaks of shapes becoming more graceful and noble, the masculine *ko-Karatsu* yielding to a feminine, luxurious appearance.

Now also a reserved "official" chamber was added to the Shiinomine kiln. By the early 1660s, Shiinomine had three climbing kilns of twenty chambers each, and the pottery village had grown to 350 houses. A five-chamber kiln easily holds three to five thousand pieces; if all the climbing kilns of Shiinomine were fired at once, the yield would have been between thirty-five and fifty thousand pieces. Since the usual firings were of everyday objects, tea things being fired only once a year, the large kilns of Shiinomine were obviously able to pick up much of the slack in production resulting from numerous kilns converting to porcelain. As long as there was demand, they supplied Japan with household wares as the Karatsu kilns had done beforehand. By the mid-1660s, Shiinomine was a thriving pottery village, some fifty years old, with second- and third-generation Korean potters. Some of the first naturalized Koreans, such as Koma no Ōna, who lived to be 106, survived to witness all these changes.

The third-generation Nakazato, Jin'emon, epitomizes the potters working in the Presentation (*kenjō*) style. His elaborate craftsmanship was apparent in pieces featuring the hallmarks of the mid-Shiinomine period—glaze under the foot, a whiter, fine clay, and a pale cream-colored, glossy glaze. About 1657, he left Shiinomine to reopen, after almost fifty years of inactivity, the kiln at Ōkawabaru that his grandfather Matashichi had closed. Why did Jin'emon leave the thriving center that he dominated? Certainly not to search for porcelain clays or for better patronage. The reason for this move remains an unanswered question; but the response of the people is well recorded—when he left they cried out, "The god of the kilns (*kama no kami*) has left us!"

Shortly after Jin'emon reopened Ōkawabaru, the enterprising Wahei arrived bearing credentials as the official Karatsu potter, with the privileges and salary of a samurai. He associated himself with Jin'emon, added a new, "official" chamber to the kiln, and established a production studio at the same place. One cannot help but wonder who actually made the official pieces for the lord. The Ōkawabaru kiln remains provide us with a variety of shards—early, simple, thick wares from Matashichi's time and later, elegant examples from the mid-seventeenth century, but there are none one can easily associate with Wahei. He had secured his status of *kachi* (comparable to samurai) by appealing to the lord and pointing out that it was difficult to work like the contemporary potters; a suitable rank and salary would let him compete successfully. Thus, Wahei was required to work a hundred days each year at Ōkawabaru, though he kept his family at Bōzumachi, Karatsu city, twelve miles or so (twenty kilometers) away.

Maeda Tōjiuemon then joined Wahei, apparently as an apprentice, thus beginning a long-term association with him. He, too, made only hand-built pieces and later was renowned as a ceramic sculptor. It was this Tōjiuemon who, early in the eighteenth century, taught Kiheiji, the fifth-generation Nakazato, the hand-building technique of Wahei. Kiheiji also learned sculpture techniques from him, eventually building a reputation of his own as a skilled sculptor. As enthusiasm for the tea ceremony, and particularly for Karatsu-style tea wares, diminished, sculptured ceramics occupied the Karatsu potters more and more.

Judging from the records, the latter half of the seventeenth century was relatively uneventful for the Karatsu potters. Shiinomine had suffered and recovered from a serious flood, and the fief changed hands twice. The Matsudaira family took control in 1678. Despite being a prominent family in tea circles, they seem to have had no particular impact on the pottery, possibly because of the brevity of their rule. They were supplanted by the Doi in 1691.

Legend says the teabowls called *hibakari* ("fire only") were made sometime during this last half of the century. Whether these teabowls made in Japan by Korean potters from clay and glaze imported from Korea are totally fictitious or have some measure of historic reality is uncertain. Ostensibly, the only thing Japanese about them was the kiln fire—*hibakari*. The ideal they represent is firm and clear. At a time when the style of Karatsu had undergone a significant change, it symbolized a yearning for the unrefined, Korean-related type formerly produced. Stories about these *hibakari* teabowls are many and undying. The most consistent tradition places their manufacture somewhere during the second generation of the Nakazato and Ōshima families. One version speaks of two potters coming to Shiinomine from Tsushima island bringing with them Korean clay and glazes. They were named Jin'emon and Shishibei, the same names as the third-generation Nakazato and one of the potters spared during the Shiinomine scandal. Of the many teabowls they made at Shiinomine, they took forty to sixty back to Tsushima and destroyed the rest. Although Hizen's eminent historian Nakajima Kōki[64] and the present Nakazato Tarōuemon XIII[65] question the story, it tells a great deal about the perceived standards for Karatsu. Wares ideal in type, specially selected, made by itinerant Korean potters bearing famous names, taken to a place between Japan and Korea and manufactured with combined elements of Korea and Japan—all show how much the Korean materials and style were revered for tea ware. Regard for Korea as the source for ideal ceramics persists to the present day, when the search goes on to find a location in Korea with remains of ancient wares comparable to early Karatsu.[66]

The impact of the seventeenth century shift to porcelain, the closing of many kilns, changes in ruling families, and altered taste all affected the affairs of the Karatsu potters.

> Porcelain rapidly was accorded preference over Karatsu for everyday food service, so that over sixty Karatsu kilns converted to porcelain during the Kan'ei

era (1624–40). At the beginning of the Shōhō era (1644–45) Sakaida Kakiemon succeeded in producing multicolored overglaze enameled wares, and most of the remaining Karatsu kilns were soon abandoned. Subsequent production of Karatsu was limited to the official kilns at Hirayama, Bōzumachi, and Tōjinmachi, and to a group of kilns manufacturing folk wares for use in local farming villages. These included Shiinomine, Kuromutayama, Kotajiyama, Yuminoyama, Kiharayama, and Nishiyama—all of which produced attractive folk wares of interest to collectors today.[67]

As the century progressed, even Shiinomine, the largest kiln complex, met with disaster. The expansion of porcelain into the domestic market brought mounting financial problems and severe economic hardships to the potters. The Shiinomine potters became indebted to the merchants of both Imari and Karatsu. Once the Imari merchants became aware of the potters' defaults, they took the case to the lord. This was the beginning, June, 1697 (Genroku 10), of the Shiinomine scandal investigation (*Shiinomineyama kuzure*; "Shiinomine collapse"), which lasted until October, 1703. It resulted in "exile" for most of the potters, who turned to farming. Some received a compensation "through the mercy of the lord" although they were dispossessed. One "died at an inn"—by his own hand?—before the hearings ended. A few were permitted to remain at Shiinomine, including Jin'emon's sons, Tarōuemon and Sakuhei, and Ōshima Kaheiji and Shichibei. The official kiln of Shiinimone was closed January 19, 1708 (Hōei 5), and by 1723 (Kyōhō 8) it was completely destroyed and abandoned. Between 1708 and 1723 some activity continued, although its nature and volume is not entirely clear. It appears to have been under the strict control of the lord. In 1707, the year prior to the closing of Ochawangama at Shiinomine, Nakazato Tarōuemon IV and Ōshima Yajihei IV were given a raise in salary. Together with Nakazato Kiheiji V, then just seventeen, and four nonpotters, they constructed a new Karatsu kiln, Ochanwangama[68] at Bōzumachi, Karatsu city. Only Presentation teabowls are believed to have been fired there, and the workers remained just seven, three potters and four nonpotters, including the caretaker of the kiln.

Closing Shiinomine was not entirely unfortunate, despite the public disgrace and personal tragedy for the potters. Kiheiji tells of its last days:

> Gradually they fired only poor products; the prices rose and the fuel stock was exhausted. In January, 1722 (Kyōhō 7), Kaemon, son of Kaheiji, and Kyūgorō (Tōemon), son of Yajihei, had to repair Shiinomine Ochawangama. In May, 1722, the order was given to fire all kinds of ware until March of the following year, when all had to be finished. In June, 1723, this kiln was closed down. Kaemon and Tōemon and the caretaker of the kiln were dismissed, Tōemon being demoted to the salary of one man [the level of an apprentice].[69]

Nakazato Kiheiji V is the last Karatsu potter prior to modern times about whom much is known. Leaving Shiinomine at seventeen, he was given a salary two years later and told to study in Karatsu. By that time Wahei and Tōjiuemon had begun to have difficulties. The suspicion that Wahei's pottery was not first quality is confirmed by Kiheiji, who wrote:

Now Wahei's handbuilt work was such that he was appointed caretaker of the lord's tea house [both a removal and a demotion], and his craftsmen were made bee keepers.[70]

Wahei and Tōjiuemon were told to stop making Presentation teabowls. Tōjiuemon left with Wahei, but later returned for a while to Karatsu, spent some time in Hirado, and finally became the caretaker of a tea house in Wataba village. It was during the time he was back in Karatsu that he taught Kiheiji sculpture techniques. His student became noted as a master sculptor and passed his skills on to his son Nichirabō—the popular name for Nakazato Ichiji.

Kiheiji is more important to us as an informant than as a potter. In the early 1720s, the shogunate conducted their investigation for which Kiheiji wrote the Nakazato family history (*Nakazatoke kyūki*; Plate 202), covering events from the time of their arrival

OLD DOCUMENTS RELATED TO KARATSU

Source	Document, Date, Paging
Nakajima *Hizen tōji shi*	Administrative Policy of Hirotaka, 11th day, 8th month, Kan'ei 13 (1637), pp. 45–46
	Matsuura Karatsu ki (Matsuura Record), Kan'ei 13 (1637), p. 47
	Komatsu family genealogy, Bunka 11 (1815); recopied Bunsei 1 (1818), pp. 47–48
	Nakazato kiroku (Nakazato Documents) by Nakazato Kiheiji, Kyōhō 5 (1721) and Kyōhō 8 (1724), 49–55. A large portion of this document with commentary appears in Harada and Nakazato, *Nihon no yakimono*, pp. 102–07.
Mizumachi *Tōsetsu 24*	*Matsuura mukashi kagami* (Ancient Records of Matsuura), Hōei (1704–11), p. 4
	Matsuura kojiki (Ancient Documents of Matsuura), Kansei (1789–1801), pp. 4–5
	Matsuura ki shūsei (Collection of Matsuura Documents), undated, p. 5
	Nakazatoke kyūki (Old Documents of the Nakazato Family) by Nakazato Kiheiji, Kyōhō 5 (1721), p. 5
Nagatake *Kyūshū ko tōji*	documents' contents stated but not reproduced except sections of the *Yakimono taigai*
	Kaitō shokokuki (Documents of Various Countries of the Eastern Sea), undated, p. 139
	Yakimono taigai, section of *Matsuura bussan zukō* (General Introduction to Pottery, in the Illustrated Study of Matsuura Products), undated, pp. 274–78

Additional ancient documents are reprinted in Mizumachi, *Ko-Karatsu*, Vol. I, 210–24.

in Japan up to his own day. The account is in two sections, for the years 1721 (Kyōhō 6) and 1724 (Kyōhō 9). It seems that on each occasion the investigating officials interviewed him as well. At the first meeting, he presented twenty-seven teabowls for examination, all but five made by himself. "This inquiry was made because the supervisor to the shogun found ancient teabowls were finer than present-day ones."[71] We are left uninformed as to just what was wrong with the current products and when the "finer ancient ones" were made. Kiheiji says the poor quality ones were too thin, "but they seem to be more appreciated even though inferior." The finer ones could be Old Karatsu wares, made in an entirely different style and closer to the Korean aesthetic.

As chronicler of the early Karatsu potters, Kiheiji was recounting events going back some 125 years. No doubt there was a mixture of tradition, legend, and blurred facts. His writing, nevertheless, is the most informative available. With the exception of the *Matsuura Karatsu ki*, 1637, all other useful records relating to the Hizen potters are of approximately the same date as Kiheiji's or later (table, page 33). In its basic information, there is no reason to question the diary. Given the importance of the investigation, it is likely that there are fewer popular anecdotes or exaggerations included than would ordinarily be found in a collection of family memoirs. Kiheiji points out that in preparing his statements he referred to all the Nakazato family documents. His account of the Shiinomine scandal is that of a participant. According to Tarōuemon XIII, Kiheiji's diary is now in the possession of the Nakazato family at Ochawangama, Tōjinmachi, Karatsu. This is where Kiheiji and Ōshima Yakichi V moved in 1734 (Kyōhō 19), ten years after the official investigation.

Between Kiheiji's time and the end of the Meiji era (1868), only birth and death dates of the official potters were recorded, and even these are not always complete (table, page 28). Two other families governed the fief during this interim, the Mizuno from 1763 and the Ogasawara from 1817. When the feudal clans were abolished in 1872, Ochawangama, although no longer a lord's kiln, continued to be operated by the Nakazato and Ōshima families. This venerable kiln continued to be used until 1919 and is now enshrined like an icon on the Nakazato property (Plate 224). The Ōshima stopped potting within ten years of the closing of Ochawangama, when the twelfth-generation Ōshima Mannosuke became a carpenter in Karatsu city. Two Nakazato brothers, Ten'yu and Keitarō, managed the kiln. They were primarily ceramic sculptors. Captain F. Brinkley, writing in 1901, mentions one of them:

> A modern Karatsu expert called Nakazato Keizō [Keitarō] is distinguished for his skill in modeling figures of men and animals. He ceased to work, some five or six years ago, owing to partial loss of sight.[72]

Ten'yu's second son, Nakazato Shigeo became interested in the history of his family and the renowned works of the past. He constructed a *noborigama* of the early Karatsu type near the former Ochawangama, assumed the title Tarōuemon XII, began looking for old kiln sites, dug among them, studied, researched, and revived the shapes and decorations of the past. His life was spent reestablishing the techniques and quality of the early Karatsu potters from Korea.

A branch of the Nakazato family under Nakazato Tokio is still in Mikawachi (Mikōchi), where Koma no Ōna moved with her son Nakazato Mouemon in 1622. It is believed some had been potters at Shiinomine and remained in that region after the closing of the kiln. Northwestern Kyushu is populated today by the descendants of the makers of Old Karatsu, but only the Nakazato family of Karatsu city claims an unbroken lineage of ceramic workers.[73]

This history of the early Karatsu potters is reconstructed from scanty information about a few among hundreds. Of those few, what is known is piecemeal; like the shards at their kiln sites, there are only fragments from which to refashion the whole. Some things are clear—that Karatsu ware was made at the Kishidake kilns before the Korean potters' arrival; that Karatsu was not only made by immigrant Koreans, but by Japanese as well, such as the former roof tile maker Masachika, various *rōnin*, and the displaced Kishidake potters. Among the latter, there probably were some of Korean descent whose families came to Japan at any number of earlier dates, possibly even as *wakō* captives. And there were enough Japanese potters to warrant the issuing of protective legislation to guard the rights of the Koreans. Throughout the seventeenth century the degree of assimilation of the Korean potters and the freedom of mobility they enjoyed varied from place to place. The discovery of porcelain affected the entire pottery population and changed the methods of production. Specialization was introduced in the form of porcelain throwers, trimmers, decorators, etc. But for Karatsu potters, the Japanese custom of a small, home industry continued even at the large kilns, so that forming, decorating, and completing pieces was the work of one person.

NOTES

1. These were: Chikuzen, Chikugo, Hizen, Higo, Buzen, Bungo, Satsuma, Ōsumi, and Hyūga. Modern Kyushu has been redistricted into seven prefectures: Fukuoka, Saga, Nagasaki, Kumamoto, Ōita, Kagoshima, and Miyazaki. It also includes the islands of Iki and Tsushima, the Gotō Islands, and Satsuran Islands.

2. Sansom 1961, p. 20.

3. Franks 1885, p. 22.

4. *Matsuura ki shūsei*, an undated collection of old documents quoted in Mizumachi 1955, p. 5.

5. Nakajima 1955, pp. 17–18.

6. Mizumachi 1955, pp. 9–10.

7. Nagatake 1963, p. 139.

8. Some Western historians include all Japanese pirates such as the tenth century looters on the Inland Sea among the *wakō*. More precisely, they were the international pirates who began raids in Korea in 1223. See Hazard 1967a, pp. 260–77.

9. In 934 the poet Ki no Tsurayuki described perils from pirates in the Inland Sea, a lament echoed six centuries later in 1581 by the Jesuit Valignano against the *wakō*. Sansom 1961, pp. 117 and 272.

10. Eileen Katō, "Toward an Understanding of the Background" in *Ryōtarō*, 1979, p. 65.

11. Sansom 1961, p. 261.

12. Sansom 1961, p. 366.

13. The *Sōtan nikki* appears in the series of tea ceremony records, *Chadō koten zenshū*. See Sansom 1961, p. 423. This same year Hideyoshi gave his famed Kitano tea party for thousands in Kyoto, five years before the first Korean campaign.

14. Nakajima 1955, p. 70.

15. Fukui 1934, p. 12.

16. Reischauer and Fairbank 1962, p. 590.

17. Nakajima 1955, p. 48, reprints the "Genealogy of the Komatsu Family." When these samurai were first dispossessed about 1589, they moved to Matsuura, became potters in the early seventeenth century, and eventually settled in Shiinomine, a production center for Karatsu.

18. Goedertier 1968, p. 235.

19. The history of the Hata family, their fall, and a complete reprint of a document dated 1595 (Bunroku 3) signed by Kurokawa Ganpachirō recounting their last days is given in Nakajima 1955, pp. 18 and 75–79.

20. Mizumachi 1955, p. 12.

21. Nakajima 1955, p. 80.

22. Harada and Nakazato 1969, pp. 109–111.

23. Fodella 1970, footnote 12, p. 5.

24. Sansom 1961, p. 430.

25. Sansom 1969, p. 30.

26. Sansom 1969, p. 37.

27. The condition of these Satsuma potters is poignantly recounted in Shiba, 1979.

28. Nakajima 1955, pp. 62–63.

29. Satow 1887, p. 202.

30. Nakajima 1955, p. 128.

31. Nakajima 1955, pp. 60, 62.

32. Jenyns 1971, 82.

33. Satow 1887, p. 202.

34. Okuda, Koyama and Hayashiya 1954, p. 3.

35. Nakajima 1955, p. 62. For a report of recent studies of Wungch'ŏn (Japanese: Komogai) in relationship to Karatsu, see Mikami 1971, pp. 1–8.

36. Nakajima 1955, pp. 70–72.

37. Nakajima 1955, pp. 70–72. Tenshō 20 and Bunroku 1 coincide, both being 1592. The resulting confusion about the date has caused both this document and a noted early Karatsu jar with this date inscribed on it to be questioned.

38. Nakajima 1955, p. 72.

39. Nakajima 1955, p. 85.

40. Miller 1960, p. 60.

41. Nakajima 1955, p. 61.

42. Nakajima 1955, pp. 85–97.

43. *Encyclopedia of World Art* 1960, v. III, col. 314.

44. Nakajima 1955, p. 94.

45. Nakajima 1955, p. 97.

46. In 1967 the death of Sampei was firmly established when Ikeda Chūichi discovered it recorded at the Ryūsen-ji temple in Nishi-Arita as September 20, 1655. John Pope, "The Beginnings of Porcelain in Japan" in Cleveland 1970, pp. 3–5.

47. Kiln excavations and shards show that porcelain and stoneware were fired simultaneously in the same kilns and chambers. Several fused stoneware and porcelain shards can be seen in the collections of the Idemitsu Museum of Arts, Tokyo and of Dr. Oliver Impey of the Ashmolean Museum, Oxford.

48. Nakajima 1955, p. 67.

49. Nakajima 1955, p. 92.

50. Harada and Nakazato 1969, p. 109. This is the same number said to have gone with Ri Sampei. It must simply indicate a large number of persons.

51. Mizumachi 1973, p. 221.

52. Harada and Nakazato 1969, p. 110.

53. Nakajima 1955, pp. 47–48.

54. Nakajima 1955, p. 78.

55. *Seto ogama yakimono narabini Karatsu gama toritate no yuraiki*, an undated old document quoted in "Karatsu gama" 1953, p. 76.

56. Nakajima 1955, pp. 47–48.

57. Harada and Nakazato 1969, p. 109.

58. The following information is compiled from the diary of the fifth-generation Nakazato, Kihei-ji, reprinted with commentary in Harada and Nakazato 1969, pp. 102–107; Mizumachi 1955, p. 5; and Nakajima 1955, pp. 49–55; and the lineage of Karatsu potters in Harada and Nakazato 1969, pp. 109–111.

59. From this time on the -*emon* ending of Kyushu potters' names appears. The Japanese characters actually read -*emon* or -*uemon*, which the majority transcribe today as a simple -*emon* with the notable exception of Nakazato Tarōuemon. -*Sae* and -*ue* mean "left" and "right" respectively, and -*mon* means "gate," referring to the officials at checkpoint gates. The origin of such names is quite old.

60. Mizumachi 1963, p. 324.

61. "Matsuura Karatsu" in Nakajima 1955, p. 47.

62. V. IV, pp. 182–183.

63. pp. 308–310.

64. Nakajima 1955, p. 51.

65. Harada and Nakazato 1969, p. 102.

66. Mikami 1971, pp. 1–8.

67. Mizumachi 1963, p. 2.

68. Literally, "Teabowl kiln." There were at least four Ochawangama—the one at Shiinomine, another at Hirado, and two in Karatsu city, first at Bōzumachi and later at Tōjinmachi.

69. Nakajima 1955, p. 55.

70. *Ibid*.

71. Nakajima 1955, pp. 49–55.

72. Brinkley 1901, VIII, p. 312.

73. Information courtesy of Igaki Haruo, Tokyo.

CHAPTER II

Examples, Influence, Problems

The phenomenal development of ceramic production in late sixteenth and early seventeenth century Japan involved the introduction of new techniques and materials. In general these techniques were rapid throwing on a kick wheel, widespread use of applied feldspathic glazes, efficient high-temperature firing and kiln atmosphere control, use of underglaze decoration, and, then, the use of kaolin to make porcelain. The new ceramic produced in northern Kyushu—which came to be known as Karatsu ware—is a high-fired stoneware with a hard, often finely crackled, feldspathic glaze. Many pieces have freely painted iron underglaze decorations—simple reeds and grasses, flowers, and patterns of crosshatched lines. All the smaller pieces are wheel thrown and have trimmed foot rims. No previous Japanese ceramic ware possessed these qualities. Karatsu ware became one of the most widely marketed and used everyday wares in Japan.

Yet, for a ceramic whose name became a household word, a large number of basic questions are asked repeatedly. When did Karatsu ware production start—after or *before* Hideyoshi's campaign? If before, how much before? This question of time relates directly to the issue of whether or not Karatsu ware production was begun by Korean potters brought back from the war, by earlier immigrant Koreans who came freely (or as hostages of Japanese pirates?), or did it start with Japanese potters influenced by the Korean style? Many say that Karatsu derives from Korean Yi dynasty wares; to what extent is this true? Most extant early Karatsu pieces were made for or incorporated into the tea ceremony; can Karatsu, then, be understood in any other context today? Finally, technique poses questions: which techniques came from Korea? Was Karatsu the first Japanese ware using them? To what extent can the remains found at kiln sites unravel Karatsu's history? Technical analysis is very useful in approaching answers to these questions. The events surrounding Hideyoshi's Korean military adventures and the immigration of Korean potters were broached in the preceding chapter, but the issue of the initiation of stoneware production in northern Kyushu is still to be resolved.

Karatsu ware was never intended for export abroad. These pots were shipped in great quantities from Karatsu to the rest of Japan. Like the Imari porcelains, which developed somewhat later, they were identified by the name of their export city—Karatsu—despite their origin in over a hundred different kilns. The word ''Karatsu'' became synonymous with household wares in western and central Japan, and in many places remains so today.

In addition, Karatsu was and still is a preferred tea ceremony ceramic. During the late sixteenth and early seventeenth century, when Karatsu production was expanding, the popularity of the way of tea was at a peak. For a favored rustic teabowl, lords surrendered rights to territory and possessions, noblemen intrigued and plotted, fortunes were flung about, lives were risked. The tea devotee was a zealot, and the tea master was all-powerful in dictating rituals and taste. The unpretentious Karatsu household wares caught the attention of influential tea masters, notably Sen no Rikyū and Furuta Oribe, who selected pieces of special character or charm to be elevated from *zakki* (household ceramics) to *chaki* (tea ceramics). Besides these items, some Karatsu pieces were made specifically for the tea ceremony. Use of Karatsu as a tea ceremony ware accounts for the careful preservation of most old Karatsu pieces known today. An examination of typical examples of Karatsu throws light on why the pieces held such attraction for the men of tea.

EXAMPLES OF KARATSU

For purposes of discussion and presentation, Karatsu ware here is broken down into two simple categories: pots made expressly for the tea ceremony and pots made for household use.

Wares Related to Tea

The semicircular shape of the late sixteenth century painted teabowl shown in Plate 35 originated with rounded bowls used for measuring rice. This thinly potted piece has a lip painted in underglaze iron (the *kawakujira* style lip), and a motif of a rapidly painted circle surrounding a cross appears on opposite sides of the pot. A single glaze covers the inside; the exterior glaze stops short of the foot, exposing the dark reddish brown clay.

Everything about this teabowl suggests a rapid, spontaneous production. The lack of symmetry, the irregular painting of the lip rim, parts left unglazed where the bowl was held while being dipped, the smudged part of the design, the exposed raw clay—all are obviously results of rapid manufacture and decoration. Some glaze, where the underglaze iron pigment was too dense, pulled away during firing, and the trimmed foot rim has been gouged on the side. The milky, semitransparent glaze is finely crackled, and here and there cracks have developed in the body. Chipped areas have been mended with gilded lacquer. Karatsu is said to be a rustic ware; at first glance, the description suits this teabowl.

Such freedom of execution, with nothing retouched, is in accord with the restraint appropriate to tea ceremony taste. The walls are refined for stoneware, thin and graceful. The rounded form avoids harsh symmetry, yet maintains a sense of poise and fullness. Both grace and strength are combined in the shape. The torn glaze spots and abrupt staining of the lip suggest something vulnerable that has endured violence. That the natural, noble, and weak can endure over that which is forceful and strong is a favorite paradox expressed in the tea ceremony concept of *wabi*. Other qualities—the softly lustrous glaze; the dense, grainy clay; the bold, rhythmically painted designs; the deft trimming of the unsmoothed foot rim—interact to stimulate and hold the imagination.

The design painted on this bowl is the *kutsuwagata*, a Greek cross within a circle. It is unusual to find such a design on Karatsu. Ordinarily, the painted designs have no iconographic or symbolic significance. This is one of the standard Japanese family crests assumed to have been used by Christian daimyo in Kyushu. The exceptional use of an emblematic design here argues for its purposefulness—a piece perhaps ordered by or made for a Christian lord. It could also be a hidden religious symbol. After 1587, the inconsistent enforcement of a ban against Christianity led to the use of the tea ceremony as a setting for clandestine worship with teabowls, often marked with a cross, functioning as chalices. This design, then, implies a late sixteenth century date, after the spread of Christianity in Kyushu.

The handsome, straight-sided, "carved" (*hori*) Karatsu teabowl in Plate 9 is attributed to the Handōgame kiln, where similar shards were excavated (Plate 182). Since it and other kilns of the Kishidake group were closed in 1594, when their lord fell from power, it must have a pre-1594 date. Unlike the painted bowl, the shape of this plain glazed teabowl has no relationship to household wares. Its plain cylindrical shape is similar to that of teabowls manufactured in Korea and the Mino district of Japan, putting this piece within the tea ceremony genre. The opaque white glaze has a small crackled pattern and is speckled with pit marks, which expose the dark clay. Unlike most Karatsu, it is glazed to the foot rim, which in turn is unglazed. This exceptionally low foot rim is rather incongruous. It is constructed as a pair of concentric ridges, an unusual device found on straight-sided, "carved" Karatsu teabowls (Plate 109).

This nonfunctional and technically inexplicable manner of carving a foot rim simulates the appearance of applied foot rims on white Shino teabowls from the Mino kilns of central Honshu. There are, for example, cylindrical white Shino pieces with unaccentuated lip rims and with a series of crossing diagonal lines painted in underglaze iron. These could be the prototypes of the diagonal incised lines seen on the Karatsu piece, even though Shino and Karatsu pots are quite distinct. The curious Karatsu foot rim appears to be an attempt to duplicate, by trimming, the appearance of the applied Shino foot rim. The Shino bowls have a warm, playful character, while the deep gouges, taller proportions, and firm, slightly concave sides give the Karatsu bowl a sense of strength and endurance. The very lack of underglaze painting adds to the nobility of this piece. There are, nevertheless, "carved" Karatsu pieces with underglaze iron painted into the gouges (Plate 112).

A third teabowl (Plate 11) is doubly derivative, inspired by Seto *temmoku* bowls, which in turn were based on *temmoku* (Jian) teabowls imported from China. The flared sides and narrow, shallow foot rim comes from the *temmoku* Chinese shapes; the creamy, opaque glaze suggests a glaze used at the Seto kilns on Honshu. Despite these borrowings, the Karatsu piece is not a copy. The trimming, the glaze, and their interaction are peculiar to Karatsu. The opaque light glaze, although similar in color, is quite different from that of Seto ware. It is fired at a higher temperature and develops a soft luster characteristic of light-colored Karatsu glazes.

The rapid fabrication at Karatsu included trimming pieces while the clay was still quite wet and dipping them in a glaze as soon as they could be handled. The untrimmed upper portion of a piece dries more quickly than the lower portion and consequently absorbs moisture from the glaze more rapidly than the wetter, trimmed area does. Also, unrefined clay trimmed when wet (and left unsmoothed) will have a "grainier" surface than clay trimmed in a dry state. Many Karatsu teabowls display this "graininess" on their lower part, which was wet when trimmed. This difference between the upper and lower sections of the teabowl affects the final appearance of the glaze. The mature glaze on the smooth, drier upper surface contrasts with that on the unsmoothed, trimmed lower area where the wetter clay and exposed grains of sand interact with the glaze during firing, causing it to "crawl"—to form small puddles or beads. The glaze on the upper section, in contrast, is smooth. These different glaze textures are often found on Old Karatsu pieces, regardless of style or shape. Invariably, the difference in the glaze occurs between the trimmed and untrimmed sections. On this teabowl, the smooth, crackled glaze of the upper part contrasts and harmonizes with the beaded crawling below—an effect never found on Seto or Chinese *temmoku* wares.

One of the best-known, most frequently published, Karatsu pieces is the tea jar in Plate 41, which shows well the characteristics and charm of Karatsu. This wheel-thrown piece, rounded and full in shape, is gracefully poised on a shallow, trimmed foot. The milky translucent glaze, finely crackled, ends just above the foot, exposing the reddish-brown, grainy clay. On each side it is decorated with a spreading, rather spiky underglaze painting of a persimmon tree. The potter used his finger dipped in iron oxide pigment to dot on fruit, in clusters of three, on the leafless branches. For Karatsu, the shape is fairly symmetrical. Above the center, the form ripples slightly up to the shoulder. The inner lip has a narrow flange, touched with underglaze iron, for a lid. Three small ears have clusters of squashed balls of clay, three below and two at the top, painted in iron oxide and harmonizing with the fruit clusters. It is a carefully made piece, thin-walled and lightweight. There is something elemental about this rounded vessel, like an air-filled balloon of clay upon which a fruiting tree appears. A strange commingling of ideas is suggested. The clay and full-blown shape evoke earth and air. The tree, spreading with crisp abruptness, devoid of foliage yet covered with fruit, suggests life, struggle, and fruitfulness. Against a white background the painted design would be too violent, but as it moves across the subdued gray of the thinly glazed clay, the spiky branches take on a staccato, rhythmic movement. Together with these images mingles a sense of elegance and refinement, implied by the carefully made ears and neck. It is the understatement of Karatsu that harmonizes the divergent moods.

If there is a secret to the charm that Karatsu has had for Momoyama period tea devotees, Edo period collectors and connoisseurs, and contemporary ceramic enthusiasts alike, it must be this very fusion of diverse elements held together in a seemingly natural way. Karatsu is a ware that can be both used and regarded as a treasure. Unpretentious and unimpressive at first glance, it has a technical harmony and visual diversity that is increasingly delightful with each encounter. Forthright in its materials and techniques, it still has an element of mystery. It cannot be completely exhausted in the way a more perfect piece can be. Nor can it be analyzed completely.

In addition to items preserved as tea ceramics and *zakki* converted for tea usage, the corpus of Old Karatsu includes excavated pieces (*hori no te*, *horidashi*) unearthed during the eighteenth century, when tea enthusiasm for Karatsu was intense. Karatsu's history, preservation, and earliest documentation are all linked to the world of tea.

The focus of a tea ceremony is on its ceramics—their harmonious selection and arrangement, individual character, and history. They are scrutinized and admired in detail, are the subject of conversation and a source of visual enjoyment. Other than its intrinsic worth, the value of a piece depends on its having been in noted collections, having been seen, used, and admired by famous connoisseurs. A tea utensil's history enhances its worth. Writings in praise of a piece are preserved, such testimonials forming part of its documents. Like all precious Japanese art, cherished tea utensils are stored in paulownia (*kiri*) wood boxes, whose lids may have dated signatures and inscriptions. Valued tea caddies have one or more brocade bags, stored over forms duplicating the caddy's shape (Plate 2). The often very precious and antique brocades act as a counterpoint to and interact with the generally somber tea caddy in subtle ways. All these increase the value of the object.

No stoneware has been valued so highly for so long a time as the tea ceremony ceramics of Japan. Among them, Karatsu has maintained a favored status from the time of its early use by tea men such as Hideyoshi and his tea masters in the last decade of the sixteenth century up to the present day.

"Hagi first, Raku second, Karatsu third," is a well-known tea circle aphorism ranking tea ceramics. The first two choices may vary—"Raku first, Hagi second," or "Ido first, Hagi second"—but Karatsu remains a constant third.

By the mid-seventeenth century renowned old tea utensils were listed in the *Ganka meibutsuki* (1660). There were *ō-meibutsu*, antedating Karatsu, selected by tea masters Nōami and Sōami for shogun Ashikaga Yoshimasa during the Muromachi period; *meibutsu* singled out by Sen no Rikyū and his contemporaries for Oda Nobunaga and Toyotomi Hideyoshi in the Momoyama period; and *chūkō meibutsu* chosen by Kobori Enshū (1574–1647) in the early Edo period. Five Karatsu teabowls are included among the *meibutsu*—four small teabowls and another large *oku-Gōrai* type, thought at that time to be Korean.

Since 1950 the Japanese National Commission for Cultural Properties has formally designated culturally important items. Among the ceramics ranked as "National Treasure" and "Important Cultural Property" are three old Karatsu pieces—a teabowl (Plate 69), a water jar (Plate 127), and a large dish (Plates 153–54). In addition, the retired Karatsu potter, Tarōuemon Nakazato XII, later called Muan, was declared a "Living National Treasure" in 1975 (Plate 217).

Such admiration was hardly the response of the first Westerners to see Japanese tea ceramics. Many expressed their dismay at the value placed on objects of such inelegant appearance. The Portuguese Jesuit, Alessandro Valignano, in Japan in 1574–75, wrote:

> The cups in which they serve the brewed *chaa* are very small but made of a certain quality recognized by the Japanese. They are prized beyond belief. . . . We would not know what to do with one in Europe except to put it in a song bird's cage as a drinking vessel. . . . Among a thousand similar cups the Japanese immediately recognize the one with the master's touch—a gift I think no European could ever acquire.[1]

Captain F. Brinkley, writing for the *Japan Weekly Mail*, was more caustic:

> At Karatsu and Bizen they excelled in the manufacture of accidents. They

could make a pot look as though it were the work of some wayward genius, who, failing to achieve a drain-tile or a sewer-pipe, had stopped short at an ewer or a flower-vase. These utensils had a sylvan aspect. They would admirably have graced a bushman's banquet spread on the stump of a decayed tree. . . . The *chajin* was born into the world an unforetold and unexpected Messiah. . . . To him the shrivelled shapes and blotched surfaces suggested beauties imperceptible to the profane crowd.[2]

Rikyū seems to have anticipated reactions like these when he said, "There are some people who loathe the slightest flaw on the utensil they use. They do not know the spirit of the tea ceremony."[3]

The esteem accorded tea ceramics was not without a political dimension. Hideyoshi, unquestionably passionate in his devotion to tea, was also shrewd enough to play upon its popularity among his daimyo for his own benefit. By awarding choice tea ceramics instead of fiefs to his vassals, he kept his subjects from amassing sufficient territorial wealth to endanger his own power over them. At the same time, he was recognizing their loyal services and conquests with objects his own tea masters had endowed with status and value. This effective policy continued during the Edo period when the Tokugawa shoguns also used tea caddies and bowls politically, limiting the period of ownership to the lifetime of the recipient. Within this context, many daimyo instituted official kilns within their territories. The reserved wares produced here were for their own personal use or to be given as gifts. The Kyushu lords who brought back potters from their Korean campaigns might well have been motivated by a blend of tea, politics, and economics.

During the eighteenth century, the status of Karatsu fluctuated, as did the popularity of the tea ceremony itself. Early in the century, Karatsu was extremely popular; the demand was so high that it led to searching abandoned kiln sites for usable ceramics. After the Tempō period (1830), interest in the tea ceremony declined, and so did the popularity of Karatsu. Throughout the Meiji period (1868–1912), the fashionable trends ignored Japanese traditions for innovations from the Western world. The following Taishō era (1912–26) was marked by a revival of interest in tea. Once again, Karatsu gained status. Particularly popular were small teabowls and those called *ishihaze*. Since World War II, Karatsu has continued as an important tea ceramic. By now, certain famous old pieces are literally priceless, their value exceeding any monetary figure. Modern Karatsu potters cater to the tea trade. Collections of Karatsu are no longer the possession of a shogun and his daimyos, but are in the hands of the rulers of the contemporary world, the business tycoons who are the successors of the Edo merchants.[4]

Tea Ceremony Records

The great tea master Sen no Rikyū (1521–91) left no written treatise of his theories. His disciples compiled his teachings, which, together with his letters, were preserved in the seven-volume *Nanbō roku* ("The Record of Nanbō" a student of Rikyū). Since Rikyū spent time in Kyushu in the service of Hideyoshi and favored unpretentious Japanese ceramics, he must have known and used Karatsu pieces. Furuta Oribe (d. 1615) succeeded Rikyū as tea master to Hideyoshi just prior to that warlord's two Korean campaigns and made the earliest known written records of Karatsu ware.[5]

One discipline of the tea master was to keep a tea ceremony diary. He recorded the date, time of day, utensils used, and their placement, together with the decorations of the room (*tokonoma* scroll and its inscription, flowers and vase used), the guest of honor, and other guests. Oribe's earliest Karatsu entry is in the *Koshoku zensho*:

23rd day, 2nd month, Keichō 8 [1603], Karatsu *hana ire* [flower vase].[6]

Additional Karatsu entries appear in the same document:

10th day, 3rd month, Keichō 8, Karatsu *mizusashi* [water jar] with feet. . . .
Morning, 20th day, 4th month, Keichō 8, *chawan* [teabowl] Karatsu. . . .
25th day, 4th month, Keichō 8, Karatsu ware *suji mizusashi* [water jar with a striped texture]. . . .

There are other entries, mostly dated eighth to fifteenth year of Keichō. Karatsu was used frequently by Oribe during this time. The *Koshoku shōden Keichō otazunesho* also notes his use of Karatsu during the same period:

Morning of the 5th month, Keichō 8, *mizusashi* of Karatsu ware, placed at one side. . . .
Chawan Karatsu ware used at night party, 11th day of the 1st month, Keichō 12 at Chōzu-no-ma [a room at Oribe's residence]. . . .
Karatsu *mizusashi* used at a daytime party, 15th of the 1st month, Keichō 12. . . .
Whale meat and *shijimi* [small freshwater mussels] placed on a Karatsu dish, morning, 6th day of the 6th month, Keichō 13, served on a footed tray in Oribe's mansion . . . *mizu koboshi* [waste water pot], Karatsu ware.[7]

These first records of Karatsu begin ten years after Oribe left Hideyoshi's Nagoya Castle in Kyushu and continue over a period of seven to eight years.

An amusing episode about a handsome Karatsu piece is related in the *Koshoku densho*. On the 13th day of the 12th month of Keichō 9 [1604], Haruta Matazaemon (a samurai) invited Oribe, Saifuku-in (a monk), and the merchant Hisayoshi for a tea ceremony. Afterward they all went sightseeing around the town of Terabayashi. In one of the shops Oribe spotted a handsome Karatsu water jar. While he was asking Haruta if he wanted it, the merchant Hisayoshi claimed it and refused to give it up. They became embroiled in a violent quarrel, even exchanging blows over it. In the end, Hisayoshi won out. Later that evening the merchant hosted a tea ceremony for the others, gracing the occasion with his newly won Karatsu piece.[8]

Besides those of Oribe, other early seventeenth century documents mention Karatsu. Kamiya Sōtan, a Kyushu merchant and tea devotee from Fukuoka, speaks in his diary, *Sōtan nikki*, of a special tea ceremony he attended during one of his travels. In this instance the most honored tea utensil, the powdered tea caddy (*cha ire*), was Karatsu ware:

At the mansion of Sōbon, son of Suda Sōkyu, in Osaka. A midday tea ceremony, 9th day of the 10th month, Keichō 11 [1606]. Calligraphy by Mian Xianjie [a Southern Song dynasty artist; Japanese: Mittan Kanketsu] in the *tokonoma*; chrysanthemums in a basket on the hearth; an iron kettle; water container of Shigaraki ware; in front of it a Karatsu *cha ire* placed in its brocade bag; black Raku teabowl; the only guest, Kamiya Sōtan.[9]

SELECTED WRITINGS OF
TEA MASTERS AND CONNOISSEURS

Date	Title and Author	Subject
mid-15th century	Sōami *Kundaikan sōchōki*	Catalogue of Chinese utensils
c. 1590	Yamanoue Sōji *Chaki meibutsushū*	Names of writings, tea caddies, and tea jars
late 16th century	Nambō Sōkei *Nambō roku* (7 vols.)	Letters and teachings of Sen no Rikyū
late 16th century	Furuta Oribe *Koshoku densho*	Tea ceremony utensils and anecdotes
	Koshoku shōden Keichō Otazunesho	Report of a government investigation of Oribe
	Koshoku zensho	Tea ceremony records
1660	*Ganka meibutsuki*	Connoisseurship and description of famous utensils
mid-17th century	Kobori Enshū *Enshū gosen jūhappin*	Tea caddies; illustrated
1704–44	Matsudaira Norimura *Meibutsuki*	Connoisseurship of tea utensils
1789-97	Matsudaira Fumai *Kokon meibutsu ruiju* (18 vols.)	Connoisseurship and description of famous pieces
early 20th century	Takahashi Sōan *Taishō meiki kagami*	Catalogue of noted tea caddies and teabowls

This was an *ikkaku ittei*, a tea ceremony for a single guest and the host. In all likelihood the *cha ire* was a gift Sōtan, the Kyushu merchant, brought to his host in the Osaka-Kyoto area, and the private tea ceremony marked its initial use by the new owner.

Besides the diaries and tea ceremony records of masters and devotees, catalogues of famous pieces were compiled (table above). In keeping with the esoteric tea taste, wares were typed according to minute distinctions, sometimes based on only a few examples. The resulting confusion of types (see page 161) was compounded because pieces were also classified according to different writers' personal inclinations—all unquestioned because of the prestige and authority accorded to tea masters and connoisseurs. These identifications are still used, compounding the difficulty of understanding the Karatsu style as a whole. Diverse terminology is not unusual for tea ceremony wares from major kiln sites, but in the case of Karatsu it suggests a variety this relatively simple ware does not possess.

Household Wares

Unquestionably the vast quantity of household Karatsu has perished, as would be expected of any everyday ware. Nevertheless everyday pieces (*zakki*) are identifiable among tea ceramics. The mortar (*suribachi*) is still a standard Japanese kitchen utensil. Spouted bowls (*katakuchi*), intended for food preparation and service, are rather awkwardly used as teabowls (Plates 13, 81, 121–26). Numerous rice bowls (Plates 7, 8, 31, 32, 34) are used as teabowls, and food storage vessels function as water jars (*mizusashi*; Plates 16, 40, 82, 94, 128). In light of intense production at over a hundred kilns, Karatsu *zakki* must have numbered tens of millions. The classical style of Karatsu made today is exclusively tea ware, and for all practical purposes everyday Karatsu crockery has become extinct. The large early seventeenth century storage jar in Plate 19 is now used as a water jar for the tea ceremony. Its shape is a classic one, found among many utilitarian objects in Japan. The strong lip and accent at the shoulder are widespread features of unglazed storage jars made at various kilns active in the Muromachi period (1333–1573) before the development of Karatsu. The combination of both a dark and light glaze on a single object, the mark of Korean Karatsu, is an unique Karatsu feature. The dark glaze is glossy and fluid when mature. The opaque white glaze is the rice-straw ash glaze called *namako* (''sea cucumber'') by Karatsu potters, which, when highly fired, becomes streaked and runny. Where the two glazes intermingle, pale blue streaks may occur, especially when the light-colored glaze is (the most common case) on the upper portion of the vessel. The two glazes mature at slightly different temperatures, so that the lower-maturing brown glaze becomes shiny and runny, while the white, maturing at a higher temperature, stays stable and matte. A pleasing interplay of opposites results—dark and light, glossy and dull, fluid and stable.

Karatsu wares were all made on the wheel, either thrown or built up with coils, then paddled (the *tataki* technique; Plates 215–19). The *tataki* process (used for this sturdy jar) produces strong walls, thinner than the size and shape suggest, resulting in a heavy appearance and light weight. The foot is a simple untrimmed slab, and glazing stops short of the foot. Patches of clay are exposed where the glaze pulled away from the body of the jar, and the dark clay shows through the thin glaze at the shoulder ridge and lip. Simple, unobtrusive, subtle variations, apparent only on close examination, were especially valued by tea devotees, and just such qualities are present in this jar.

The small Korean Karatsu salt storage jar in Plate 18 was converted into a ceremonial tea caddy. Despite its diminutive size—less than three inches (8.6 cm.) high—this piece has the same simplicity and strength as the storage jar described above. The shape, as a matter of fact, is found in larger jars. It was thrown on the wheel, has a flat, untrimmed foot, and two slight ridges at the shoulder. The poured glazes are irregular, and in this case the dark glaze is the upper one. The surface is covered with subtle textures—the glaze at the lip is so thin that the coarse graininess of the clay emerges; the dark glaze forms slick pools at the base of the neck; the fine ridges at the shoulder interplay with the dense concentration of pinholes over much of the body glaze; and the rough clay just above the base is touched here and there with thin white glaze. The shape has been fashioned to appear soft and gentle. Wherever the contour shifts—at the lip, the flow of the neck to the shoulder, the merging of the body and foot—each harsh edge has been rounded. Attractive and pleasant in appearance, the small tea caddy is like a sculpture that invites touching and handling. Most Karatsu pots have this appeal. They are of a scale usable by people, and even the finest pieces are sufficiently unpretentious to encourage holding, their light weight and surface textures making the experience a pleasant one.

The tiny milky-glazed saké cup (*guinomi*) pictured in Plate 51 needs to be handled and scrutinized to be fully appreciated. The lip is painted with an iron underglaze. It was indented on one side while the clay was still moist, making the slightly flared lip bend inward without altering the full roundness of the poised body. A touch of elegance has been added to the mend on the lip, where, on gilded lacquer, an exquisite relief of a bee is accentuated with black lacquer eyes and body. The underglaze iron on the lip (known as *kawakujira*—"whale skin") blends into the milky glaze in an irregular, fuzzy line. At the upper ridge of the lip, the underglaze is a rich golden brown, which turns black-brown in the lower sections. The grainy clay texture shows through the thin, milky glaze. A deeply cut foot rim was fashioned with two or three quick gouges into the pliant clay.

There is a vital quality to this tiny cup. The graceful dent in the lip, variations in the underglaze iron, and fresh character of the foot rim all suggest that, rather than being a mended piece a few centuries old, it has just come from the potter's hands and might still be evolving into its final form.

Spontaneous details such as these make Karatsu ware appear to be still developing. Although complete, they are never finished. It is as though the potter barely brings the piece into existence and then releases it into a life of its own. Each person who sees the piece is free to delight in the evident display of how and of what it was made. A more refined, finished piece leaves little to the imagination. Karatsu shows its clay body, how it reacted to the potter's hands and tools, how it was glazed and decorated—all uncontrived and without retouching. If an aesthetic theory was to be developed for Karatsu, it would be one related to process, equally satisfying to contemporary and traditional connoisseurs. The strength, vulnerability, and approachability that made tea devotees recognize the *wabi* spirit in Karatsu is superseded today by the appeal of its forthright use of materials and undisguised display of its fabrication process. These marks can be seen even in the most self-conscious Karatsu pieces, the Korean Karatsu made specifically for the tea ceremony.

Korean Karatsu

Two vases (Plates 19, 97) show the farthest extent to which stylistic preoccupation affects Karatsu. Both are Korean Karatsu types, strong shapes decorated with dark brown and opaque white glaze. The vase in Plate 19 has a sleek appearance for Karatsu ware, with its satin-white upper section, paddled hexagonal shape, and tall lines. The undulating profile of the heavy lip breaks the severity of the body contour. A horizontal incised line on the base harmonizes with the horizontal ridges of the lip. The six sides of the body are freely incised with vertical lines. Touches of pale blue emerge where the heavy,

46 KARATSU

white glaze flows into the translucent brown. Two ears, protruding from the short neck, act as a transition between the firm body and rolling lip. This piece lacks some of the spontaneity seen in Plates 17 and 20. The gouging of the body, foot trimmings, vertical shape, and heavy lip all suggest an influence from the innovative Iga ware of Japan. Iga potters made fashionable tea ceremony vases and water containers for a brief time in the early seventeenth century, the probable date for this vase. The Karatsu piece is more symmetrical and smooth than Iga ware, yet the proportions, shape, lip, gouges, and foot—all unrelated to other types of Karatsu—echo details found on Iga pots.

The vase shown in Plate 97 is even more flamboyant. Here the dark and light glazes are dripped in irregular patterns over the body, much of the clay being left unglazed. All sleek lines and surfaces vanish, as the object becomes a blending of blatant textures and movement. The expressive momentum becomes completely externalized. There is a self-conscious, almost baroque thrust to the surface. The glazes trail across the vase in a heightened, almost frenzied rhythm. Such Korean Karatsu pieces stand alone in the entire repertoire of Karatsu. Just as an Iga influence can be detected in the previous vase, inspirations from Bizen ware appear here. A popular type of unglazed Bizen had brilliant, linear red patterns winding over the surface. These *hidasuki* (fire-flashed) marks came from wrapping green (unfired) pots in brine-soaked straw to induce streaked patterns during the firing. Although not totally imitative, it seems the Karatsu potters sought to capture these random patterns by trailing dark and light glazes over vases and jars. There are still other details relating to Bizen: the exposure of much raw clay; combed, dented, incised, and gouged surfaces; undulation and distortion of the body. Two coils twisted together form the ears, adding dynamism to the irregular shape. The random drippings of the light and dark glazes intensify the sense of an unstable, dramatic surface. The lip, coated with white glaze, has an unusually high incidence of blue, possibly deliberately induced, quite in keeping with the total planned effect of this vase.

Karatsu and Korea

Since these and other two-glazed pots are known as Korean Karatsu, just what is Korean about them? Certainly nothing related to their appearance, since no known Korean ceramic has the two glazes these do, nor are shapes like these two vases found among Korean wares. If resemblances cannot explain why such wares are called ''Korean Karatsu,'' how can it be explained?

Calling an entire type of Karatsu ware ''Korean'' is only one facet of the tradition, as long as the history of Karatsu itself, that links Karatsu with Korea. In early Edo period Japan, the influx of Korean potters into Japan at the close of Hideyoshi's 1590s Korean campaigns fostered the assumption that all Karatsu ware was Korean in style. It became customary to define Karatsu as a Korean-style stoneware. At a time when Japanese-made pots were still relatively recent arrivals in tea ceremony usage, an association with Korea, whose ceramics (together with Chinese) had a well-established association with tea in Japan, would certainly lend prestige to any piece. Thus, it was advantageous to associate Karatsu with the much-admired ceramics of Yi dynasty Korea. The tradition linking the Karatsu style to Korea endured in part because of the validation and prestige such a link ensured. The dominant position of ceramics in the tea ceremony assured the situation's continuation.

Indeed, large numbers of Korean potters working in Kyushu brought technical innovations and improvements with them. And certain shapes produced at Karatsu kilns, especially simple rice bowls, are quite like Korean shapes. In fact, a popular Karatsu teabowl called *oku-Gōrai*, a name associating it with the interior of Korea, was originally a large rice bowl. These were believed to be from Korea, until Karatsu kiln remains showed them to be Japanese. Repeatedly the relationship of Karatsu ware to Korean potters, techniques, and ceramics was disproportionately stressed.

"Korean Karatsu" was a name once applied to a wide variety of Old Karatsu, but it eventually came to be used to designate wares having two glazes, dark and light. This is one of those ironic cases in the development of nomenclature, which, ultimately, is not only inappropriate but markedly so. The group of Karatsu now called "Korean" has less resemblance to Korean ware than all other Karatsu. While there are similarities between some Plain and Underglaze Decorated Karatsu pots and those manufactured roughly at the same time in Korea (Plates 209–12), Korean pieces displaying combined dark and light glazes are unknown. In fact, the technique of dark and light glazes applied in the Karatsu manner could be a local innovation. Kyushu ceramics show many influences—from Japan, Southeast Asia, China, and Korea—at this period, but prototypes for the dark-and-light glazed type have yet to be found. While there is no reason a genuine innovation should not be credited to the Karatsu potters, it was customary for them to be inspired by other ceramics and to develop a style or technique that betrayed the source of inspiration.

Overemphasis on Karatsu being "Korean" persists to the present. Searches continue—potters and scholars looking for the kiln site and Korean pots that will validate calling Karatsu a Korean-type ware. The kilns of Korea—particularly those in the north at Hoeryŏng, the source of the opaque white rice-straw ash glaze—have not been subjected to the intensive, scholarly investigations conducted in Japan. It is possible but unlikely that the "missing link" will be discovered. Professor Mikami Tsugio of the Idemitsu Museum of Arts led Korean kiln excavations; the late Mr. Choi Sunu, former curator of Oriental ceramics and director of the National Museum of Korea, collected shards "resembling" Karatsu from Korean sites; the Karatsu potter Nakazato Tarō-uemon XII studied kiln sites and pots only to find that, unlike the Japanese Sue ware, which is easily confused with Korean Silla ceramics, Karatsu and Yi pieces remained distinguishable. Foot rims were glazed in Korea but not in Japan, and other technical variations betrayed the origin of each.

This writer also joined in the search. One small bowl in the Honolulu Academy of Arts with a handsome *namako* glaze and unglazed foot rim (Plate 83) was identified as Yi ware. Among hundreds of examined pieces of Korean ceramics, it stood alone as a concrete link with the Karatsu style. It looked more like Karatsu than Yi ware. When this was pointed out to Robert Griffing, then curator at the Academy, he searched into its history. The donor had given it to the museum as a Korean ceramic from Hoeryŏng. When asked to check his records, it was discovered that the Tokyo dealer who sold the piece had said it was "of a type often found of Korean manufacture in Hoeryŏng, but in this case is the Japanese, Kyushu-made variant, known as Chōsen [Korean] Karatsu."[10] Although the small bowl would hardly be classified as Korean Karatsu today, it is a fine example of Plain Karatsu.

The experience with the Honolulu bowl emphasizes how the desire to favor Korean ceramics blurred a clear view of Karatsu. There are undeniable influences in forming and firing, in knowledge of glaze and underglaze materials, but, valid as these influences are, they are limited. The disproportionate emphasis on Korean ceramics has hampered the clear understanding of Karatsu as a distinctly Japanese style of ceramics with identifiable characteristics.

Excavated ceramics from Handōgame and other Kishidake group kilns show that the Karatsu style existed before the coming of Korean potters at the end of Hideyoshi's campaigns. A kiln type, techniques, and glazes, all of which derive from Korea, were already employed to fabricate an innovative Japanese-style ceramic.

Karatsu differs from Korean ceramics in shape, decoration, and glazing. There are fourteen basic Karatsu shapes, all related to the function of the objects (see page 162). Their scale is quite limited, the largest dimension of the vast majority not exceeding one foot (30 cm). All are usable either as utilitarian ceramics or tea ceremony wares. In contrast, Yi wares have been classified into 144 shapes by Gompertz and include groups of ceremonial ware, table ware, stationery ware, toilet ware, furniture, implements, containers, building materials, etc.[11] Korean pieces also have a corresponding variety of sizes and include molded and slab-fashioned pieces, square and polygonal shapes, lidded pieces, and objects of complex shape with many sections luted together. Bulbous forms, such as jars and bottles, were made by Yi potters in two sections joined in the middle to form smooth, full forms (Plate 212), whereas Karatsu potters threw these shapes as a unit, seldom achieving the precision or fullness seen in Korean pieces. Thus, even for comparable shapes, Korean and Karatsu pieces differed because of the mode of manufacture.

There are similar shapes found among Karatsu and Korean teabowls. The Ido (Plate 209) and cylindrical teabowls (Plates 210–11) of Korea have shapes found in the Karatsu repertoire. Such Korean pieces were admired by tea devotees and were even ordered from Korea by the Japanese. When Karatsu potters adopted these shapes, it could have been a conscious production of popular shapes rather than a carry-over of Korean tradition.

Karatsu decoration differs from Yi ware in technique, subject matter, and style of painting. White slip was an important material for the Yi potter, especially in the Korean *punch'ŏng* ware. Slip was simply and roughly brushed on for decorative effect (*hakeme*), brushed into incised and impressed designs (*mishima* type inlay), and, as a dipped or brushed-on engobe, was carved into bold patterns and used as a base for sgraffito and painted underglaze iron designs. Only Karatsu *mishima* and *hakeme* relate to the Korean *punch'ŏng* wares; these Karatsu types are far less numerous and less skillfully made than *punch'ŏng* ceramics (Plates 31, 39, 104, 105). The Yi Koreans painted designs in underglaze iron, copper, and cobalt on porcelain and stoneware, often over a white slip ground. Although a white slip base is never used for Karatsu underglaze painting, it is among those Korean underglaze designs on slip that an occasional similarity to painted Karatsu exists (Plate 212). Most often the Korean motifs are painted around the entire piece, whereas Karatsu has isolated designs, usually two or three separate units. In general, similarities between Karatsu and Yi underglaze decorations exist, but are rare.

Even the subject matter of the designs differs. Korean designs painted on white slip include stylized borders with plants, flowers, birds, fish, clouds, and geometric motifs;

underglaze painted directly on the clay body includes subjects totally foreign to Karatsu: tigers, dragons in clouds, bamboo, trailing grape vines, lotus, and medallions. Yi wares exhibit a Korean, and ultimately Chinese, iconography; the simple or highly stylized grasses, reeds, flowers, trees, birds, and nonrepresentational decorations of Karatsu are without the weight of iconographic meaning.

The high-fired, feldspathic glazes Karatsu potters used had their origin in Korea. But their method of glazing, by dipping or pouring, leaving the foot rim and usually the lower, outer portion of the object unglazed, was Japanese.

When comparing the physical appearance of Karatsu and *punch'ŏng* ceramics, it is apparent that the similarity between them is minimal indeed. No Korean prototype for Korean Karatsu is known, and Karatsu shows little relationship to Yi ware in size, shape, decoration, or glazing. The indebtedness to Korea for techniques is unquestioned, but the final products of the potters in Japan are quite distinct.

Korean potters coming to Japan at the time of Hideyoshi's campaign began making ceramics according to a style already established in Hizen Province, as remains at Kishidake kilns such as Handōgame show. Korean fabrication techniques and glazes were already in use. The decorative innovations introduced at this late date seem isolated to the opaque white rice-straw ash glaze and slip inlay, and even these may already have been in use. Yi Korean ceramics show no promise of yielding a Karatsu prototype. So Karatsu must be regarded as a Japanese-style ceramic, with indebtedness to Korea for techniques and materials alone.

This not only removes the ambiguity about Karatsu's relationship to some unknown Yi type, but also dispels the problem of the absence of substantial quantities of *hakeme* or *mishima* Karatsu. If the Korean potters at Karatsu kilns worked in the Korean style, inlaid or brushed white slip pots should be abundant. The South Korean *punch'ŏng* potters were probably among those who came to Japan. Nevertheless, the potteries where Koreans settled in Kyushu did not produce wares in the *punch'ŏng* style, although they did experience a heightened production of the already established Karatsu style.

GENERAL CHARACTERISTICS

The examples examined here show the scope of Karatsu, from simple, household utensils to select tea wares, yet they only hint at the diversity of Karatsu ceramics. Within each of the types—Plain, Underglaze Decorated, and Korean, found at nearly every site, there is great variety, and each object is unique. Even within matching sets of saké cups or *mukōzuke* dishes, there are no two identical pieces. No wonder writers keep describing Karatsu as a "diverse" ceramic ware—a useless criterion for identifying and classifying objects. The common description of Karatsu as rustic and crude is no more helpful. Japanese domestic stoneware and pottery, as well as most tea ceremony wares, also fit this description.

Relating pieces to kiln sites would be an insurmountable problem; there were over one hundred kilns producing Karatsu, many remains being no longer identifiable. If Karatsu is indeed a valid ceramic style, there must be a set of characteristics that identify it.

A look at forming techniques is helpful. Wheel-throwing is the most common process. Karatsu was thrown on lightweight, rapidly turning kick wheels derived from Korea (Plate 223). The majority of thrown pieces have trimmed foot rims. An exception is the group of tiny powdered-tea caddies, one of the smallest groups in the Karatsu corpus, which ordinarily have flat bases (Plates 58–59). Even large water jars, when thrown on the wheel, are trimmed.

The other forming technique, paddling (*tataki*), involves forming a pot by coiling, smoothing the coils together with the fingers, then refining the body by using a wooden block (anvil) on the inside of the pot while paddling the clay on the outside (Plates 215–19). A pattern of overlapping arcs is left by the anvil on the inside of the pot (Plate 191). The wheel is used as a revolving platform during the paddling and is kicked for finishing pieces with thrown necks and lips (Plate 190). *Tataki* pieces tend to be large in scale, but the paddling process produces thin, dense walls; bases are flat, untrimmed, and lightweight.

The shapes of Karatsu ceramics are limited to a small group of simple, unadorned forms. The potters avoided assembling parts, making their pots in one piece. Certain vases and jars have small ears added; pouring vessels were given simple spouts. The only handles are on rare ewers. The majority of Karatsu pieces—teabowls, plates, jars, etc.—are simple shapes with no structural or decorative clay additions.

Karatsu is also distinguished as a high-fired, reduced stoneware, using feldspathic glazes. There are three basic glazes—an opaque white, a milky transparent, and a dark, iron glaze. The appearance of each glaze changes with materials and firing conditions. Karatsu clays are all sandy and highly refractory.

Whatever their intent or origin, Karatsu pieces in general display the following characteristics:

1. Clay dug from local sites, with minimal preparation before fabrication.

2. Three basic feldspathic glazes.

3. Wares glazed without bisque firing and completed in a single firing.

4. Kilns fired to stoneware temperatures using some reduction.

5. Pots formed on the wheel either by throwing or by coiling and paddling.

6. Trimmed foot rims on thrown wares.

7. Unglazed foot rims

8. Underglaze decoration brush painted or applied in iron oxide, consisting of simple or highly stylized plant, bird, animal, or nonrepresentational designs. Lip rims sometimes painted with or dipped in iron oxide.

9. Pieces made without added parts or with uncomplicated slab-fashioned spouts and simple handles.

10. A variety of pots fired at a single kiln: all three types of Karatsu; both household and tea ceremony wares; at Handōgame, the early nonfeldspathic glazed Pre-Karatsu and Karatsu; at later kilns, Karatsu and porcelain.

Too much skill is evident in Karatsu ware to call it rustic; too much freedom and spontaneity to call it sophisticated. Its style lies somewhere between these poles. The undisguised display of natural materials—the clay and its textures, glazes and designs applied rapidly and freely; crackled and pocked glazes; unglazed, trimmed foot rims and irregular shapes—makes Karatsu immediately appealing to the senses without demand or pretension. In the late sixteenth and early seventeenth century, Karatsu was unique. The style of Karatsu ceramics was the direct result of the potters' techniques and materials; closer examination of these will tell more about the wares and their makers' skills.

NOTES

1. Quoted in Jenyns 1971, pp. 125–126.

2. Quoted in Bowes 1890, p. 554.

3. Ueda 1967, p. 91.

4. There probably are about fifteen hundred Old Karatsu pieces extant. In addition, shards have become collectors' items. Businessmen from Kyushu amassed the two largest collections. The late Idemitsu Sazō established the Idemitsu Museum of Arts' collection in Tokyo, with some four hundred pieces and an extensive shard collection. It is fully catalogued and is published in Mizumachi's *Ko-Karatsu*, Vol. II. The partially published collection of the late Tanakamaru Zenpachi of Fukuoka has about three hundred pieces. It is divided between the Tanakamaru Foundation collection and a private family collection. Third in size is the Morse collection, Museum of Fine Arts, Boston. The 122 Karatsu pieces, acquired in the late nineteenth century by Edward S. Morse, are published in his *Catalogue of the Morse Collection of Japanese Pottery* (Cambridge: Riverside Press, 1901, reprinted by Tuttle in 1979). Some Karatsu is in Kyushu museums: The Arita Ceramic Museum, Karatsu Castle Museum, Kyushu Ceramic Museum in Arita, and Saga Culture Center, Saga city. Non-Japanese museums with Karatsu ware include the Freer Gallery of Art, Washington, D.C.; The British Museum and Victoria and Albert Museum, London; and Asian Art Museum of San Francisco. Other museum holdings, although small, may include one or two famous pieces (Seattle Art Museum; Baur Collection, Geneva). Pieces are scattered in private collections in Japan (70 percent of the Karatsu Castle Museum display belongs to the Nakazato family) and in the West (Gerry Collection, Long Island, N.Y.).

5. There are three documents by Oribe: *Koshoku zensho* (Koshoku is another name for Oribe), a set of tea ceremony records; *Koshoku shōden Keichō otazunesho*, a report of a government investigation of Oribe; and *Koshoku densho*, concerned with tea ceremony utensils and anecdotes.

6. Quoted in Satō 1963b, p. 71.

7. *Ibid.*, pp. 70–71.

8. *Ibid.*

9. *Ibid.*

10. Letter from Mr. Robert P. Griffing, Jr., Honolulu Academy of Arts, March 23, 1973.

11. Gompertz 1968, pp. 81–85, based on Asakawa Takumi's *Chōsen tōji meikō*.

1. Plain Karatsu tea caddy, rice-straw ash glaze. H. 4.9 cm. Idemitsu Museum of Arts.

2. Plain Karatsu tea caddy, name: Tama Tsushima (''Beautiful Islet''). H. 8.9 cm. Two brocade bags. Idemitsu Museum of Arts.

3. Plain Karatsu teabowl, *oku-Gōrai* shape, rice-straw ash glaze. H. 9.2 cm. Tanakamaru Collection.

4. Plain Karatsu teabowl, name: Haku-ō ("White Seagull"), rice-straw ash glaze with streaks of blue, attributed to Hobashira kiln. H. 12.2 cm. Tanakamaru Collection.

5. Plain Karatsu teabowl, *oku-Gōrai* shape, name: Aki no Yo ("Autumn Night"). H. 9.0 cm. Idemitsu Museum of Arts.

6. Plain Karatsu teabowl, *oku-Gōrai* shape, name: Sazare Ishi ("Pebble"). H. 8.1 cm. Idemitsu Museum of Arts.

7, 8. Plain Karatsu teabowl, traces of *nameko* blue in interior bottom glaze.
H. 8.2 cm. Idemitsu Museum of Arts.

9. Plain Karatsu teabowl, incised with bold diagonal crosshatched lines (*hori* Karatsu type). H. 9.6 cm. Private collection, Japan.

10. Plain Karatsu teabowl, heavily crackled glaze. D. 12.6 cm. Idemitsu Museum of Arts.

11. Plain Karatsu teabowl, shape and glaze called Seto Karatsu, attributed to Shiinomine kiln. H. 6.7 cm. Idemitsu Museum of Arts.

12. Plain Karatsu teabowl, black glaze under a crawling white glaze (*jakatsu*—snakeskin—effect), attributed to Shōkoya kiln. H. 7.7 cm. Idemitsu Museum of Arts.

13. Plain Karatsu spouted bowl, name: Hanare Goma ("Stray Horse"). H. 7.0 cm. Tanakamaru Collection.

14. Plain Karatsu water jar, dark iron glaze. H. 20.8 cm. without handle. Tanakamaru Collection.

15. Korean Karatsu vase, ''carp'' mouth; excavated from the Fujinkawachi kiln. H. 20.3 cm. Tanakamaru Collection.

16. Korean Karatsu water jar, opaque white glaze, lip dipped into dark iron glaze and marked with heavy drippings of white glaze. D. 20.1 cm. Private collection, Japan.

17. Korean Karatsu water jar, name: Robaku ("Waterfall on Mt. Lu"), opaque white glaze on upper section forms a run over dark iron glaze on body, attributed to Fujinkawachi kiln. H. 17.1 cm. Fujita Art Museum.

18. Korean Karatsu tea caddy, name: Roku-ji ("Temple at the Foot of the Mountain"). H. 8.6 cm. Idemitsu Museum of Arts.

19. Korean Karatsu vase, glossy finely crackled white glaze over a speckled dark iron glaze, two ears and two holes for hanging drilled in the lip rim. H. 23.6 cm. Idemitsu Museum of Arts.

20. Korean Karatsu water jar, blue streaks occur where the rice-straw ash glaze runs into the dark glaze. H. 20.2 cm. Idemitsu Museum of Arts.

21. Korean Karatsu saké bottle, thick iron glaze on neck, thin rice-straw ash glaze on body, decoration on body sometimes identified as a peony. H. 20.2 cm. Tanakamaru Collection.

22. Korean Karatsu bottle, a household pot used in the tea ceremony as a vase. H. 20.5 cm. Idemitsu Museum of Arts.

23. Korean Karatsu water jar, dark iron glaze and white rice-straw ash glaze trailing on body. H. 19.0 cm. Tanakamaru Collection.

24. Korean Karatsu water jar, concave body with two small lugs, dark and light glazes trailed on body, attributed to Fujinkawachi kiln. H. 20.3 cm. Idemitsu Museum of Arts.

26. Korean Karatsu ewer, blue streaking formed by white rice-straw ash glaze running over most of the vessel. H. 20.6 cm. Idemitsu Museum of Arts.

25. Korean Karatsu ewer, white rice-straw ash glaze shows slight traces of blue where it feathers into the thin, translucent iron glaze, attributed to Fujinkawachi kiln. H. 23.8 cm. Idemitsu Museum of Arts.

27. Korean Karatsu ewer, twisted handle, dark iron glaze runs into the lower white glaze. H. 15.8 cm. Freer Gallery of Art.

28. Underglaze Decorated Karatsu tea caddy, underglaze iron decoration of wild grape spray, attributed to Dōzono or Matsuura Kame-yanotani kiln. H. 8.8 cm.

29. Underglaze Decorated Karatsu teabowl, name: Ayame ("Iris"), provenance unclear. H. 9.2 cm. Tanakamaru Collection.

30. Cylindrical Underglaze Decorated Karatsu teabowl, horizontal combing on body, freely painted design of a shrine. H. 8.4 cm. Idemi-tsu Museum of Arts.

67

31. Underglaze Decorated Karatsu teabowl, incised and impressed patterns filled with white slip (*mishima* technique), high foot rim. H. 7.5 cm.

32. Underglaze Decorated Karatsu teabowl, name: Suehiro ("Folding Fan"), *kawakujira* style lip. H. 9.1 cm. Tanakamaru Collection.

33. Underglaze Decorated Karatsu teabowl, *tokusa* (horsetail) design. H. 9.0 cm. Tanaka-maru Collection.

34. Underglaze Decorated Karatsu teabowl, *kawakujira* style lip, spiral designs. H. 7.8 cm. Idemitsu Museum of Arts.

35. Underglaze Decorated Karatsu teabowl, *kawakujira* style lip, two designs of cross within circle (opposite sides of bowl). H. 9.0 cm. Idemitsu Museum of Arts.

36. Underglaze Decorated Karatsu water jar, flowers and bamboo fence decoration on facing side, linked curling vines on opposite side. H. 16.1 cm., D. body 23.0 cm. Idemitsu Museum of Arts.

37. Underglaze Decorated Karatsu water jar, name: Tsu no Kuni ("Harbor Kingdom"), reed design in iron oxide; attributed to a kiln of the Kishidake group. H. 15.8 cm., D. body 19.3 cm. Idemitsu Museum of Arts.

38. Underglaze Decorated Karatsu water jar. H. 13.0 cm., D. body 18.3 cm. Idemitsu Museum of Arts.

39. Underglaze Decorated Karatsu water jar, incised and impressed patterns filled with white slip (*mishima* technique), two lugs at the neck. H. 17.5 cm. Tanakamaru Collection.

40. Underglaze Decorated Karatsu water jar, roundels made by dipping jar into iron oxide. H. 17.1 cm., D. body 18.9 cm.

41. Underglaze Decorated Karatsu tea jar, three ears, persimmon tree decoration, fruit painted by fingertips dipped in iron oxide. H. 17.1 cm., D. body 17.5 cm. Idemitsu Museum of Arts.

42. Underglaze Decorated Karatsu *mukō-zuke* dishes, raised corners accentuated by the underglaze iron painting, attributed to Dōzono or Kameyanotani kiln. H. 7.1 cm.

43. Takeo style plate, brushed white slip, pine design in underglaze iron and copper glaze, attributed to Kawagokamanotani kiln. D. 28.4 cm.

44. Underglaze Decorated Karatsu food dish, central floral motif, attributed to Kameyanotani kiln. D. 7.5 cm.

45. Underglaze Decorated Karatsu dish, pine design, attributed to Dōzono kiln. D. 18.0 cm. Tanakamaru Collection.

46. Underglaze Decorated Karatsu platter, pine design. D. 36.3 cm.
Idemitsu Museum of Arts.

47. Underglaze Decorated Karatsu *mukō-zuke* dish, design of pair of crossed arrows and the Japanese character for ''bow'' (弓). D. 15.6 cm.

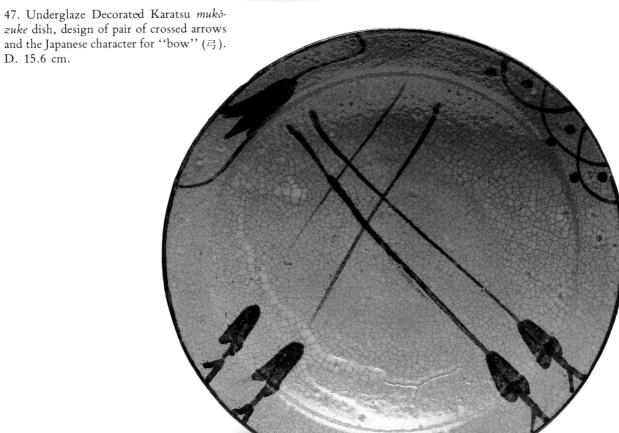

48. Underglaze Decorated Karatsu plate, paired crossed arrows principal motif, finely crackled glaze, attributed to Kameyanotani kiln. D. 18.5 cm. Collections Baur, Geneva.

49. Underglaze Decorated Karatsu *mukōzuke* dish, crackled
glaze, underglaze iron decoration. D. 12.3 cm.

50. Underglaze Decorated Karatsu large bowl, two handles,
design of birds flying over rushes (shown), a hilly landscape
(opposite side), and flowering plants (interior), spotted decoration on rim. D. 26.5 cm. Mr. Sakamoto Gorō.

51. Underglaze Decorated Karatsu saké cup, *kawakujira* style lip (mended rim). H. 5.1 cm. Idemitsu Museum of Arts.

52. Underglaze Decorated Karatsu hemispherical water dripper, design of hilly landscape, attributed to Takeo Uchida kiln. H. 3.1 cm., D. 6.2 cm. Idemitsu Museum of Arts.

53. Unglazed Karatsu bottle, called Bizen Karatsu. H. 24.0 cm.

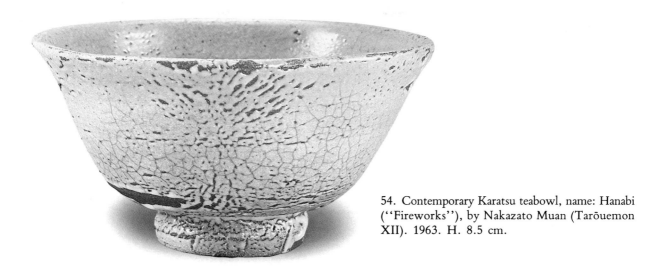

54. Contemporary Karatsu teabowl, name: Hanabi ("Fireworks"), by Nakazato Muan (Tarōuemon XII). 1963. H. 8.5 cm.

55. Contemporary Karatsu water jar, incised and impressed designs filled with white slip (*mishima* technique), by Nakazato Tarōuemon XIII. H. 18.4 cm.

56. Jar by Nakazato Shigetoshi, 1975, unglazed, burnished surface with white clay rubbed into the body. H. 32 cm.

57. Jar by Nakazato Takashi; unglazed Tane-gashima style, all colors resulting from oxides within the clay or kiln atmosphere. 1970. H. 20.8 cm. Photograph by Jim Eckberg.

58, 59. Plain Karatsu tea caddy, name: Tama Tsushima ("Beautiful Islet"). H. 8.9 cm. Idemitsu Museum of Arts. (See Plate 2)

60. Plain Karatsu tea caddy, name: Omoigawa
("River of the Heart"), deep amber glaze on
upper portion. H. 8.6 cm. Hatakeyama
Collection.

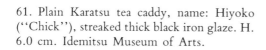

61. Plain Karatsu tea caddy, name: Hiyoko
("Chick"), streaked thick black iron glaze. H.
6.0 cm. Idemitsu Museum of Arts.

62. Plain Karatsu tea caddy, name: Kaku-daishi
(" Priest Kaku"), runny iron glaze. H. 8.0 cm.
Idemitsu Museum of Arts.

63. Plain Karatsu tea caddy, brown iron and white rice-straw ash glaze intermingled during firing. H. 11.5 cm. Gemeentelijk Museum het Princessehof, Leeuwarden.

64. Underglaze Decorated Karatsu tea caddy, evenly crackled light glaze and spots of iron underglaze. H. 4.0 cm., D. body 7.8 cm. Freer Gallery of Art, Washington, D. C.

65. Plain Karatsu teabowl, *oku-Gōrai* shape, crackled light glaze with irregular spotting, attributed to Handōgame kiln. H. 9.9 cm. Idemitsu Museum of Arts.

66. Plain Karatsu teabowl, name: Yamazato ("Mountain Village"), finely crackled opaque white glaze with irregular spotting, attributed to Hobashira kiln. H. 8.5 cm. Idemitsu Museum of Arts.

67. Plain Karatsu teabowl, *oku-Gōrai* shape, opaque light glaze with numerous pinholes, stain on lip is attributed to tea. H. 8.2 cm. Idemitsu Museum of Arts.

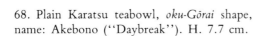

68. Plain Karatsu teabowl, *oku-Gōrai* shape, name: Akebono ("Daybreak"). H. 7.7 cm.

69. Plain Karatsu teabowl of the type known as *Zekan* Karatsu, name: Sambō ("Three Jewels"); designated National Treasure. D. mouth 15.5 cm., D. foot 6.6 cm. Kubōsō Memorial Art Museum.

70. Plain Karatsu teabowl, name: Sanshō ("Mountain Happiness"), heavily crackled opaque white glaze of almost pure feldspar, attributed to Handō-game kiln. H. 9.6 cm. Idemitsu Museum of Arts.

71. Plain Karatsu teabowl, name: Haku-un (''White Cloud''), heavy opaque white glaze with crawling on the lower portion. H. 6.8 cm. Idemitsu Museum of Arts.

72. Plain Karatsu teabowl, *oku-Gōrai* shape, thin, opaque light glaze with fine crackle and scattered pinholes. H. 7.9 cm. Idemitsu Museum of Arts.

73. Plain Karatsu teabowl, attributed to Matsuura Dōzono kiln. H. 8.2 cm. Idemitsu Museum of Arts.

74. Plain Karatsu teabowl, *oku-Gōrai* shape, glaze drippings formed at time of glazing. H. 8.7 cm. Idemitsu Museum of Arts.

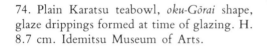

75, 76. Plain Karatsu shallow teabowl, name: Kiri-Hitoha ("Paulownia Leaf"). H. 4.0 cm. Idemitsu Museum of Arts.

77. Plain Karatsu shallow teabowl, attributed to Kojirōkaja kiln. H. 4.6 cm. Idemitsu Museum of Arts.

78. Plain Karatsu teabowl, textured black iron glaze. H. 7.3 cm.

79. Plain Karatsu teabowl, rolled lip and deformed (*kutsu*) shape, black glaze under a crawling white glaze (*jakatsu*—snakeskin—effect); attributed to Shōkoya kiln. H. 8.0 cm. Idemitsu Museum of Arts.

80. Plain Karatsu teabowl, rounded lip indented at
three points, *jakatsu* effect (see preceding). H. 8.4 cm.
Idemitsu Museum of Arts.

81. Large Plain Karatsu spouted bowl, squat deformed
(*kutsu*) shape. D. 25.5 cm. Idemitsu Museum of Arts.

82. Plain Karatsu water jar and ceramic lid, soft rice-straw ash glaze. H. 11.4 cm., D. body 16.7 cm. Idemitsu Museum of Arts.

83. Plain Karatsu jar, "abacus bead" shape, feathery lines of blue just below lip. D. 14.0 cm. Honolulu Academy of Arts.

84. Plain Karatsu water container, attributed to Handōgame kiln. H. 15.9 cm. Idemitsu Museum of Arts.

85. Plain Karatsu water jar with two small loop handles, runny dark iron glaze; attributed to Shōkoya kiln. H. 18.2 cm., D. body 19.1 cm. Idemitsu Museum of Arts.

86. Plain Karatsu water jar with two handles and three added feet, mottled reduced iron glaze called *ao* Karatsu. H. 19.7 cm., D. body 22.6 cm. Idemitsu Museum of Arts.

87. Lidded Plain Karatsu water jar with two handles and three small feet. H. 19.1 cm., D. body 18.6 cm.

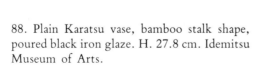

88. Plain Karatsu vase, bamboo stalk shape, poured black iron glaze. H. 27.8 cm. Idemitsu Museum of Arts.

89. Small Plain Karatsu bottle used as a shaker for sweets (*furidashi*) in tea ceremonies. H. 11.2 cm. Idemitsu Museum of Arts.

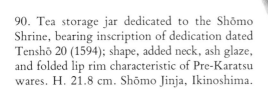

90. Tea storage jar dedicated to the Shōmo Shrine, bearing inscription of dedication dated Tenshō 20 (1594); shape, added neck, ash glaze, and folded lip rim characteristic of Pre-Karatsu wares. H. 21.8 cm. Shōmo Jinja, Ikinoshima.

91. Plain Karatsu pedestalled dish, finely crackled opaque white
glaze speckled with pinholes and patches of crawling. H. 8.4 cm.,
D. 18.7 cm. Idemitsu Museum of Arts.

92. Plain Karatsu saké cup, rice-straw ash glaze,
scattered pinholes. H. 5.0 cm., D. 5.8 cm.
Idemitsu Museum of Arts.

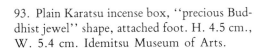

93. Plain Karatsu incense box, "precious Buddhist jewel" shape, attached foot. H. 4.5 cm.,
W. 5.4 cm. Idemitsu Museum of Arts.

94. Korean Karatsu water jar, streaks of opaque
white glaze cascading over translucent brown iron
glaze. H. 16.0 cm., D. body 15.7 cm. Idemitsu
Museum of Arts.

95. Korean Karatsu vase, bulbous ridged lip and
two loop handles at narrow neck; attributed to
Fujinkawachi kiln. H. 24.8 cm. Idemitsu Museum
of Arts.

96. Korean Karatsu vase, name: Saru ("Monkey"), opaque white rice-straw ash glaze showing strong traces of blue, dark iron glaze trailed on body. H. 21.7 cm. Idemitsu Museum of Arts.

97. Korean Karatsu vase, undulating body contour and two twisted handles, lip dipped in white rice-straw ash glaze over iron glaze, white and iron glaze tailed on body. H. 21.7 cm. Idemitsu Museum of Arts.

98. Korean Karatsu vase with two loop handles, flared, irregular lip rim, heavy dark iron glaze with matte surface, white rice-straw ash glaze trailed on body. H. 22.1 cm. Freer Gallery of Art, Washington, D. C.

99. Korean Karatsu vase with two handles, trailings of iron and rice-straw ash glaze on body; attributed to Fujinkawachi kiln. H. 18.5 cm. Idemitsu Museum of Arts.

100. Small Korean Karatsu bottle, name: Yomogigashima ("Island of Sagebrush"), used as a shaker for sweets (*furidashi*) in the tea ceremony; attributed to Fujinkawachi kiln. H. 21.3 cm. Idemitsu Museum of Arts.

101. Korean Karatsu bottle, dipped in white rice-straw ash glaze to shoulder ridge, body dipped in black iron glaze, wiped off on bottom section. H. 22.2 cm. Idemitsu Museum of Arts.

102. Underglaze Decorated Karatsu tea caddy, opaque rice-straw ash glaze crawling in large patches. D. 6.0 cm. Idemitsu Museum of Arts.

103. Underglaze Decorated Karatsu tea caddy, name: Yakiyama (''Burning Mountain''), metallic patches where iron underglaze painting has bled into the white glaze, dense crackle in opaque body glaze. H. 10.3 cm. Idemitsu Museum of Arts.

104. Underglaze Decorated Karatsu shallow teabowl, stamped and incised designs filled with white slip (*mishima* technique), stenciled central medallion of white slip. H. 5.0 cm., D. 18.5 cm.

105. Underglaze Decorated Karatsu shallow teabowl, stamped and combed designs filled with white slip (*mishima* technique), milky glaze. D. 15.24 cm. Museum of Fine Arts, Boston; Morse Collection.

106. Underglaze Decorated Karatsu teabowl, simple iron underglaze decoration under a translucent rice-straw ash glaze. D. mouth 13.4 cm. Tanakamaru Collection.

107. Underglaze Decorated Karatsu teabowl, spiral design; attributed to Matsuura Dōzono kiln. H. 8.3 cm.

108, 109. Underglaze Decorated Karatsu teabowl, straight sides and central bulge, double foot rim similar to that found on *hori* Karatsu teabowls, dark iron glaze in interior, opaque white rice-straw ash glaze on exterior. H. 9.7 cm., D. foot rim 7.6 cm. Idemitsu Museum of Arts.

110. Cylindrical Underglaze Decorated Karatsu teabowl, *kawakujira* style (iron-dipped) lip, fisherman motif. H. 9.5 cm. Idemitsu Museum of Arts.

111. Underglaze Decorated Karatsu teabowl, random decoration of iron underglaze beneath an evenly crackled rice-straw ash glaze. H. 7.2 cm. Idemitsu Museum of Arts.

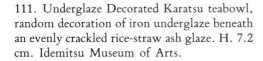

112. *Hori* (carved) Karatsu teabowl with underglaze decoration, opaque white rice-straw ash glaze with crawling on the entire exterior. D. 12.3 cm.

113. Underglaze Decorated Karatsu teabowl, *temmoku* shape, playful underglaze iron painting. H. 8.5 cm. Idemitsu Museum of Arts.

114, 115. Underglaze Decorated Karatsu teabowl, *temmoku* shape, "bamboo node" foot rim, painted design of paired arrows and an arrow striking the bull's eye, a thick opaque rice-straw ash glaze. H. 6.2 cm. Idemitsu Museum of Arts.

116–118. Underglaze Decorated Karatsu tea-bowl, heavy lip and squat deformed (*kutsu*) shape, underglaze iron wash on exterior and drippings on interior, white rice-straw ash glaze, double foot rim. D. 11.6 cm. Idemitsu Museum of Arts.

119. Underglaze Decorated Karatsu teabowl, heavy folded lip, squat irregular (*kutsu*) shape. D. 15.6 cm. Idemitsu Museum of Arts.

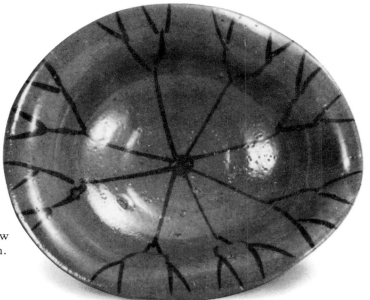

120. Underglaze Decorated Karatsu shallow teabowl, lotus leaf design. D. mouth 16.2 cm.

121. Underglaze Decorated Karatsu spouted bowl, radiating lines in underglaze iron below lip, characteristic of Old Karatsu from Michinayatani kiln. H. 13.1 cm. Idemitsu Museum of Arts.

122, 123. Underglaze Decorated Karatsu spouted bowl, "C" motif on each side, rice-straw ash glaze alternating between crackling and crawling. H. 10.7 cm. Idemitsu Museum of Arts.

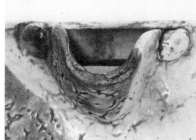

124–126. Underglaze Decorated Karatsu spouted bowl, sides and tip of spout dipped into iron oxide, pronounced crawling of rice-straw ash glaze over areas of underglaze iron and trimmed area above foot. Details reveal spout-making technique: a clay slab is bent over a finger and its edges joined onto the vessel at the lip. H. 9.9 cm. Idemitsu Museum of Arts.

127. Underglaze Decorated Karatsu water jar, six splashes of underglaze iron at shoulder and touches of underglaze iron on lip; registered Important Cultural Property. H. 17.3 cm., D. body 12.9 cm. Private collection, Japan.

128. Underglaze Decorated Karatsu water jar, underglaze painted decoration of reeds, milky glaze speckled by iron content of clay. H. 17.0 cm. Asian Art Museum of San Francisco, The Avery Brundage Collection.

129. Underglaze Decorated Karatsu water jar, top view of Plate 36, showing the curling vines motif and gilt lacquer lip mends decorated with wave patterns. D. mouth 16.6 cm. Idemitsu Museum of Arts.

130. Underglaze Decorated Karatsu water jar, "abacus bead" shape, underglaze iron painting of reeds, crawling of glaze in trimmed area above foot. H. 14.7 cm., D. body 22.1 cm. Idemitsu Museum of Arts.

131. Underglaze Decorated Karatsu water jar, thick rice-straw ash glaze, underglaze iron on lip (*kawakujira* style) running in streaks over upper body, attributed to Hobashira kiln. H. 13.8 cm. Idemitsu Museum of Arts.

132. Underglaze Decorated Karatsu water jar, modified "abacus bead" shape, crisp underglaze iron painting on body and shoulder softened by milky glaze. H. 15.7 cm., D. body 20.2 cm. Idemitsu Museum of Arts.

133. Underglaze Decorated Karatsu flower vase, underglaze iron painting of rushes and two bands on neck, matte rice-straw ash glaze; attributed to Uchida kiln group. H. 41 cm. Nezu Art Museum.

134. Takeo style bottle, brushed white slip, underglaze iron painting of a pine tree with accents of green copper glaze covered with clear glaze. H. 30.1 cm. Saga Prefectural Museum.

135, 136. Underglaze Decorated Karatsu vase with two loop handles near foot and two holes drilled in the sides for hanging, underglaze iron painting ignores shifts in contour of the body, undeciphered carved characters on fold inside lip (detail); attributed to Fujinkawachi kiln. H. 24.0 cm. Idemitsu Museum of Arts.

137. Underglaze Decorated Karatsu *mukōzuke* dish, shape and design influenced by Shino ware of Mino, thick matte rice-straw ash glaze. Tanakamaru Collection.

138. Underglaze Decorated Karatsu *mukōzuke* dishes, flared lips shaped into
outline of Japanese folding fan, *kawakujira* style (underglaze iron) lips and
diagonal striped border below, trailing grapevine design; painting similar to
shards found at Taku Kōraidani. H. 8.2 cm. Idemitsu Museum of Arts.

139. Underglaze Decorated Karatsu *mukōzuke* dishes with flared lips pinched
into a square. H. 7.5 cm. Idemitsu Museum of Arts.

140. Underglaze Decorated Karatsu lobed *mukōzuke* dishes, *kawakujira style* (underglaze iron) lips and trailing vine designs. H. 8.0 cm. Idemitsu Museum of Arts.

141. Underglaze Decorated Karatsu fluted *mukōzuke* dish, underglaze iron decoration forming scallops linking flutes, attributed to Takeo Oyamaji kiln. H. 9.2 cm. Idemitsu Museum of Arts.

142. Underglaze Decorated Karatsu tall and square *mukōzuke* dish, each side painted with a flowering plant, thick rice-straw ash glaze. H. 11.4 cm. Dr. and Mrs. Roger Gerry Collection. Photograph by Eric Pollitzer.

143. Underglaze Decorated Karatsu tall *mukōzuke* dish, *kawakujira* style (underglaze iron) lip, heavy pattern of pinholes in glaze. H. 9.9 cm. Freer Gallery of Art, Washington, D. C.

144. Underglaze Decorated Karatsu tall square *mukōzuke* dish, *kawakujira* style (underglaze iron) lip, underglaze iron painting of wild grass, attributed to Dōzono kiln. H. 10.4 cm. Idemitsu Museum of Arts.

145, 146. Underglaze Decorated Karatsu beaker used as a *mukōzuke* dish, *kawakujira* style, (underglaze iron) lip, motif of fisherman on one side, three pines on the other. Tanakamaru Collection.

147. Underglaze Decorated Karatsu deep *mukōzuke* dish, design of circle, crosses, and lines, opaque glaze. H. 9.3 cm. Idemitsu Museum of Arts.

148. Takeo style platter, combed patterns filled with white slip (*mishima* technique), painted underglaze iron vine tendrils, shiny amber and runny copper green glazes. D. 41.9 cm. Museum of Fine Arts, Boston; Morse Collection.

149. Takeo style large dish, combed white slip, transparent glaze with trailed copper green glaze; unearthed at Ayutthaya, Thailand. H. 10.0 cm., D. 28.8 cm.

150. Takeo style large bowl, combed and tooled patterns in white slip, scattered areas at rim and center not covered by slip, transparent glaze. H. 16.0 cm., D. 52.2 cm. Idemitsu Museum of Arts.

151. Underglaze Decorated Karatsu plate, slip-painted stencil patterns, brushmarked (*hakeme*) background, dark lacquer mends. H. 3.7 cm., D. 14.8 cm.

152. Underglaze Decorated Karatsu dish, stamped designs filled with white slip (*mishima* technique), transparent glaze over dark brown clay. H. 6.0 cm., D. 25.4 cm. Idemitsu Museum of Arts.

153, 154. Underglaze Decorated Karatsu large dish with fluted rim, underglaze iron painting of pine tree, painted border band with two clusters of tapered lines, milky translucent glaze; attributed to Kameyanotani kiln; registered Important Cultural Property. H. 13.5 cm., D. 43.5 cm. Umezawa Memorial Museum.

155. Underglaze Decorated Karatsu shallow dish, underglaze iron painting of millet stalk flanked by paired diagonal lines, slight crawling of glaze with scattered pinholes. D. 33.1 cm. Seattle Art Museum, Eugene Fuller Memorial Collection.

156, 157. Underglaze Decorated Karatsu large dish, underglaze iron painting of pine tree, finely crackled glaze with scattered pinholes, glaze starting to crawl in center. H. 8.1 cm., D. 36.3 cm. Idemitsu Museum of Arts. (See Plate 45)

158. Underglaze Decorated Karatsu dish, painted underglaze iron rim and plant design. H. 4.1 cm., D. 18.0 cm. Idemitsu Museum of Arts.

159. Underglaze Decorated Karatsu dish, painted underglaze iron rim and plant design. H. 4.3 cm., D. 18.5 cm. Idemitsu Museum of Arts.

160. Underglaze Decorated Karatsu large dish; painted underglaze iron plant design. H. 11.7 cm., D. 37.2 cm. Idemitsu Museum of Arts.

161. Underglaze Decorated Karatsu dish, metallic sheen in areas of heaviest underglaze iron; design influenced by Mino ceramics. H. 5.4 cm., D. 17.5 cm. Idemitsu Museum of Arts.

162. Underglaze Decorated Karatsu square dish with cut rim, underglaze iron painting of flowering stems, stylized horsetails at corners, broad strokes at edge; shape and decoration influenced by Oribe ware. H. 5.7 cm., W. 16.5 cm. Idemitsu Museum of Arts.

163, 164. Underglaze Decorated Karatsu large bowl with two handles, delicately painted thin underglaze iron design of plants. H. 13.2 cm., D. mouth 26.5 cm. Mr. Sakamoto Gorō. (See Plate 50)

165, 166. Underglaze Decorated Karatsu square dish, underglaze iron painting of mountains and trees in interior, stripes on folded rim appear to have been painted directly across. H. 8.6 cm., W. 26.6 cm. Idemitsu Museum of Arts.

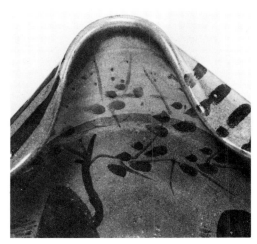

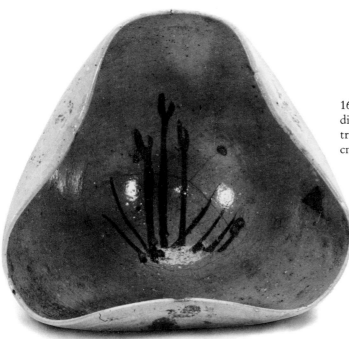

167. Underglaze Decorated Karatsu triangular dish, painted underglaze iron plant design; attributed to Dōzono kiln. H. 9.3 cm., W. 17.2 cm. Idemitsu Museum of Arts.

168. Underglaze Decorated Karatsu lobed conical dish, painted underglaze iron design of fishnets, a basket, and two small fish. H. 7.4 cm., D. 20.3 cm. Idemitsu Museum of Arts. (See Plates 169, 177)

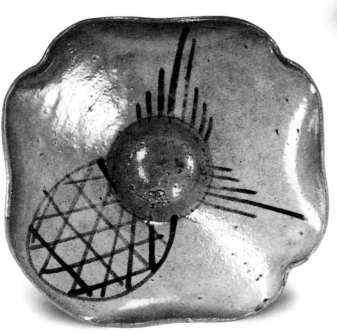

169. Underglaze Decorated Karatsu square dish, painted underglaze iron design of basket and two sets of stylized horsetails, simple bowl-shaped contour with slight buldge above foot rim. H. 8.4 cm., D. 17.8 cm. Idemitsu Museum of Arts. (See Plates 168, 177)

170. Underglaze Decorated Karatsu large shallow dish with broad rim, underglaze iron painting of iris and reeds, small areas of glaze crawling. H. 11.2 cm., D. 41.2 cm. Idemitsu Museum of Arts.

171. Underglaze Decorated Karatsu stemmed bowl with attached thrown stem, painted underglaze iron simple spiral design, except for smudges and drippings, the stem is unglazed; attributed to Michinayatani kiln. H. 11.9 cm., D. 15.5 cm. Idemitsu Museum of Arts.

172. Underglaze Decorated Karatsu saké cup, deep dip of underglaze iron at lip (*kawakujira* style), attributed to the Matsuura group kilns. H. 3.8 cm. Idemitsu Museum of Arts.

173. Underglaze Decorated Karatsu saké cup, underglaze iron painting of wild grass, finely crackled glaze. H. 5.0 cm. Idemitsu Museum of Arts.

174. Underglaze Decorated Karatsu saké cup, underglaze iron painting of paired plants. H. 7.4 cm. Idemitsu Museum of Arts.

175. Underglaze Decorated Karatsu saké cup, underglaze iron painted character for "big" (大) shown and character for "small" (小) on opposite side. H. 5.1 cm. Idemitsu Museum of Arts.

176. Underglaze Decorated Karatsu saké cup for use while riding a horse, underglaze iron painting of plant. H. 8.0 cm. Idemitsu Museum of Arts.

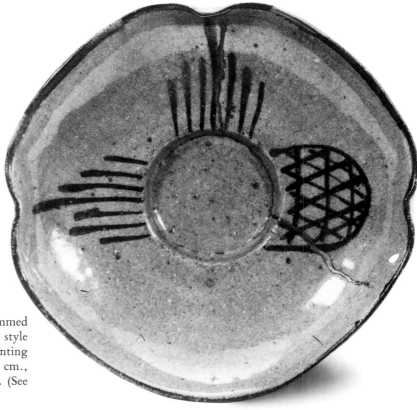

177. Underglaze Decorated Karatsu stemmed saké cup stand (interior), *kawakujira* style (underglaze iron) lip, underglaze iron painting of basket and stylized horsetails. H. 8.3 cm., D. 20.5 cm. Idemitsu Museum of Arts. (See Plates 168, 169)

178. Small Underglaze Decorated Karatsu fire container in the shape of fish basket, underglaze iron painting of a cormorant. H. 5.5 cm. Tanakamaru Collection.

179. Underglaze Decorated Karatsu square fire container, underglaze iron design; shape and glaze show influence of Shino ware of Mino region. H. 9.2 cm. Idemitsu Museum of Arts.

180. Underglaze Decorated Karatsu incense burner (Presentation Karatsu), carefully potted cylinder with three attached feet, underglaze iron painting of reeds and wheels, two herons and a scroll on opposite side. H. 8.5 cm. Idemitsu Museum of Arts.

181. Underglaze Decorated Karatsu incense burner, hexagonal at the lip rim, three added feet, underglaze iron painting of crossed rice stalks. H. 9.0 cm. Tanakamaru Collection.

182. Plain Karatsu shard excavated from lower Handō-game kiln, *hori* (carved) Karatsu type, fashioned to be a teabowl. (See Plates 9, 112)

183. Underglaze Decorated Karatsu shard excavated from the Takeo Kawagokamanotani kiln bearing the painted underglaze iron inscription *Genna yonnen, ni gatsu, jūhachi hi* (2nd month, 18th day, 1618). Inscriptions of characters are unusual in Karatsu; dating is even rarer.

184. Base of a paddled Plain Karatsu water jar (such as in Plate 87), three balls added as feet; unearthed from Kameyanotani kiln remains.

185. Shard of Underglaze Decorated ware showing the erosion of glaze caused by condensed moisture dripping within the kiln in the early stages of the firing. (See Plate 46)

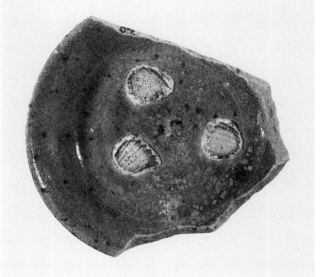

186. Shard showing marks of seashells used as spurs. Although this is not a Karatsu shard, this practice was found at Karatsu kilns.

187. Shard from Fujinkawachi kiln showing the marks of shells used as spurs.

188. Shard from Dōzono kiln remains; foot of *tataki* (paddled) jar showing mixture of two clay bodies; bloating and porosity of Karatsu clay is evident.

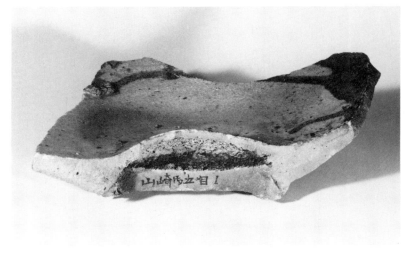

189. Shard from Yamasaki Omedate kiln remains showing the typical bloating of Karatsu clay.

190. Shard from the Matsuura Kameyanotani kiln remains; interior of *tataki* (paddled) bottle showing pattern of overlapping arcs resulting from the use of an "anvil" inside the pot.

191. Shard from the Takeo Shōkoya kiln remains; interior of *tataki* (paddled) jar clearly reveals pattern of overlapping arcs left by "anvil" used inside the pot.

192. Underglaze Decorated shard from Kōraidani kiln remains in the Taku group; the shard section verifies that the Karatsu technique was to paint iron oxide under rather than on the glaze.

193. Lip rims excavated from Handōgame kiln showing the technique of folding over clay to produce a thick rim. This technique was used for large objects of the style preceding Karatsu and is not seen in Karatsu wares.

194. Evidence of porcelain and Karatsu ware being fired together; fused shards of Karatsu stoneware and porcelain (top) found at Mukaie no Hara kiln site, Arita, by Dr. Oliver Impey. H. 7.7 cm. Department of Eastern Art, Ashmolean Museum, Oxford.

195. Shard excavated from Shiinomine kiln remains, underglaze decoration in white slip applied through a stencil, eight spur marks.

196. Shard of Underglaze Decorated teabowl, *oku-Gorāi* shape, stylized horsetail (*tokusa*) decoration. (See Plate 33)

197. Shard of plate with painted underglaze iron grass design.

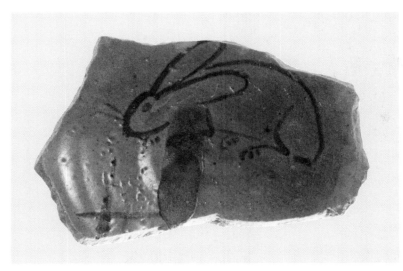

198. Karatsu shard with underglaze painting of a rabbit; other than birds, animals are rare decorations on Karatsu ware and are seen primarily on shards. Examples of rabbits, shrimp, fish, and horses are known.

199. Shard from Takeo Kameyanotani kiln remains; flying birds painted in the manner seen on wares produced at the Mino kilns.

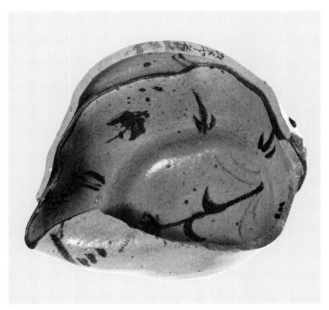

200, 201. Two views of shards fused together during firing; underglaze decoration shows influence from Mino wares; excavated from Takeo Kameyanotani kiln remains.

202. Page from the diary of Kiheiji V written as a partial defense during the government investigation of the Shiinomine kilns (1697–1703); now in possession of the Nakazato family, Karatsu city.

203

204

205

206, 207. Large blue-and-white porcelain plate depicting the preparation of clay and steps involved in the fabrication, decoration, and firing of ceramic ware; registered Saga Prefectural Cultural Property. Arita Ceramic Museum.

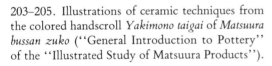

203–205. Illustrations of ceramic techniques from the colored handscroll *Yakimono taigai* of *Matsuura bussan zuko* ("General Introduction to Pottery" of the "Illustrated Study of Matsuura Products").

208. Oribe bottle showing Karatsu influence in Mino area: light, crackled opaque glaze, Karatsu inspired underglaze iron design, upper section dipped in copper green glaze; attributed to Otami kiln. H. 17.7 cm. Dr. and Mrs. Roger Gerry Collection. Photograph by Eric Pollitzer.

209. Korean Ido teabowl, Yi dynasty, name: Nara, glazed foot rim; designated Important Art Object. H. 7.1 cm. Idemitsu Art Museum.

210, 211. Korean rice bowl, Yi dynasty, glazed foot rim. H. 8.8 cm., D. 14.4 cm. National Museum of Korea, Seoul.

212. Korean celadon oil jar, Koryŏ dynasty, showing underglaze painted design comparable in style to painting seen on Karatsu ware. H. 9.5 cm. Honolulu Academy of Arts. (See Plate 44)

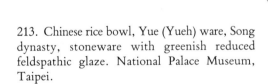

213. Chinese rice bowl, Yue (Yueh) ware, Song dynasty, stoneware with greenish reduced feldspathic glaze. National Palace Museum, Taipei.

214. Spotted Longchuan (Lung-Ch'uan) celadon spouted bowl, Yuan dynasty, shape influenced by metal prototypes, bowl lip behind spout left intact. National Palace Museum, Taipei.

215

217

216

218

219

215–219. *Tataki* (paddling) technique demonstrated by Nakazato Muan (Tarōuemon XII). 215. Ash is sprinkled on wheelhead. 216. Clay for the base is pounded onto wheelhead; the clay beyond circle of ash holds the piece to the wheel. 217. Vessel sides formed by joining coils of clay. 218. Coiled wall is paddled on outside while wooden ''anvil'' used against inside; overlapping arcs made by ''anvil'' can be seen. 219. Pot given final shape and exterior texture, and lip is thrown.

220. View of a *noborigama* chamber showing the loading of the kiln with greenware that has been decorated and glazed. Ochawangama, Karatsu city.

221. Handmade tools used to make Karatsu ware; (l. to r.) above: three paddles used on pot exterior (*tataki* technique); fourth paddle used for pounding flat pot base on wheelhead; cutting cord. below: three "anvils" for pot interior (*tataki* technique); wiping cloth; two ribs for shaping, smoothing, and cutting. Ochawangama, Karatsu city.

222. Underglaze iron being painted on greenware by Nakazato Tarōuemon XIII. Before firing, each piece will be dipped in glaze. Ochawangama, Karatsu city.

223. Lightweight, fast-turning kick wheel used for throwing Karatsu ware; the small flywheel is kicked counterclockwise; potter's seat can be seen in the left corner; trimming, decorating, and measuring tools are on the counter; the *hera*, always kept wet, is in the bowl of water. Ochawangama, Karatsu City.

224. Remains of the Ochawangama kiln opened in 1831; located on the premises of the present Ochawangama studio and kiln, these overgrown remains have been dedicated as a sacred Shintō site.

225. Remains of the Handōgame kiln; the fire mouth is in the distance under an added shelter; the stepped ascending levels of the kiln floor are still evident beneath the overgrowth; each level was a separate kiln chamber; no superstructure of the kiln remains. (See Plate 205)

226. Fire mouth of Handōgame kiln remains; the low fire ports and their supports remain.

227. View of Karatsu city from Karatsu Castle. The Matsuura River is in the foreground; Ochawangama in front of foothills left of the central canyon.

228. Pottery studio, Nakazato home and gallery, Ochawangama, Karatsu city. The Nakazato home is the first large building beyond the long train platform in the center of the picture; the potter's studios and kiln are clustered to the left of the home; the gallery is among the group of buildings to the right of the home.

229. Karatsu Castle now functions as a historic museum.

230. The ramparts of Karatsu Castle.

231. Roof tiles of Karatsu Castle, showing the clan crest of overlapping diamonds.

232, 233. Torii and stone lantern designating a sacred site for Korean potters. 232. Beyond the torii are remains of an ancient kiln; Korean potters are reputed to have assembled here for festivals in the past. 233. Ceramic plaque inscribed "Korean deity."

234. Shards from the Yamase kiln imbedded in the wall of the Nakano ceramic shop in Karatsu city, evidence both of the abundance of Karatsu remains in the area and of the nonsystematic early excavations of the Karatsu kilns.

CHAPTER III

Kilns and Techniques

When the late Edo period tea enthusiasts dug into the remains at Karatsu kiln sites, they were busy searching for buried masterpieces and had no interest in the exacting task of a systematic excavation. Since the beginning of the Shōwa era (1926), Japanese, from private individuals to research groups, have been excavating and documenting ancient sites. An excavation on November 21, 1931 by Kurahashi Tōjirō of the Tokyo Engineering Administration Association "studied Handōgame, Hobashira and others . . . guided by Kimbara Koichi of Takeo and Nakazato Tarōuemon XII of Karatsu who had been studying the sites beforehand."[1] A 1939 excavation of Handōgame by Nakazato Tarōuemon XII, Furudate Kyūichi and Kimbara postulated a Kamakura period origin for the kilns,[2] and there were the independent, clandestine excavations of four Kishidake sites, upper and lower Handōgame, Hobashira, and Saraya, by Iwao Matsuo in 1939–40.[3] Similar excavations were taking place at Seto, Mino, and Bizen, leading, as did the Karatsu digs, to renewed interest in the ancient wares, research into their technical processes, and attempts to reestablish production within the same tradition. The most important postwar Karatsu investigation was undertaken in April, 1956 by the Hizen Tōji Kenkyū-kai (Hizen Pottery Research Association).[4]

Kiln remains showing vast quantities of household wares reflect the total production of Karatsu more accurately than extant examples, which are predominantly tea ceremony wares. The style of kiln construction and methods of firing can be determined from the ruins. Although the old kilns do not hold answers to all questions about Karatsu, they do show the relationship of the Karatsu type kiln to Korean prototypes, and the shards are evidence of the diversity and evolution of ceramic types within the total repertoire. By relating the remains to historic events, kiln remains help clarify dating.

The first kiln type that produced Karatsu was the simple, vaulted, linked-chamber, climbing kiln—the *waridake noborigama* ("split-bamboo climbing kiln"). Handōgame (Plates 225, 226) is a typical example. It was a single, long, semicircular vault broken into smaller chambers by walls made completely of clay. In later Karatsu kilns, the walls were of coarse clay bricks coated with clay. Korean kilns used slabs of granite protected by a layer of clay. In the Karatsu kilns, the clay functioned both as a surface and a binder. At the base of the baffle walls that separated the chambers were a series of vents. These created a downdraft, forcing the fire to climb from chamber to chamber.

Fig. 1

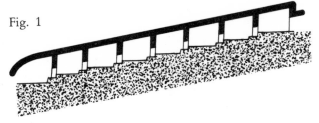

Axial cross-section of a split-bamboo (*waridake*) climbing kiln; fire chamber at left.

Cross-section of climbing kiln baffle wall; fire ports (vents) at bottom.

There is no evidence of shelves having been used. Instead, as in Korea, wares were stacked on top of each other, using shells (*kaigara zumi*; Plates 186, 187) or clay balls (*me*; Plates 170, 195) as spurs to separate the pieces. Later, simple clay stilts (*tōchin*) were introduced. Bases of some large vessels have marks from being fired on rice husks or sand on the floor of the kiln.

Fig. 2

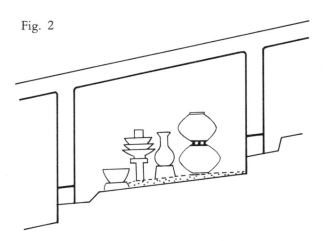

Kiln chamber with wares stacked for firing.

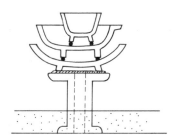

Stacked pots separated by clay balls (*me*) and placed on a clay stilt (*tōchin*) resting in sand.

Of the two kilns at Handōgame, Upper Handōgame had eight chambers and was approximately fifty-four feet long, seven feet wide, and four feet high. The kiln was built on a hillside, and the floor of each chamber was leveled. The slope was such that the step rise from chamber to chamber was three and one-half to four inches (Plate 225). Lower Handōgame was of roughly the same proportions, about sixty feet in length with seven chambers.

There were some variations in dimensions and number of chambers from kiln to kiln. Michinayatani, in the same Kishidake group as Handōgame, had fourteen chambers and was almost 130 feet in length, and the three kilns at Shiinomine of the Matsuura group extended to twenty chambers apiece. But the plan of Handōgame, constructed from the earth of the vicinity, constituted the basic Karatsu kiln. The linked chambers made it possible to utilize the fire efficiently, to obtain high temperatures, and to control reduction. This contrasted with earlier Japanese kiln styles and those used outside Kyushu: the *anagama*, essentially a totally or partially sunken tunnel in a hillside with no inner partitions, or the *ōgama*, which arched over a shallow trench with one or more flame-dividing pillars.

The Karatsu kilns made high-fired, reduced stoneware possible, and pottery remains validate that the potters used this potential to the full.[5] All three types of Karatsu—Plain, Underglaze Decorated, and Korean—have been found at practically every site. Differences from kiln to kiln involve variations in the clay body (sandiness, percentage of iron, degrees of coarseness and plasticity), the development of one type of Karatsu more than others, and occasionally unique shapes, sizes, and decorative motifs. Japanese scholars, particularly Mizumachi, Nakajima, and Satō, have attempted to identify some characteristics with specific kilns. Although there is some validity in this effort, considering the stylistic similarity of products from several sites, the focus in this book is more on major variations and trends among *groups* of kilns. (See pages 191ff, where notes on the products of certain individual kilns are given.)

The diversity of Karatsu production is evident in the kinds of wares fired in both the early and later kilns. Those kilns that later converted to porcelain manufacture went through a period of simultaneous firing of stoneware and porcelain. The practice of firing wares of different styles together in the same kiln was not unusual. Pre-Karatsu products from early Kishidake kilns, especially from Handōgame, were fired together with Karatsu, and later, Takeo style stoneware was fired together with Karatsu. Both the Pre-Karatsu and Takeo stonewares differ from all varieties of Karatsu in their shapes and size, and the Takeo wares have completely different decoration. Since Pre-Karatsu, porcelain, and Takeo style products were all fired at kilns that at the same time were producing Karatsu style ware, it is apparent that assigning a piece to a specific kiln site is not sufficient to validate it as Karatsu; the characteristics of the pots themselves, more than their place of manufacture, establish their identity.

Shards from the earliest Karatsu kilns, those that closed in 1594 with the fall of the Hata, show the basic Karatsu characteristics,[6] involving a then new approach to both glazing and decoration. Kishidake potters applied feldspathic glaze to high-fired stoneware and fired it to maturity and decorated with underglaze iron and white slip. Prior to Karatsu, the Japanese use of feldspathic glaze was limited to the lower-firing Seto and Mino kilns, where underglaze iron painting was in use by the Momoyama period.[7]

Iron oxide painted decoration was a striking development and became a part of the Japanese ceramic genre. From early Karatsu on, it is evident that painting was done by the potter rather than a specialist decorator. Always simple and direct, the painting sometimes reaches heights of spontaneous vitality.[8]

The multitoned rice-straw ash (*madara*; ''mottled'') glaze, popularly known as *namako* (''sea cucumber''), and the translucent, milky feldspathic wood ash glaze, commonly used on painted wares, were introduced. Iron glazes firing in a wide range of tones from amber to green to brown and a bluish black also appeared. These basic glazes and underglaze techniques, seen at the earliest kiln remains, were consistent characteristics of the ware.

Handōgame, recognized with Hobashira as the earliest kilns where Karatsu was made, exemplifies the oldest Japanese *noborigama*, the prototype of the "split-bamboo," barrel-vaulted style climbing kiln. It is situated at the base of Kishidake Mountain, where Lord Hata had his castle. The Handōgame shards are of a coarse, sandy clay with moderate iron content, fired to a buff, gray, or brown color—all variants of a single clay body used in an unrefined state. Both Karatsu fabrication techniques—throwing and paddling (*tataki*)—are evident. Thrown pieces have unglazed, shallow feet trimmed from the pot body. Many shards display the *chirimen-jiwa* effect, a rough texture resulting from rapid trimming (Plate 118) that is admired in tea circles.

Almost all Handōgame pieces are utilitarian household wares (*zakki*)—rice bowls, dishes, spouted bowls (*katakuchi*), plates, and large water and food storage jars. Lips of large vessels are heavy and folded over (Plate 193). There also are plates with fluted rims (*fuchi-naburi zara*). These become less common at later kiln group sites (Plates 153–54). The *hori* Karatsu ("carved" Karatsu) teabowls, with their unusual double foot rims, are found at Handōgame, evidence that at this earliest kiln at least some pieces were specifically made for the tea ceremony (Plate 182).

The Handōgame shards show the three basic Karatsu glazes—the feldspathic wood ash glaze, feldspathic rice-straw ash glaze (*namako*), and the dark iron glaze produced by adding iron-oxide to the wood ash glaze. The milky translucent feldspar glaze appears in both its pale amber oxidized and greenish reduced state. The glazes crackle in a fine pattern. Iron oxide underglaze painting of simple motifs and painted lip rims (*kawakujira*) are prevalent. In addition to these are a number of simple nonfeldspathic ash glazes, seen especially on large containers of a style developed before Karatsu. Some of these pieces were glazed only from the deposits of kiln ash.

Handōgame remains range from the white *hori* Karatsu teabowls to the simplest everyday pieces. The quality reflects a sure, rapid, manufacture. Mechanical precision, resulting in exact symmetry or multiple, identical pieces was of no concern. With the possible exception of certain slip-decorated types and the rare *jakatsu* glaze (Plates 12, 79, 80), all types of Karatsu are found at this early site, including the two-glazed Korean Karatsu.[9] The rice-straw ash glaze, not seen at Handōgame, occurs on shards from Hobashira.

The ancient Karatsu potters used unrefined clays from the vicinity where they built their kilns without mixing different clays or adding other materials. Abundant clay deposits are found in relatively small veins throughout Hizen Province. Although these vary in iron content, sandiness, and degree of plasticity from site to site, all are highly refractory stoneware clays with a coarse, sandy, even-grained body. In choosing a site, the potter considered the availability of clay and water, a slope for the *noborigama*, and sufficient timber to fire his kiln. The feudal lords moved potters or limited their production because of depletion of the forests, but the potters moved about in search of good clay. Today's Karatsu potters maintain the same focus on clay. According to Nakazato Tarōuemon XIII, "masterpieces are products using the natural potentials of the clay to the fullest." He values the qualities of a good clay as: 1) plasticity; 2) a high firing range, around 1270° C [2318° F; Seger cone 8–9]; 3) sufficiently low iron content to leave the glaze unaffected; and 4) low percentage of shrinkage.[10] By these standards, Karatsu clays are less than ideal. All have, due to their sandiness, a limited degree of plasticity. Their high refractory level is evidenced at kiln remains, where one rarely finds shards of sagging pots that began to vitrify during firing. In fact, at Ochawangama, some of the modern Karatsu potters experimented with shards from ancient kiln sites, refiring them to cone 13 (1380° C; 2516° F)[11] without warping or melting the clay body. Variations in iron content account for some of the differences in the color of fired Karatsu clay; the degree of reduction and the duration of firing also affect the final color.

CHEMICAL ANALYSIS OF CLAY BODIES

	Kishidake kilns			Kishidake group		Matsuura group
	Handōgame	Michinayatani	Saraya	Yamase	Kojirō-kaja	Abondani
Silica (SiO_2)	72.58	77.76	74.75	55.26	73.41	74.25
Aluminum Oxide (Al_2O_3)	18.50	14.43	14.38	35.11	18.64	16.66
Ferric Oxide (Fe_2O_3)	1.60	1.07	1.38	2.40	1.11	1.43
Calcium Oxide (lime) (CaO)	.67	.45	2.01	.45	.45	.45
Magnesium Oxide (MgO)	.48	.48	.80	.97	.64	.80
Feldspar (aluminum silicate) with sodium and potassium	5.25	5.41	6.04	5.46	.15	5.85

adapted from Mizumachi 1963, pp. 207–12.

To assess shrinkage rates of Old Karatsu wares, the Nakazatos at Ochawangama experimented with clay deposits dug from old kiln sites. They found a relatively high shrinkage rate, 7 percent to 14 percent, in the clay of Fujinkawachi of the Matsuura group.[13] The unfiltered clay used for Old Karatsu could have had an even higher shrinkage rate. The limited plasticity permitted pieces to be thrown in rapid succession on the fast-turning kick wheel only if the clay was kept relatively dry, a process made possible by a special Karatsu tool, the Korean style *hera*. The paddling (*tataki*) technique was also tailored to accommodate the limited plasticity. The wheel-trimmed foot rim, another characteristic of Karatsu, was easily fashioned from the grainy clays.

Despite being a hard, high-fired stoneware, old Karatsu pieces have the light weight and low thermoconductivity characteristic of porous earthenware bodies. This results from the character of the clay—its sandy porosity and the limited compression from wedging. In addition, the unlevigated clays contained impurities, which burned out in the firing process, leaving walls with small inner air pockets, which, in turn, functioned as insulators. Thus, Karatsu was ideal for both domestic and tea ceremony usage, since the vessels maintain the heat of their contents while remaining lightweight and comfortable to handle.

Other than the removal of large pieces of foreign matter—stones, roots, etc.—the ancient potters seem to have done little to prepare or refine the local clay before beginning to use it. Honey, in discussing the clay processing of Yi dynasty Korean potters, associates simplified procedures with a low economic status, a condition probably shared by the potters of Karatsu:

> The poor man cannot afford the time required to refine the materials of his pottery, for the long-continued grinding and repeated levigation needed to produce a dense smooth jadelike ware. Nor has he time for a careful precision in painted work. . . . His pottery must be strong and durable in use, but will not necessarily pay much regard to neatness or cleanliness; these are apt to be the luxuries for the well-to-do.[14]

Besides small particles of organic matter—insects, leaves, etc.—some small stones that absorbed water and might explode during firing also remained in the clay. Sometimes they erupted gently towards the surface, creating an effect called *ishihaze* ("burst stone"), greatly admired in tea circles. Karatsu *ishihaze* differs from that seen on other wares, which result from small bits of feldspar in the clay rising to the surface. Later potters, including some working today, implant small stones into thrown pieces in order to induce this effect.

Foreign matter presents a hazard in firing since, once it burns out, it leaves a pocket in which steam collects. Intense pressure creates a bloating, which, with increasing steam pressure, may explode. Bloating of this sort is common in Karatsu wares (Plate 189). The incidence of explosions, however, is retarded by the long, slow initial heating of the kiln, which allows considerable moisture to be released through the porous clay before the glazes become molten. Drops of condensed moisture falling on the unfired glaze leave erosion marks (Plates 44, 185). With such a highly refractory clay, distortion, due to vitrification of the clay body, a common cause of warping, is rare (Plate 15). In Old Karatsu, air pockets, bloating, and high shrinkage in firing contributed to producing irregular pots. The method of fabrication also contributed to this result, but here only the influence of scanty preparation and the composition of the clay body is noted.

The mobility of the potters and relatively brief period of peak production indicate that ageing of the clay was minimal, probably a few months or less. Unlike Chinese potters, whose ideal was for one generation to prepare clay for the next, the Karatsu potters had a sense of expediency comparable to the Yi potters of Korea.

Even though the potters used clay in a relatively raw state, it was systematically wedged. First the masses of unearthed clay were foot-wedged. Then, taking a large mass, the potter kneaded it into spiral folds ("chrysanthemum wedging"—*kiku momi*), forcing his weight on it with the palms of his hands, folding it over, and repeating again and again. After one to two hundred compressions, the moist clay would be smooth, even-textured, and cone shaped (Plate 207, lower left). The cone of clay is ready without any further shaping for throwing off the hump. When twentieth century Western potters learned this wedging method, now used throughout the country, they identified it with Japan, unaware that it was one of many techniques that originated in Korea.

The potter's wheel was used for all types of Karatsu. As early as the Yayoi period, a simple, hand-turned wheel had come to Japan from Korea, and over the centuries Korean wheel innovations followed. By the early sixteenth century, Kyushu potters were using a kick wheel. The fast-turning kick wheel (Plate 223) used at the peak of Karatsu production in the early seventeenth century appeared in Japan either with the Korean potters who came at the time of Hideyoshi's Korean campaigns or slightly before. It is the wheel used throughout Kyushu today, in contrast to the stick-propelled hand wheel common in other parts of Japan. It is essentially the same as the Yi dynasty wheel:

> The Korean potter's wheel is commonly made by cutting the central part of a solid piece of timber—perhaps a section of a tree trunk—in such a way as to form a double "T" [工]. . . . This is set on top of a shaft, which is sunk deep in the ground and revolves in a socket at the base. It is a kick wheel, turned by direct action of the bare feet, and thus its primitive character is compensated by perfect control.
>
> . . . The Korean potter's wheel was described by Pierre Louis Jouy in 1888 as follows:
>
> The Korean potter's wheel consists of a circular table from two to three feet in diameter and four to six inches thick, made of heavy wood so as to aid in giving impetus to it when revolving. In general appearance it is not very unlike a modeler's table. This arrangement is sunken into a depression in the ground, and revolves easily by means of small wheels working on a track underneath, the table being pivoted in the center. The wheel is operated directly by the foot, without the aid of a treadle of any kind. The potter sits squatting in front of the wheel, his bench or seat on a level with it, and space being left between his seat and the wheel to facilitate his movements. With his left foot underneath him, he extends his right foot and strikes the side of the wheel with the bare sole of the foot, causing it to revolve.[15]

Propelled with a backward foot stroke, the wheel revolves in a clockwise direction, which is peculiar to Korea and Western Japan. Whereas most Western kick wheels rely on the momentum of a heavy flywheel, the Karatsu wheel has a small flywheel of wood, spins rapidly because of its light weight, and responds easily. This relative delicacy and sensitivity of response makes it more like a hand tool than a machine.

The Karatsu *hera*, a long, broad, curved, interior rib, is essential for throwing (Figure 3, page 152; Plate 207, lower left).[16] It is used only in Kyushu and Korea. Although other ribs may be used, the *hera* is the basic tool and accounts for interior depressions commonly found in Karatsu bowls and broad *mukōzuke* dishes (Plates 168, 169). The *hera*-makers were specially skilled Korean craftsmen, some of whom came to Japan. A serious problem for modern Karatsu potters has arisen since the death of the last Japanese *hera* craftsman and their increasing scarcity in Korea. Attempts have been made to cast *hera* in fiberglass, but the nonabsorbent surface makes for a less satisfactory tool. Basically,

Fig. 3

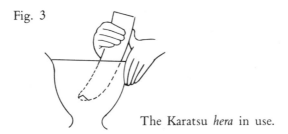

The Karatsu *hera* in use.

it is the *hera* that makes the throwing of the sandy Karatsu clay possible. The high sand content and consequent limited plasticity make it necessary for Karatsu pots to be thrown quickly, with as little added water as possible, in order to avoid collapse of the walls. The *hera* provides an inner support against which the potter can quickly raise the shape while compressing, and thus strengthening, the clay. In addition, slip, not water, is sufficient lubricant, so weakening through addition of moisture can be minimized. This compressing of clay by throwing with the *hera* accounts for the relative thinness of the walls of this stoneware. Using this tool, the potter throws pieces in rapid succession. Once the clay has been opened, the *hera* is inserted and the clay compressed and pulled up along its curved ridge. In one or two strokes, a piece is thrown, the clay narrowed near the base, and with a twisted reed or a horse hair, is cut free. The cutting thread, tied to a stick handle at one end only (Plate 221, upper right), twines around the base of the spinning piece and, with a slight pull, easily releases the thrown piece from the clay mass. Because of the clockwise revolution of the wheel and the style of the cutting thread, a distinctive shell-like pattern on the pot bottoms swirls from left to right. Japanese call this the *karamono itokiri* ("Chinese—i.e., continental—cutting").

When the freshly thrown pot is lifted from the hump, the upper part of the remaining clay is centered and a new piece begun. This rapid technique allows the Karatsu potter to produce five hundred or more pieces a day. As each piece is removed, some natural warping of the circular form occurs. In most thrown pieces, shape distortions result from the rapid process of manufacture. Such distortions are perceived as inner expressions of the material. The potter lets the clay itself speak.

Decorative shaping occurs on some thrown wares. Among the shards of Handōgame and other Kishidake kilns, fluted rims can be seen, the edge obviously pinched as the object turned on the wheel. Deep insets in the center of bowls, as previously noted, are created by compressing the central area with the *hera*. When emulating the Oribe style, pieces were patted into polygonal shapes with wooden paddles, at times appearing to have been molded unless one notices the telltale rounded base and circular trimming of the foot rim (Plates 49, 144, 181). Oribe wares also inspired making extended lips on tall *mukōzuke* dishes, which could then be formed into a variety of shapes while still leaving the body cylindrical (Plates 138, 139). Often lips were just pinched in at four corners, or rims were folded over. Occasionally rims of plates and dishes were even carved into irregular shapes (Plate 162). Deliberate distortion was used to form the squat, irregular bowl and dish shape known as *kutsu-gata* (Plates 116–19).[17]

The undulating upper profiles of many narrow-mouthed wheel-thrown jars result from the throwing method and demands of the sandy clay. This can be seen on larger pieces that have been narrowed in the upper half and is evidence of the problems the potters face in forming this shape. Irregularities appear even on very finely potted pieces such as the Idemitsu persimmon jar (Plate 41). Koreans even when making the smallest oil jar, threw shapes that narrowed towards the top in two sections, joining the two parts along the bulging edge. Karatsu potters consistently resisted making pots that could not be fashioned as a single, wheel-thrown piece. Whenever a jar was so narrow that the *hera* could not be inserted, the upper section was formed quickly by hand only. Thus, even though narrowing is awkward on a clockwise-turning wheel, the potters chose this way of working, leaving the rippled upper silhouette as evidence of this solution (Plate 132). When the bulbous, "abacus bead" shaped jars are smooth on the upper, narrowed part, they usually have been trimmed smooth (Plates 130, 131); this is the only case of trimming the upper portion of a pot.

The potter trims his thrown wares in rapid succession on a clay chuck. For trimming, the wheel rotates counterclockwise. His trimming tool is a single, untapered, right-angled metal piece (Plate 223). The excess clay is removed from the lower section of the body, and the foot trimmed in two or three deft strokes. The speed of trimming, more than the degree to which the clay has hardened, results in the admired wrinkled effect (*chirimen-jiwa*) inside the foot rim (Plate 118). Speed also accounts for most Karatsu foot rims being slightly off center. Some are sufficiently varied in width to be called "crescent-shaped" and have great appeal for tea devotees. Precise pieces with carefully rounded foot rims exist, but most are irregular and unsmoothed.

The spouted bowl and ewer are the only Karatsu shapes for which functional parts are added to the thrown shape. Occasionally vases or large jars have small lugs (*mimi*) added. The spouted bowl, a rounded bowl with a pouring spout is a household utensil for which there are Chinese prototypes (Plate 214). The opening for the pouring spout is a rough hole poked through the upper wall, leaving the pot lip intact (Plates 125–26). The spout is simply a flat piece of clay shaped around a finger and attached to the body. The ewer spout is also a flat clay piece folded over to form a tube and fused to the pot with the seam facing the body (Plates 25–27). Handles are neither pulled nor shaped, but are simple coils or slabs, sometimes grooved or twisted (Plates 25–27, 97). The casual handling of pieces added to the spouted bowl and ewer tells us again that the Karatsu potter was interested in rapid production.

Of those Karatsu pieces with decorations carved into the clay, the majority were carved while on the wheel, probably at the time of throwing or trimming. Examples are the carvings on *hori* Karatsu teabowls (Plates 9, 112), combed decoration on some Korean Karatsu (Plate 97), and horizontal engravings occasionally seen on thrown wares (Plates 14, 85, 87, 88, 94, 97, 103). Vertical carvings on large paddled vessels and certain Korean Karatsu vases were done both on and off the wheel.

Added clay decorations are rare; springing and molded decorations are unknown. Small, squashed clay balls are used where functional parts—spouts, handles, etc.—are affixed, usually placed at points of stress (Plates 41, 124–26). Some say these strengthen such points, but actually their function is primarily ornamental.

Large bowls, jars, and bottles are generally made by paddling (*tataki*) process (Plates 215–19). To begin, the potter flattens a ball of clay into a circular pad, which is an inch or so bigger than the diameter of the intended base. On the wheelhead he sprinkles ash, scrapes it into a circle the size of the planned base, and over this affixes the larger clay pad, which adheres to the wheel head only along the outer perimeter where it extends beyond the ash. The potters realized that clay with high shrinkage shifts and undergoes intense stress during firing, causing bases of large vessels to crack. To compensate, the Kishidake potters intermixed a relatively stable white sandy clay with the body clay for these pads, thus lessening the danger of cracks in the base without risking an incompatibility between the base and body of the vessel (Plate 188). Coils of clay are built up on the base, compressed and shaped by paddling on the outer surface while moving a wooden block against the inside. The potter slowly revolves the wheel in a clockwise direction by the rhythmic pull of the paddling strokes. Both paddling tools have textured surfaces to prevent sticking to the wet clay and to increase the surface area in contact with the clay so as to more efficiently join the coils (Plate 221). The "anvil" used inside is usually made from the central core of a large branch, round and scorched or carved into a series of concentric arcs. The paddle may have any number of textures, either from scorching to etch out the wood grain, carved designs, or wrapping with cord. The *tataki* technique results in sturdy, thin-walled large vessels that combine the strong tensions typical of coiled ware with the added strength of the forcefully compressed clay walls.

Once the body is formed, the potter adds coils from which the lip or neck are thrown (Plate 190), the outer surface is smoothed to the desired degree, and the extension of the clay pad at the base is cut away. The *tataki* technique thus eliminates the heavy bottoms often found on large pieces. The finished pot can be lifted off easily, since the layer of ash has prevented the pot's base from adhering to the wheel. Traces of ash seen on *tataki* pot bases are the result of this technique rather than from the piece's being placed, as has been suggested, on an ash bed in the kiln. The even flat base is usually tapped to make it slightly concave. Inside, the characteristic arc impressions of the "anvil" remain apparent, but the exterior surface is generally smooth (Plates 190, 191).

Tataki antedates Karatsu, having originated in northern Korea, where the two beating tools evolved. Some Sue ware pieces appear to have been made in this manner. Although paddling tools for shaping hand-built pottery are common throughout the world, *tataki* is distinguished by the simultaneous use of wooden tools both inside and out, which gives thinness, strength, and compression to the pottery wall.

Glaze is the main decoration for all Karatsu ware. It is often applied over quickly brushed touches of iron oxide or white slip. On two types of Underglaze Decorated Karatsu—*hakeme* (brushmarked) and *mishima* (slip inlay)—the potter applies a runny white slip made of impure porcelain, which occurs in small pockets or narrow veins within Hizen clay deposits. For *hakeme*, slip is brushed on as the piece revolves on the wheel, using a coarse brush, often made of rice stalk ends, thus depositing a swirling, streaked trail of thick slip. The more complicated ware, *mishima*, has patterns impressed or incised into the clay. Wooden or bamboo stamps carved with simplified floral or geometric designs are used to create borders and allover patterns. Sometimes simple linear patterns are incised into the raw clay. Then the entire surface is coated with a mixture of the white clay suspended in a fish or seaweed gum. After the surplus is scraped away, white slip remains deposited in the impressions, and the whole is covered with a clear glaze. The *punch'ong* wares of Korea were masterpieces of this technique, but among Karatsu products these are the least numerous, and they lack the quality of prime Korean pieces. In relation to other Karatsu types, the technique is painstaking. Its limited manufacture again emphasizes the Karatsu potters' interest in rapid, free production. Related to this is the occasional decoration, possibly intended as a bold imitation of *mishima*, with white clay patterns stenciled onto uncarved wares, examples of which have been found at early Matsuura and Takeo kiln sites.

Underglaze Decorated pieces are the most numerous of the Karatsu types. The casual freedom of the painted iron oxide decorations made these pots attractive not just to tea devotees but to the general populace as well. When Karatsu ware is mentioned, this type comes to mind first. Underglaze iron-decorated Korean wares were being made in the late sixteenth and seventeenth centuries, at the same time that Old Karatsu was flourishing. Some Karatsu and contemporaneous Korean pots have similar shapes or painted decorations (Plates 209–12). The Korean designs were usually painted on slip.

These early Japanese underglazed stonewares were painted when they were about leather hard and had been trimmed. The potter used a form of *fude*, the long-bristled brush used for writing. Karatsu shards show iron oxide bleeding into the raw clay (Plate 192). On some, the design is not completely covered by a glaze (Plates 34, 40, etc.), verifying that the designs were painted directly onto the clay body under the glaze rather than being applied, as could have been done, on top of the unfired glaze. The spontaneity of the designs displays the freedom and rapidity of the potter's deft strokes. The pots tell their own story of this process. There is a particularly revealing bowl in the Idemitsu collection with the lip bent over to form a square shape. Stripes decorate the bent-over sections of the folded lip, obviously brushed on quickly, touching all four sections of the lip in a single series of continuous, quick strokes (Plates 165–66). A more restrained decorator would have painted each lip separately, but the impetuous Karatsu potter continued each stripe across the bowl. Other examples of the potter-painter's almost expressionistic vigor are when zones of pots, such as rims of plates or everted lips of bowls, are completely ignored, the design uncontained by physical or implied borders (Plates 47, 153–54, 156–57, etc.). Under the influence of Furuta Oribe, more careful and studied painting and the intrusion of borders, medallions, or panels appear (Plates 138, 161, 162). Silhouetted flowers, reeds, fruits, birds, or just abstract designs done in small, firm strokes or dots in carefree array are the usual designs. Again, Oribe influence led to outlined shapes, especially among the products of the Takeo group of kilns, typified by Oyamaji.

The potters did not bisque fire,[18] but completed their products in a single firing. Saggers were never used. Glaze was applied either by dipping or pouring, the foot rim and lower part of the body being left unglazed. For all but Korean Karatsu and special teabowls with different glazes on the interior and exterior, only a single glaze was applied. The two-glazed Korean Karatsu commonly has a dark glaze covering the lower portion, while the upper section is dipped into an opaque white glaze. Korean Karatsu pieces with dark and light glazes freely trailed over the surface (Plates 23, 24, 96–99) form an exceptional, dynamic group. Although the Karatsu feldspathic glazes were introduced from Korea, the Karatsu method of glazing is different from Korea. Korean wares are totally glazed, foot rim and all.

Glazes were simple in composition and limited in number. The table below of glazes in use now at Ochawangama shows the batch proportions of glaze materials. There are, according to Nakazato Takashi, three basic Karatsu glazes: a milky translucent glaze (feldspar; Japanese, *chōseki*); a multitoned, unstable rice-straw ash glaze called *namako* (also *madara*, ''mottled''), with a range from opaque white to runny transparent; and a dark iron glaze (*temmoku*). More simply, these can be thought of as two basic glaze recipes, one having a higher percentage of feldspar than any other ingredient, the other of silica-bearing rice-straw ash. The dark *temmoku*[19] is merely one of these with iron oxide added. The iron oxide, in addition to creating a dark color, fluxes the glaze, lowers its melting point, and thus accounts for the runny, often thin, Karatsu *temmoku*. While today's potters at Ochawangama add iron to the milky translucent glaze, there is reason to believe that some of the ancient potters used the rice-straw ash glaze with iron. Thus, at Fujinkawachi, where large quantities of Korean Karatsu glazed with both rice-straw ash and iron glazes were produced, it is likely that a single glaze recipe, the *namako*, served for both the white and dark glaze, the latter depending on a simple addition of the coloring iron oxide. Since the ancient potters worked with materials found in natural deposits, they had no need to add clay to their glazes to make them adhere well to the pots; an amount of clay would have been present in the feldspathic deposits they mined.

Traces of iron oxide in all Karatsu clays make the milky translucent glaze found on Plain and painted Karatsu fire a pale yellow-brown when oxidized, a greenish gray when reduced. If wood ash is increased, the underglaze iron bleeds (Plate 161); an increased clay content maintains firm lines in the underglaze design (Plate 158). Pine-wood ash supplies more iron content, darkening and fluxing the glaze; a hardwood ash supplies more calcium and increases the glaze's opacity.

The iron-rich black glaze, *temmoku*, is amber to brown in color if oxidized; when reduced, it turns a dark blue-black. For all the glazes, as the chemical composition varies, the glaze color, translucency, and melting point fluctuates.

BASIC GLAZES IN USE AT OCHAWANGAMA

appearance / chemical / Japanese name ＼ ingredient	feldspar	clay	wood ash	rice-straw ash	iron	cone
milky translucent feldspar *chōseki*	40	30	30			8–12
opaque white, mottled rice-straw ash *namako, madara*	30	30	40	30		9–12
black, brown iron *temmoku*	40	30	30		5–15	8–12

The opaque white rice-straw ash glaze—the multitoned *madara*—is also called *namako* ("sea cucumber"). Mizumachi say *namako* is found only in North Korea, while the other glazes appear throughout Korea.[20] Silicic acid in the rice-straw ash causes the streaked, shifting coloring and induces occasional traces of bright blue (Plates 1, 4, 19, 25, 26). Bamboo, which also contains silica, was sometimes used as fuel. The resultant bamboo ash deposited on wares during the firing process could account for blue spots and streaks appearing on wares not having the rice-straw ash glaze. This occurrence is referred to as the "*namako* phenomenon" (*namako genshō*). The appearance of blue streaks in rice-straw ash glaze is of interest. They appear only in glaze with silica content, or, as just suggested, on pots exposed to ash bearing silica. Silica itself is not a colorant. The blue traces must come from reduced iron oxide particles either in an adjacent glaze, as in Korean Karatsu, or from the clay body. The blue traces occur where the glaze has become fluid during the firing, running in streaks, in fat drips or rolls, or caught in puddles. Potters believe this blue is triggered by a rapid increase in temperature under reduction conditions while the oxides are in a molten state, the silica catalyzing the iron to produce the striking blue color. If more wood ash is added, this glaze becomes greener and more translucent, like a runny celadon. When there is more rice-straw ash, it becomes white and opaque.

Despite their simple basic formulas, extensive variety in the Karatsu glazes resulted from the chemical compositions of the natural materials, the proportions of each material in a glaze, and firing with fluctuations between oxidation and reduction atmospheres. The range of appearance possible for the milky, translucent feldspar glaze and the rice-straw ash glaze makes glaze identification difficult for all but obvious examples. The limited number of natural glaze materials were and are identifiable and readily available to both ancient and contemporary potters. What is constant is the simplicity of the materials used and that all the glazes, including those at early Kishidake sites, are high-fired feldspathic glazes.

It appears that the use of such glazes on stoneware originated in Japan with Karatsu ceramics. Mino wares were also using feldspathic glazes by the mid-sixteenth century on lower-fired wares. It is debatable whether feldspathic glazes were first used at Mino or Karatsu, since they seem to have appeared within a relatively short time of each other, if not simultaneously. Hayashiya Seizō believes that a white feldspathic glazed teabowl owned by the great tea master Takeno Jōō (d. 1555) was made in Mino,[21] and today it is generally assumed that feldspathic glazes with underglaze painting began at Mino. The efficient Karatsu kilns fired them at higher temperatures.

Karatsu glazes range from black to white with warm and cool colors in between, extend from clear transparent to opaque glazes, display matte and glossy surfaces, and vary from a thin, runny glaze, clinging tightly to the clay, to thick, viscous glaze sagging into heavy drops. The glazes are both stable and fluid, crackled and crawling, smooth, rippled into ridges, bubbled, and pock-marked. In short, the Karatsu glazes introduced an entire repertoire of high-firing effects, a contribution that has remained and expanded throughout Japan.

All Karatsu ware was fired in linked-chambered, climbing kilns. The barrel-vaulted early kilns like Handōgame (*waridake*; "split bamboo"; Figure 1, page 146) and the later dome-chambered type ("beehive"; Plates 204, 224) differ principally in their external construction, the dome kiln giving more even temperatures within the chambers. Ascending from the fire box and its chamber at the lower end are chambers separated by vertical baffle walls. Each is perforated at the bottom by a row of fire holes or vents (Plate 205, left) that force the draft and fire to ascend from chamber to chamber. The floor of each chamber is horizontal, being cut into the hillside like a series of deep steps. On one side of each chamber is an opening to allow ware to be stacked and removed (Plate 204). This is sealed up during the firing. Portholes with removable plugs are opened to add fuel to each chamber and to observe the development of the firing.

The early Karatsu pots were stacked inside each other, with minimal use of kiln furniture (Figure 2, page 146). Marks on *oku-Gōrai* types of teabowls indicate they were fired upside down. Most other small pieces were loaded in an upright position.

The fire rose and fell within each chamber in a serpentine pattern, entering at the floor-level fire holes, rising to the chamber top, and being drawn down to the back fire holes leading to the next chamber. This produced variations of temperature and atmospheric pressure in the chamber, the section by the front fire holes being the hottest, and that by the back fire holes the coolest. The chamber floor remained relatively cool. The quantity and placement of pots in the chamber also influenced the path of the fire. Ceramics near the front fire holes received the most intense force of the flames, were most subject to atmospheric pressure, and were most likely to receive flame-borne ash. Thus, bloating and ash deposits occur most frequently on vessels stacked near the front wall of the chamber. Underglaze painted Karatsu more often was stacked near the back wall, a more protected and cooler part of the chamber. The chambers in the center of the kiln, at times reserved for tea vessels, had the most even temperatures. To obtain a rich deposit of natural ash, a limited number of pieces can be stacked in the fire box. We cannot tell to what extent the Karatsu potters of the past availed themselves of these subtle controls, but it would be naive to assume they were unaware of them.

Once the wares were stacked, the portal of each chamber was closed and sealed with wet clay. The fire chamber was stoked first with large logs. The kiln was gradually heated over a long period of time. This allowed the potters to fire pieces that had not dried completely, the final drying process taking place in the kiln. The sandy porosity of Karatsu clay permits steam to escape easily from the pieces and diminishes the incidence of explosions from this otherwise risky procedure. The complete kiln is heated by this firing, but not sufficiently to bring each chamber to maturity. After the first chamber reaches cone 7 (1100° C; 2012° F), successive addition of fuel to each chamber begins. Small logs are fed through the ports (Plate 204). Most parts of the chamber have wares stacked to the top, but in the port areas only the lowest part of the chamber is stacked, to avoid damaging pieces when the wood is fed into the incandescent chamber. The degree of oxidation or reduction is controlled by the rate of stoking fuel. If fuel is added before combustion of the previous amount of fuel is complete, an oxygen-choked reduction fire results. With this controlled stoking, it is possible to have an oxidizing firing for lower chambers and a reduction firing for upper ones in a single kiln firing. Fuel is added to the first chamber at frequent intervals until it reaches the desired temperature; then stoking of the second chamber begins, and so on until the entire kiln reaches maturity. Firings extend over several days and nights. Japanese cypress (*hinoki*), red elm, and oak were the usual fuels. Repeated complaints and regulations arising from the potters' deforestation of the hillsides lead to the conclusion that, under the pressure of firing, anything combustible—hardwoods, softwoods, bamboo, etc.—was used, always altering the chemical atmosphere and the type of free ash in the kiln.

Potters today gauge maturity by using pyrometric cones and pyrometers. Lacking such precise devices, Japanese potters until quite recently gauged temperatures by observing the color of the incandescent kiln chamber. A cone 1 chamber is a bright yellow-orange; a cone 7, an intense yellow; a cone 10, white.[22] The firing range of ancient Karatsu ran between Seger cones 1 to 11, roughly 1100° C to 1300° C (2012° C to 2372° F).

Pottery reaches the desired maturity through a combination of temperature and time. The color of heat, cones, and pyrometers indicate temperature only. Although the clay matures on reaching the required temperature, it will have different appearances depending upon how long it takes for that temperature to be reached and the degree of reduction firing. Coloring resulting from metallic oxides in the clay body intensifies, and the surface of the glaze will be altered by a longer period of firing. Some experiments the Nakazatos conducted with fragments from ancient kiln sites have revealed accommodations the ancient potters made to control their results. Old shards from Yamase, a clay erroneously thought to be low in iron because of its buff color, have been refired, with the result that the exposed raw clay darkened significantly. This confirms Mizumachi's analysis of Yamase clays as being high in ferric oxide content, more than twice the amount found in clay from Michinayatani, whose products are usually darker. The ancient potters at Yamase kiln prevented excessive darkening of the clay body by firing with an oxidizing flame for a minimum duration. When clay is fired in a heavily reduced atmosphere over an extended duration, the presence of even small percentages of iron causes darkening, and clay with moderate amounts can turn dark brown. Assumptions that all Karatsu clays were high in iron content have disappeared now that the effects of prolonged reduction firing on the iron oxides is recognized.

Glazes of some pieces of Karatsu, especially those with feldspathic iron glaze, resemble salt glaze. Introducing salt into the atmosphere of the kiln during firing was not common in Japan, and there is no evidence that Karatsu potters did any salt glazing. They did, however, use seashells as spurs. If a supply of shells is placed in the kiln chamber during firing, an atmosphere-deposited glaze is formed, much like a salt glaze and similar to the amber-colored glaze called *ame* found on some early Karatsu. Nakazato Tarō-uemon XIII has used this source of glaze on handsome jars, and Nakazato Takashi has induced stunning natural glazes by introducing quantities of shells into the Tanegashima style kiln he fired for durations of five to seven days (Plate 57). These glazes derived from shells range in coloring from an intense, shiny black, through browns, to greenish and transparent tones.

More than anything else, Karatsu ceramics were determined by the Kyushu clay. The potter prepared it, responded to its potentials and limitations, shaped and decorated it, and finally fired it. In the finest pieces, the natural qualities of the earth are enhanced by the mastery of the potter's hands. Throughout the process there was a constant interplay between potter and clay.

Few cultures have appreciated this balance between the nature of a material and the artist's intervention as much as the Japanese. It is not surprising, then, that they have produced some of the finest wares from limited materials. Handling the clays in a knowledgeable, uncontrived manner resulted in pieces that are both simple and sophisticated. Karatsu is representative of this manner of ceramic production.

The Karatsu potters worked with minimal materials, equipment, and techniques. The diversity of Karatsu pots occurred when these limitations were coupled with the potters' skill and resourcefulness. Beyond this, there always is an element of the unpredictable in making ceramics. The dialogue of the potter with nature—with the clay, the fire, and the atmosphere—has a mystery and excitement that is revealed in the pots themselves. If some of the materials and their treatment remain obscure, the concrete results coming from the kiln, the wares themselves, remain available for our study and appreciation.

NOTES

1. Nakajima 1955, p. 20.

2. Satō 1957c, p. 38.

3. Satō 1957b, p. 47.

4. Satō 1957c, p. 38.

5. For photographs and descriptions of shards and kiln remains see: Mizumachi 1963, pp. 240–92, and 1973, Vol. I, pp. 93–204 and 231–342; Nakajima 1955, pp. 22–32, 34–44, 59–81, 85–97, and 125–36; Satō 1963a, pp. 166–87 and 290–328.

6. Mizumachi 1973, pp. 94–110.

7. Faulkner 1981, p. 28.

8. A renowned example is the teabowl called Ayame, attributed to the Hobashira kiln (Plate 29).

9. Mizumachi 1963, fig. 118, p. 248.

10. Harada and Nakazato 1969, p.131.

11. Pyrometric cone citations refer to Seger cone numbers, the system most commonly used in Japan.

12. These percentages are only relatively precise, since the unprocessed clays had some chemical variations. Harada and Nakazato 1969, p. 132 show a similar analysis, grouping the three Kishidake kilns together.

13. The writer is indebted to Tarōuemon XIII and Nakazato Takashi for much of the information reported in this section. The continuing search for more understanding of the ancient Karatsu wares from the point of view of the artist-potter has made the Nakazato family a unique authority on Karatsu materials and processes. Their generous sharing of theories and information, and the opportunity to work at Ochawangama with them, have been invaluable. The American potter, Richard Bresnahan, who apprenticed for several years in Karatsu, has also shared technical information about clays and firing.

14. Honey 1944–45, p. 13.

15. P. L. Jouy, "The Korean Potter's Wheel," *Science*, New York, Vol. XII, 1888, p. 144, quoted in Gompertz 1968, p. 76.

16. Other Japanese potters use tools also called *hera*, but these are usually thin, pointed wooden or bamboo tools made for trimming.

17. One theory claims that the name was inspired by the shape of footwear worn in an ancient imperial kickball game introduced from China in the Nara period.

18. Only at Fujinkawachi kiln site are any quantity of bisqued shards found.

19. The word *temmoku* in Japan usually refers to a dark, saturated-iron glaze, often spotted or streaked with brown. *Temmoku-jawan* may mean a teabowl with *temmoku* glaze or a particular teabowl shape with sloping sides and small trimmed foot rim, associated with Song dynasty Jian (Chien) wares. For Karatsu it simply identifies the dark iron glaze.

20. Mizumachi 1955, p. 8. This apparently is a reference to Kainei ware, which is the Japanese rendering of Hoeryŏng, a northeastern Yi dynasty kiln site near the Tumen River operated by resident Buddhist monks. The glaze "was an oxidized feldspathic type containing silica . . . much the same ware was made at Puryŏng, Kyŏngsŏng, and Chuŭronjang." (Gompertz 1968, pp. 71–72).

21. "Ceramics of the Momoyama Period," *International Symposium* 1973, p. 82.

22. Watanabe 1971, Appendix, p. 10.

CHAPTER IV

The Karatsu Style

What exactly constitutes Karatsu ware is clarified by a scrutiny of history and the examination of materials and potters' techniques, but these fall short of defining Karatsu. Kiln site remains show the scope, quantity, and variety of products, yet are insufficient to identify the ware. Lives of potters, tea men, and lords indicate the human role in making and using Karatsu, but provide nothing to help identify it. In the end, it is the ceramics themselves, the actual examples of Karatsu, that must be turned to for answers. Karatsu cannot be identified as the product of certain kilns or potters, but rather as a *style* of such popularity and endurance that it has been and continues to be widely emulated.

This began when seventeenth century Mino potters used motifs and shapes derived from Karatsu.[1] Karatsu potters at the same time were adopting motifs and shapes from Mino ceramics. The Kyoto potter Ogata Kenzan made pots decorated in underglaze iron, "Kenzan Karatsu," adapting designs from Karatsu. Today, individual Japanese potters exhibit wares in their own personal style side by side with pieces in traditional Japanese ceramic styles, including Karatsu. The Underglaze Decorated Karatsu and Korean Karatsu are particularly popular types. Some modern potters from the Karatsu area as well as other parts of Japan attempt to duplicate famous Old Karatsu. Duplication of ancient art classics is common in Asia; it is a way of mastering ancient techniques and preserving the spirit of masterpieces. Imitation of Karatsu style pots is part of this aesthetic attitude; the modern potter validates his skills by emulating a traditional style and is free to use these same skills in exploring new personal expressions. The Karatsu model, Old Karatsu from the late sixteenth and seventeenth centuries, sets the standard for this ware. Pieces of Old Karatsu, then, must be scrutinized to discover elements of Karatsu style.

Tea men and Japanese ceramic historians classify Karatsu in so many different categories that the result often is more confusing than clarifying. Some are typed according to glaze (*madara* Karatsu, *kuro* Karatsu, *jakatsu* Karatsu, *ki* Karatsu, *ao* Karatsu). Others are grouped according to resemblance to Japanese or Chinese wares (Seto Karatsu, *temmoku* Karatsu), relationship to Korea (*oku-Gōrai*, *Chōsen* Karatsu), decoration (*hori* Karatsu, *mishima* Karatsu, *hakeme* Karatsu, *e*-Karatsu), shape (*kutsu* teabowls or bowls, *temmoku*), etc. Such an abundance of names and categories, not unusual for Japanese tea ware, emphasizes the diversity of Karatsu. However it belies the underlying simplicity of the ware, a simplicity that becomes apparent through a systematic examination of a large quantity of extant Old Karatsu.

Only the broadest groupings of Karatsu have been used in this publication, those based on the manner of glazing—Plain, Underglaze Decorated (painted and slip decorated), and Korean Karatsu (dark and light glazes on a piece). When a study of a broad, representative sampling of about one-third of the extant early Karatsu pieces was made,[2] it was shown that each of these three groupings contains similarities beyond just the manner of glazing—each has certain characteristic sizes and shapes, underscoring the logic of classifying Karatsu ware according to these basic types.

The broad sample of early Karatsu pots was first divided according to the three basic glaze types. These were then separated according to the fourteen basic Karatsu shapes: teabowl, water jar, spouted bowl, *mukōzuke* dish (tall and shallow), dish, plate, bottle, vase, jar, incense box, incense burner and fire container, ewer, saké cup, and tea caddy. Their dimensions were compared, proportions recorded, and contours noted. If the clay body had been decorated (incised, molded, sprigged) it was noted. Glazes were recorded as opaque, translucent, or transparent; dark, medium or light-toned. Painted decorations on Underglaze Decorated Karatsu were tabulated as to frequency, subject, and placement. The study provides an overview of Karatsu ware characteristics as well as the specific characteristics of each group. Some of the findings verify popular assumptions about Karatsu; others provide new information:

> The largest number of pieces are Underglaze Decorated; Plain Karatsu is next; Korean Karatsu numbers less than half as many as either of the other types.
> Teabowls are far more numerous than any other shape.
> Plain Karatsu teabowls are the most numerous of any shape in any type; Korean Karatsu teabowls are extremely rare.
> Water jars, the second most numerous shape, are almost equally represented among all three types.

The study augments information that the examination of kiln sites has yielded regarding the proportion of household wares to tea ceramics. Only a few of the fourteen shapes are specifically tea ceremony shapes: *mukōzuke* dishes, vases, incense containers, and incense burners. All others could have originated as household wares. Even among the Karatsu powdered tea containers—the tea caddies—there are examples that were made to be small jars (Plate 18). Although the Old Karatsu extant today has been preserved principally as tea ware, shapes specifically made for the tea ceremony amount to about 15 percent of all pieces. The remainder originated as obvious household ceramics or are sufficiently ambiguous in appearance to be either *chaki* or *zakki*. Every Karatsu shape could be converted to tea use (teabowls, water jars, etc.), used for the *kaiseki* meal preceding the tea ceremony (*mukōzuke* dishes, plates, bottles, etc.), or act as part of the tea room decor (vases). Since the greater part of extant Old Karatsu is common pieces later used as tea ware, it is quite possible, then, that the Old Karatsu known today is a fair representation of the total corpus and a representative sample of the Karatsu style.

Plain Karatsu (Plates 1–14, 58–93). Among Plain Karatsu a decided predominance of certain shapes exists. Over three-fourths are teabowls, water jars, saké cups, and bowls; two-thirds are teabowls alone. No other Karatsu type shows such a strong predominance of a particular shape. In fact, the most numerous items of any shape in any Karatsu type are these Plain teabowls. Plain Karatsu teabowls include many traditional classifications: *madara* Karatsu (Plate 4), Black Karatsu (Plate 78), *muji* Karatsu (Plate 66), Seto Karatsu (Plates 11, 71), *oku-Gōrai* (Plates 3, 5), *soba* type, *temmoku*, etc. Yet, Plain Karatsu teabowls, and indeed the entire corpus of Plain Karatsu, show more homogeneity than either of the other Karatsu types. Regardless of shape, the majority are between 5 and 11 centimeters (2–4¾ inches; over 85 percent being between 7 and 11 centimeters) in height. Glazes are usually opaque, white or light tones predominating. Almost all are broader than tall and have foot rims cut in plain contours placed vertically to the bowl. There are also common finishing touches the potter gave before removing the pieces from the wheel. The majority have gently shaped lip rims (Plates 3–6), only a few have plain lip rims (Plate 7, 8), and not one in the study group has a cut lip rim, a mark found on only one Plain Karatsu piece. No other Karatsu type shares so many general characteristics.

Karatsu literature often mentions a "bamboo" foot rim (one trimmed at a double angle, suggesting a bamboo node; Plate 77), giving the impression that this is a common Karatsu feature. Yet only three examples are seen within this large sample of Plain teabowls, a reminder that publications on Karatsu, both photographs and writing, frequently focus on the exceptional rather than the typical.

Other Plain Karatsu shapes are strongly homogeneous also. Water jars, almost all between 11 and 21 centimeters (4⅜–8¼ inches) high, are predominantly broad in proportion (Plates 82–84). Their large size would suggest being made by the *tataki* technique, with the consequent flat, untrimmed feet; to the contrary, almost 85 percent are wheel-thrown pieces with trimmed foot rims and shaped lips, usually formed to accommodate a lid.[3] Light, opaque glazes predominate.

The tiny saké cups have the Plain Karatsu marks also—limited range of size, broad proportions, shaped lip rims, light opaque glazes. Plain Karatsu saké cups outnumber those in the other two Karatsu types. About half have untrimmed foot rims.

On Plain Karatsu only are carved or relief markings found on untrimmed foot rims (Plates 59, 184). Although extremely rare, these are of special interest. The mark on the shard unearthed at Kameyanotani kiln (Plate 184) is also on the lidded water jar in Plate 87. The mark on the tea caddy of Plate 59 is carved into the clay; that on the water jar and shard are in relief, the result of carving into the wheelhead. Beyond the obscure meaning of the symbol itself, there is the question of the function of such markings. An obvious interpretation is that they are kiln marks, although the Karatsu kilns did not use identifying marks. They may identify pieces ordered by a particular merchant or dealer. Whatever their purpose and meaning, the markings are found on pieces that are unquestionably Karatsu, and—yet another mystery—are seen only on Plain Karatsu.

Underglaze Decorated Karatsu (Plates 28–52, 102–81). Karatsu pots with either iron oxide or slip underglaze decoration form the largest group of Old Karatsu. Slip-decorated pieces (Plates 31, 39, 104, 105, 151, 152), although numerically small, have sizes, shapes, and glazes in common with the painted pieces. Underglaze Decorated Karatsu alone has each of the fourteen shapes represented within the study. Teabowls are more than twice as numerous as any other shape. Plates, dishes, and the shallow *mukōzuke* dishes are understandably popular shapes with their ample surfaces for painted and slip decoration.

Like Plain Karatsu, the Underglaze Decorated type has broad proportions; straight, trimmed foot rims and shaped lip rims are found on most pieces. Underglaze Decorated pots in all shapes tend to be somewhat larger than the Plain Karatsu. The widest of all Karatsu pots are plates and bowls of this type. Shapes one would expect to be made in the *tataki* technique are often thrown. On all shapes, the glaze is a medium toned, translucent, often milky glaze or an opaque glaze. One might expect a transparent glaze to enhance the underglaze designs, but Karatsu potters preferred effects that are subtle or muted, softening the underglaze decorations by their choice of glazes.

Underglaze Decorated water jars (Plates 36–40, 127–32) are large, over half being between 15 and 18 centimeters. (6–7⅛ inches) high. They are thrown and have trimmed foot rims. Many have small mouths and feet, with wide bellies, resembling abacus beads, after which this type gets its name (*soroban dama*) (Plates 36–38, 130–32). Lips are shaped, but frequently lack flanges for lids (Plate 129).

Dishes and plates of the Underglaze Decorated type have a wider range of size than any other Karatsu shape of any type—5 to 30 centimeters (2–11¾ inches) or larger (Plates 155–57, 160). No other shape exceeds 30 centimeters in any dimension. Often dishes were reshaped after throwing. Rims were folded or indented to create noncircular forms (Plates 47, 165–69). Fluted rims (Plate 154) followed an old practice going back to the Kishidake sites. Widespread alteration of thrown shapes is seen only in Underglaze Decorated Karatsu and is most prevalent among dishes, though plates and tall *mukōzuke* dishes were also reshaped (Plates 42, 137–42, 144–46). Attempts to imitate molded Shino or Oribe shapes are seen (Plates 49, 137). Lips were sometimes cut (Plate 162), but more often reshaping consisted of stretching, folding, or indenting. Some reshaped tea-oriented pieces attempted precious effects, as seen in the set of *mukōzuke* dishes with lip rims in the shape of the Japanese fan (Plate 138).

The charm of Underglaze Decorated pots lies in the fresh, spontaneous paintings. No two are identical, yet all belong to the same genre (c.f. Plates 158–60, 168, 169, 177). One of the most ambitious attempts to classify the subjects in underglaze painting was conducted by Katō Hajime. He identified forty-nine subjects and still added a miscellaneous category. The paintings for him were "not so much the paintings of the tip of a brush but rather are so sensitive I would like to call them pictures painted by the heart."[4]

Taking a more general view of the painting on these pots, some characteristics are obvious. Designs are isolated; they lack confining borders or medallions; they are not used as repetitive, allover designs; the subjects are strictly decorative. Without making the detailed analysis of subjects Katō did, there are questions about the manner of painting and type of subject that can be asked: where are the designs positioned? are they isolated or connected? how many units are on each piece? are they of the same subject? are they linear designs, silhouettes, outlines? what general subjects are painted and with what frequency?

The position and frequency of repetition vary according to the ceramic shape. On teabowls, two or three isolated designs are customary, not necessarily of the same subject. No teabowl in the study group has only a single design, and just one water jar does. In contrast, the designs on cylindrical *mukōzuke* dishes are more often continued around the piece (Plates 138, 140, 141). Both isolated and continuous designs are found on dishes. Paintings on the interior of dishes and plates often extend over borders clearly defined by the shape (Plates 46, 153, 156–59, 170). The lip rim painted or dipped in underglaze iron (the *kawakujira* effect) is most common on teabowls (Plates 32, 34, 35) and *mukōzuke* dishes (Plates 138, 140, 143–46); it is rarely seen on water jars, dishes or plates.

Many designs are highly stylized: for example a simple subject such as horsetails is reduced to a decorative series of lines (Plates 33, 196). In this and other instances where there could be ambiguity, the traditional identification of subjects is honored. The painting falls into several broad groups: abstract or geometric designs; plants; birds and animals; landscapes and scenes; human figures; objects; and the underglaze iron lip (*kawakujira*). Plants are by far the most common subjects—reeds and grains, flowers, vines, trees and grasses. The simplest—reeds, grains, and grasses—predominate (Plates 130, 155, 160, 173). Nonrepresentational lines, dots, and crosshatchings are the next most common. Only one-seventh of the study group depicts birds or animals, mostly birds patterned after paintings on Oribe ware (Plates 199). There are a few sketchy human figures, usually fishermen (Plates 110, 146), and objects such as arrows and targets (Plates 47, 48, 114–15). The arrow was used by Ogata Kenzan on his Karatsu style pieces. It is a common Oribe ware motif, having been popular with daimyo for textiles, crests, and the like in the Edo period. Rarest of all are landscape scenes (Plates 50, 52, 165–66) and calligraphy (Plates 175, 183). Paintings of animals other than birds—rabbits, shrimp, a horse—are known only on shards (Plate 198). The crest of a feudal lord may be the subject on some pieces, but the liberty and freedom of the Karatsu painting prevents clear identification as a crest.

If a rationale must be found for the Karatsu underglaze painted decoration, simple ornamentation would seem to be the answer. When one makes Karatsu pottery, as I have, sitting for hours at the wheel, looking outside the studio to the grasses, reeds, tiny flowers, and leafy bushes of the rolling Kishidake and Matsuura hills, it is obvious that these are the wisps of grass, silhouetted leaves and flowers seen on Karatsu pots. The ancient potters were uncomplicated artists producing good ceramics in just a few shapes of limited size, and they decorated them with the images they saw around them. When they saw designs painted on white Shino and Oribe ware, they painted them as well in the same way they painted the grasses and flowers of their own countryside—freely, as remembered images. They used no patterns, leaving such exactitude for the painters of the blue-and-white porcelains.

Underglaze Painted Karatsu from the south Takeo kilns shows the greatest Oribe influence both in subject and manner of painting (Plates 138, 161, 162). Using outlining rather than silhouettes, framing designs, applying borders—all are Oribe derivations. Despite the strong Oribe influences, the Takeo kilns also produced Karatsu with the bolder painting the Japanese call the "Korean style," and made pieces resembling another Mino ware—Shino. These have an underglaze painting covered with an opaque glaze (Plates 49, 137) and are the closest Karatsu parallels to any Mino ware. In spite of all the borrowings and outside influences, Karatsu paintings have their own style and subjects, a blend of derived inspiration and creative interpretation quite suited to the nonsymmetric shapes on which they appear.

Slip decorated Karatsu (which is included in the Underglaze Decorated type) is the smallest Karatsu group. It tends to be freer and less skilled than the Korean *punch'ŏng* ware on which it is based. From shards at early Kishidake kiln sites, it is clear that Karatsu pots were made with inlaid, brushed, and stenciled slip decoration before *punch'ŏng* production ceased in Korea. The slip inlay (*mishima*) technique is a time-consuming, exacting one. For Karatsu potters, pressured to produce quickly in large quantities, it was a tedious and detailed process. The time demanded by the slip inlay technique must have been a factor contributing to the small quantity of *mishima* made at Karatsu kilns. Brushed slip decoration (*hakeme*) is a more common and certainly more facile technique (Plate 151). Stenciled slip decorated examples have been unearthed at early Kishidake sites (Plate 195). Stenciled Karatsu is scarce, but the technique was refined and used extensively by painters of the underglaze cobalt decorated Japanese porcelains made in Kyushu.

Korean Karatsu (Plates 15–27, 94–101). Korean Karatsu, the most vigorous and striking Karatsu type, is less numerous than either Plain or Underglaze Decorated Karatsu. It has strong identifying characteristics, the most obvious being the combined use of dark and light glazes, a widespread but not universal feature. It is the only Karatsu type showing much decorative carving of the clay body (Plates 19, 24, 99). There is a predominance of large, thrown and reshaped objects, the most numerous being tall shapes—water jars, vases, and bottles. Shapes scarcely seen among Korean Karatsu are the spouted dish, *mukōzuke* dish, incense container, saké cup, teabowl, and bowl. Of the fourteen Karatsu shapes, half play minor roles in the Korean Karatsu corpus—the shapes usually small in size.

Quantities of Korean Karatsu were produced for use in the tea ceremony and the ornamentation of the tearoom. Vases and water jars with elaborate glazes and contours were never meant to be household vessels (Plates 19, 24, 95, 97). The shapes made simply enough to have once been *zakki* are the bottle and jar (Plates 17, 20–22, 94, 100, 101), examples of which come from early kiln sites. Many Korean Karatsu pieces seen today are attributed to the Fujinkawachi kiln, renowned both for tea ceramics and Korean Karatsu.

Characteristics of the entire Korean Karatsu corpus include tall shapes (water jars range between 13 and 21 centimeters [$5\frac{1}{8}$–$8\frac{1}{4}$ inches]; bottles 18–24 centimeters [$7\frac{1}{8}$–$9\frac{1}{2}$ inches]; vases 18–30 centimeters [$7\frac{1}{8}$–12 inches]), the *tataki* technique, flat bases, and accentuated, often elaborately shaped lip rims. The two glazes—the opaque white rice-straw ash glaze and a dark iron glaze with variations from opaque to transparent, amber brown to a bluish black—provide the dramatic appearance of Korean Karatsu. When only one glaze is used, it is the iron glaze. The few unglazed pieces, the so-called Bizen Karatsu (Plate 53), also fit into this group. Usually, the lip and upper portion are dipped into the white rice-straw ash glaze (Plate 19), but there are some well-known Karatsu pots with iron glaze on the upper section (Plate 16, 18). When the white glaze fluxes and runs into the iron glaze, light blue streaks occur, a sufficiently subtle and attractive effect to inspire the placement of the white glaze at the top.

Korean Karatsu bottles have simple contours (Plates 21, 22), but other shapes tend to be reshaped and manipulated; their surfaces carved, combed, incised, and marked with impressions from carved paddles. On some, glazes are intertwined into a mesh of trailed patterns (Plates 23, 24, 97–99). Water jars and vases often have nonfunctional lugs or small loop handles. The vigorous decoration was a response to a shift in tea taste from an understated style associated with Sen no Rikyū to a dramatic one influenced by Furuta Oribe.

The inspiration for the combined use of a dark and light glaze is a puzzle. There are traceable sources for all Karatsu types, prototypes quickly being altered and made distinctive at the hands of the Kyushu potters. In addition to the connection with Korean wares, there are designs adapted from Oribe and Shino ware, the distortion and heaviness of shapes from Iga, etc. But anything comparable to the Korean Karatsu combination of dark and light glazes was not a part of Japanese or Korean ceramic ornamentation during the time Old Karatsu was produced. In fact, only in earlier wares can such a combination be seen, and then the effect is from white slip combined with an iron oxide painting or a glaze. Some Chinese pieces as early as the later Song (1127–1279) and Yuan (1279–1368) dynasties exist. They could have been brought into the Karatsu region at an early date on the ships navigating the Matsuura River, the source of the Song shards excavated at Onizuka. But there are no shards to verify this. In Southeast Asia, jars with a dipped white slip in the upper section and a thin, dark iron glaze below were produced during the Khmer period (A.D. sixth to ninth century). George Kuwayama has suggested these might be the "source of stylistic influence on Chōsen [Korean] Karatsu with its brown and white glaze,"[5] had they been imported to Japan from the Philippines. Actually, in the late sixteenth century, when the Karatsu style was being produced, Japan was conducting a lively trade, both legitimate and pirate, with Southeast Asia. Seventeenth century Japanese Takeo pieces have been dredged from the Chao Phya River at the site of the ancient Thai capital, Ayutthaya, 72 kilometers (45 miles) north of Bangkok (Plate 149). These Japanese pieces have been identified by Dean Frasché with wares produced at the Takeo Kotōge, Kotaji, and Niwagi kilns. If Japanese ceramics were taken to Southeast Asia, Southeast Asian wares could have entered Japan. In fact, underglaze decorated Thai ceramics were imported. But examples of the seventh century Cambodian Khmer ware have not been found in Kyushu. It is unlikely, although not impossible, that the combination of the dark and light glaze was an invention of the Karatsu potters. Until evidence of a source is found, this definitive mark of Korean Karatsu remains another Karatsu puzzle.

While the survey study does not identify all Karatsu, it does define the boundaries within which the vast majority of pieces fall. It further shows differences other than glazing between types of Karatsu. Although Karatsu has the reputation of being a confusing, unidentifiable ware, the study defines its limitations of size, shape, and decoration. Some famous frequently published and exhibited Karatsu pots, although well within the general parameter of the ware, are popular because of their uniqueness. The Tanakamaru Collection Ayame teabowl (Plate 29), the Idemitsu persimmon tea jar (Plate 41) and others are singular. Such pieces make Karatsu seem too diverse to classify. Other well-known pieces are more representative—the Seattle dish (Plate 155), the teabowl named Sambō (Plate 69), the Idemitsu water jar with reed decoration (Plates 36, 129). The study group embraces both singular and representative Karatsu pieces and, therefore, indicates the basic features of the style. Karatsu's variety is not unlimited, its glazes are few and used in specific ways, its painted decorations are extremely limited in subject and manner of application. The limited repertoire of motifs and decorative techniques is blended with a freedom that does not admit duplication. Each pot is totally itself; pieces with the same decoration (so-called sets) display a delightful and refreshing disregard for the conventions of making things look alike.

Non-Karatsu products from Karatsu kilns (Plates 43, 90, 134, 148–50). The early blue-and-white Japanese porcelain made at Karatsu kilns has never been called "Karatsu porcelain" but is identified as a separate ceramic genre. This has not been the case with stonewares outside the Karatsu style. Stoneware called "Pre-Karatsu" here includes large jars and bottles, part of the tradition of Japanese utilitarian folk ware, made not so much for table use, as was Karatsu, but for storage. It has a natural glaze resulting from the deposit of ash falling on the pot during firing, or is covered with a simple, nonfeldspathic ash glaze. Pieces are of a scale larger than that characteristic of Karatsu and are formed by the *tataki* process. Foot rims are untrimmed, and lips frequently are made by folding over the clay (Plate 193). Some have cylindrical necks added to a bulbous body (Plate 90), a shape found in earlier domestic Japanese ware, but neither this process or shape are characteristic of the Karatsu types.

There is a well-known tea jar of this type having a dedicatory statement inscribed into the clay, including a date—Tenshō 20 (1592)—and the name of the donor (Plate 90). It was made as an offering jar and now is in the possession of the Shōmo Shrine on Iki Island. It differs from Karatsu in shape, manner of fabrication, glazing, and scale. It further has an engraved inscription and was intended as a temple jar, both foreign to Karatsu. It has, nevertheless, been identified as Karatsu. While it quite likely was produced at an early Kishidake kiln using the same clays as Karatsu, perhaps even being fired with objects in the Karatsu style, it does not fit into the Karatsu repertoire. Its inscribed date has made it a focus for the dating of Karatsu, a condition complicated by the fact that there was no Tenshō 20 Japanese reign date, the Tenshō period having lasted but nineteen years. Such an error could be innocent enough at a provincial kiln; continuing to call it "Karatsu" would be a mistake. The jar cannot be used to give a date for Karatsu's origin since it lies outside the Karatsu style. It is far more accurate to call this and other like pieces "Pre-Karatsu," not so much because they were all made before Karatsu but because they antedate Karatsu stylistically. The Tenshō 20 jar and the group it belongs to relate to medieval Japanese ceramics; Karatsu is an early example of the modern Japanese style.

The stoneware called Takeo Karatsu also has qualities differing from Karatsu's style. It has larger shapes—wide-mouthed jars with heavy lip rims, bulbous bottles with long, slender necks (Plate 134), large platters (Plates 43, 148–50). Slip brushed over the body characterizes this group. It may be combed, incised, have underglaze iron painted on it, be painted with brown and green glaze, or have a combination of these (Plate 43). A recurring subject is a sprawling Japanese pine tree accented with iron amber and copper green glazes (Plate 134). This style seems to have evolved in the mid-seventeenth century at the Takeo kilns and is here called Takeo ware. The later Futagawa ware stems from this style. As in the case of Pre-Karatsu, there is no reason to believe the potters produced these or Karatsu exclusively. They probably made both styles simultaneously. It is this ware that has been found at non-Japanese sites: Thailand, the Celebes, North Borneo, and Okinawa. While it may have been export ware, its presence in locations overseas could also have resulted from being used by the large number of Japanese living at foreign trading posts, by traders, and by pirates. Japanese export porcelains are well documented, but no records are known for export Takeo ware.

When Pre-Karatsu and Takeo wares are isolated from the Karatsu corpus, the Karatsu style becomes clear, and both Pre-Karatsu and Takeo pots can be easily distinguished. The Takeo wares differ from Karatsu in contour, size, use of slip, number of underglaze pigments, glazes, and motifs used for decoration. They were not made for the domestic table or tea room as were Karatsu pieces and belong to a different genre. Pre-Karatsu also stands outside the Karatsu style. In scale, use, style of glazing, and even in contour it relates much more to the traditional Japanese stonewares that were produced from the twelfth to seventeenth centuries. Separating Karatsu from Pre-Karatsu permits a fair assumption to be made regarding the date of Karatsu's origin.

Date of Karatsu's origin. When Furuta Oribe made his 1603 entries regarding Karatsu ware in his tea journal, the style was well established. In fact, each type of Karatsu is seen among the remains of the Kishidake kilns, which closed in 1594 (Bunroku 3), two years after the date inscribed on the Shōmo Shrine's tea jar (see Note 37, page 35). One Underglaze Decorated shard is dated 1618 (Plate 183). These scattered dates are not sufficient to date Karatsu, and it is unlikely new data will be coming from the Karatsu kilns, since they have been sifted through again and again.

Now it is outside the Hizen region that Japanese archaeologists are finding Karatsu. In Fukui Province, the remains of Ichijōdani Castle, which burned in 1573, have yielded an informative group of ceramics. Included are Chinese *temmoku* and blue-and-white porcelain, Korean glazed stoneware, and Karatsu, some of a high quality, such as *soba* type teabowls. As the date of destruction suggests, no Arita porcelains are within this group. The Ichijōdani Castle remains provide the earliest firm date for Karatsu. At the later Toda riverside excavations in Shimane Prefecture, many Karatsu pieces have been found as well as Chinese celadons and blue-and-white porcelain, some Korean wares, and Arita porcelain. Similar deposits have been unearthed at Sakai near Osaka. While these verify the tradition that Karatsu was widespread throughout western Japan, the Ichijōdani excavations are the most useful. They show that by the third quarter of the sixteenth century Karatsu was used in western Japan. The presence of Karatsu means that the rapid-turning kick wheel, high-fired feldspathic glazes, and the multichambered, efficient *noborigama* were already in use in Kyushu. The Matsuura group of kilns developed after the fall of the Kishidake kilns (1594), so the Ichijōdani wares must be Kishidake products. At Kishidake Hobashira, the opaque white rice-straw ash glaze, identified with the North Korean Hoeryŏng ware, is found. According to Gompertz, until more exploration of Hoeryŏng kilns can be made, the "consensus of expert opinion is that none of these is older than the middle Yi period, or about 1500–1650."[6] Karatsu, then, must have originated sometime between 1500 (the ostensible earliest date for the Korean rice-straw ash glaze) and 1573 (the burning of Ichijōdani Castle).

A mid-sixteenth century origin of Karatsu is plausible. Interchange with Korea was then heightened both legitimately and illicitly. There was interest in Japanese ceramics at home, fanned by the enthusiasm for tea. The change of taste and style included an acceptance and even preference for Japanese wares by merchant tea men and tea masters alike.[7] A mid-sixteenth century date for the evolution of the Karatsu style still allows for the possibility of an earlier origin of the Kishidake kilns themselves and the beginning of a Pre-Karatsu style ware. The origin of Karatsu cannot be dated from the opening of kilns likely to have produced another prior style, nor from an atypical inscribed jar, but from Karatsu's observed relationship to the people and history of Japan—from the remains of a burned castle and from the records and remains of a period of ceramic innovations and social ferment. The mid-sixteenth century date places Karatsu's beginnings at the close of the medieval period of Japanese ceramics and at the forefront of modern ceramics. The innovations of Karatsu—underglaze decorated, high-fired, trimmed stoneware—are consonant with the emergence of modern Japanese ceramics.

Old Karatsu, that embodiment of new shapes, glazes, and decoration that characterize the Karatsu style, may have been produced for as little as seventy-five to one hundred years. The style has enjoyed periodic revivals up to and including the present. The closing of many kilns, or conversion of their production to porcelain as the result of the discovery of kaolin, altered the demand for Karatsu and, eventually, appears to have affected its style as well. Takeo kilns began making the large, slip-covered pieces. At kilns continuing to make Karatsu, such as Shiinomine and the official kilns, in response to the mid-seventeenth century shift in taste, a refined Presentation Karatsu (Plates 152, 180) prevailed. It contrasted stylistically with Old Karatsu, being made from refined, levigated clay covered with a glossy, transparent glaze. Often there were stamped or inlaid decorations. Presentation Karatsu is dated to the late seventeenth and early eighteenth century. When a revival of tea enthusiasm stirred the desire for the Old Karatsu style in the late eighteenth century, digging for cast-offs ensued at the old kiln sites. Subsequent revivals of Karatsu always turned to Old Karatsu as a model. The early wares thus became the most enduring example of the ideal Karatsu style.

Relation of Karatsu to other Japanese ceramics. The more other Japanese wares are known and understood, the more precisely Karatsu is understood. The kilns established by lords returning from Hideyoshi's campaigns—Agano, Hagi, Takatori, Satsuma—originally made ceramics like Karatsu. Careful excavations at the Nogata kiln site of Takatori ware are not only informative about Takatori products but Karatsu as well. Because the style of Takatori, especially early Takatori, is now understood more accurately, questionable pieces once identified as Karatsu are being reclassified as Takatori. As more serious exploration of early Edo sites in Hizen occurs, only more exact identification of all Kyushu wares can result.

The relationship between Mino wares—particularly white Shino and Oribe—and Karatsu is becoming more refined as well. Karatsu kiln construction and firing techniques in the Mino area and Shino and Oribe motifs on Karatsu have been known all along. Motoyashiki, the first *noborigama* in the Mino region, resembled Handōgame in construction and, like the Karatsu kilns, fired a variety of different style wares—Oribe, Black Seto, Black Oribe, Yellow Seto, Shino, and Shino Oribe. Furthermore, just as Karatsu potters were influenced by other contemporary Japanese wares—Mino, Bizen, Iga—the early Mino *noborigama* produced Mino Iga, Mino Karatsu (Plate 208), and Mino Bizen.[8]

Shards have become particularly important in knowing more about Mino wares and their relationship to Karatsu. These fragments can be identified with kiln sites and show the scope of wares from specific sites. Not far from the remains of the Mino Motoyashiki kiln, the Toki City Mino Ceramic History Research Center has been studying and organizing materials from the Mino kilns. There, in the heart of Mino country, they mounted an exhibition of sixty-five representative Old Karatsu pieces accompanied by a comparative display of Karatsu and Mino shards.[9] This landmark exhibition placed Karatsu and Mino shards with the same motifs together. It was apparent that the sharing of subjects goes far beyond flying birds and outlined flowers, including an extensive array from bamboo shoots to arched bridges, sprouting seeds to abstract designs. The shards show that the migration of motifs from Mino to Karatsu and Karatsu to Mino was not just a seventeenth century phenomenon, but continued into the eighteenth century, when stamped designs on Presentation Karatsu had counterparts in stamped and sprigged Mino ornamentations. While the extent of common painted decorations is impressive, even more striking is the difference between the Mino and Karatsu modes of painting. While Mino painting is hardly precise, in contrast to the Karatsu versions of the same subject, the Mino style seems controlled and detailed.

Increased understanding of Karatsu, resulting from studies such as those of the Takatori kiln sites and Mino excavated materials, can only continue as other studies develop. Kō-zuru Gen of Kyushu and Boston has been examining Agano ceramics for years, leading to a finer discrimination between certain Karatsu and Agano pieces. In addition, there is a growing interest in the effect Southeast Asian wares had on Japanese stoneware and early porcelain decoration; studies in this area could prove relevant to Karatsu.

Karatsu style, extension and duplication. Imitation and cross-influence are characteristics of early modern pottery production in Japan. The practices at Mino and Karatsu were usual and continue to the present day. Among works made by the Kyoto potter Ogata Kenzan (1663–1716) are some in the Karatsu style. Decorated with a radiating pattern of arrows painted in underglaze iron, the Kenzan Karatsu have a muted coloring atypical of Kenzan's usual work.

It is common for contemporary potters to work in the Karatsu style. Murata Gen, an artist-potter of Mashiko and prize winner in the annual exhibition of the Japanese Art Association (Nitten), held a Tokyo exhibition of works done completely in the Karatsu style. Another Nitten prize winner, Katō Mineo of Seto, has experimented widely with traditional styles—Karatsu, Bizen, Old Seto, Shino, Oribe, Chinese celadon, Korean and Chinese blue-and-white porcelain. Kitaōji Rosanjin, the potter exhibited when the new Japan Society building was dedicated in New York, worked in ten different styles, including Karatsu—Plain, Underglaze Decorated (*hakeme* and painted), as well as adaptations of the Takeo style. Such emulation of recognized ceramic styles by established potters and experimenting amateurs is widespread. Many adapt a style to their own interpretation, while others attempt to duplicate famous old pieces in detail. Thus the Asian artistic tradition of emulation of the classics continues in the world of Japanese ceramics.

Karatsu today. In and around Karatsu city a lively ceramic industry continues to flourish. The tourist map shows some twenty-nine kilns in the city and vicinity. Every type of Karatsu can be seen in all parts of the city, from traditional shapes to new ones developed to attract modern buyers. Nishikawa Ikkō, president of the Karatsu Pottery Association, points out:

> Today, instead of just carrying on the tradition set by olden makers, we are also eager to improve and make our own designs, thus continuing the old customs and traditions with a modern touch.[10]

Ceramics remain an important enterprise for the little port city. Only the Nakazato family traces its origins to the migration of potters at the time of Hideyoshi's campaign. Within the area are a number of independent potters who at one time worked at the Nakazato kiln. Nishioka Satoru, who excavated old kiln sites for many years, unearthed many of the items now in the Nakazato family collection. He assisted the ceramic art historian Mizumachi Wasaburō as well. His long-time association with Old Karatsu has made him a keen connoisseur of old wares and has equipped him to re-create the ancient products with remarkable accuracy. Others include Kojirō, an expert on glazes, who worked with the Nakazatos and now operates an independent kiln overlooking Nishi-Karatsu. At the foot of Mt. Kagami, about seven kilometers (eleven and one-half miles) east of Karatsu, the potter Inoue operates Kyōzangama, producing Underglaze Decorated Karatsu, both painted and *hakeme*, and Korean Karatsu.

Other than the Nakazatos, whose claim to fame and tradition is unquestioned, the Nakano family has made the most serious effort to be identified with traditional Karatsu potters. Even the characters for their name are similar to those of the Nakazatos (Nakano, 中野; Nakazato, 中里). Their published history states the family goes back four "generations" (two of these were brothers). In late Edo, about 1860, the family founder, Yatsushima Yagorō, made ceramic molds for sculpture. His son, Nakano Eirin, worked with the Nakazato family, eventually founding his own kiln. His third son, a farmer and barber, succeeded him. Upon the latter's death in 1945, his brother Nakano Tōji, a former businessman, took over the potting, "keeping the classic and authentic tradition while almost all others make new forms."[11]

After a century or more of moderate production and a focus on making ceramic statuary, pottery making has increased in the latter half of the twentieth century. Not even when Hideyoshi and his tea masters Sen no Rikyū and Furuta Oribe were in Karatsu was the market so good. The quantity of pieces demanded for household wares was larger then, but the status of the ware today, the demands from tourists, and the orders from large department stores and businesses in urban centers have made production of Karatsu more profitable for the potters than it has ever been. Indeed, it has been only since the Meiji Restoration (1868) and the abolishing of feudal clans (1872) that the potters owned their potteries free of lordly control.

Those contributing most to the revival of interest in Karatsu were Nakazato family members. They also have benefited most from it. They continued to make Karatsu while exploring old kiln sites in order to understand and reproduce more accurately the techniques, forms, and decorations of Old Karatsu.

The revival began at Ochawangama, a kiln dating back to the time of the fifth Nakazato generation—Kiheiji's time. This was the Tōjinmachi Ochawangama, built after the potters fled from Shiinomine (1707), a beehive type kiln with linked, domed chambers. The remains of Ochawangama (Plate 224) are just a few feet from the kilns now in use.

The old Ochawangama was closed in 1919. Over fifty years later it was dedicated as a Shintō sanctuary at the Nakazato Tarōuemon Ceramic Studios in Tōjinmachi, now the Chōda section of Karatsu city. It is overgrown with the local grass and field flowers seen so often on Karatsu pottery.

The present Ochawangama is sheltered by a roofed shed. It has the early *noborigama* form of Kishidake kilns, a "split-bamboo" (*waridake*) vaulted kiln with linked chambers (Figure 1, page 146). While traditional wheels, tools, and equipment predominate, electric wheels and pyrometers are also used, and there is an electric bisque kiln. For the most part, the rhythm around the studio is simple and uncluttered, probably not too unlike the early days of Karatsu manufacture.

In the first quarter of the twentieth century there was a widespread movement to restore ancient techniques. Then the early Karatsu kiln, the "split-bamboo," replaced the retired kiln. Clays from ancient veins were dug, and research on ancient glazes resulted in reviving the rice-straw ash and milky translucent glazes and the *kohiki* technique (slip-coated pots covered with translucent or transparent glaze).[12] The arc patterns inside large Old Karatsu pieces inspired new interest in the *tataki* technique. *Tataki* as practiced at Karatsu today has technical details attributable to Tarōuemon XII. The paddling method unquestionably was used for Old Karatsu, and indeed has roots in much earlier Asian ceramics. Nevertheless, the process of turning the wheel by the rhythmic striking of the vessel and the effective but unusual way of affixing the base appear to have been processes developed by Tarōuemon XII in his efforts to reproduce the quality and appearance of early paddled wares.

Nakazato Tarōuemon XII (1895–1985) (Plate 217) was the right potter, digger, researcher, and developer at a time of Japanese ceramic growth and revival, a movement that eventually reached beyond the confines of Japan. This second son of Nakazato Ten'yū (see page 34), Shigeo, was given the title Tarōuemon XII in 1927, just three years after his graduation from the pottery faculty of the local technical institute, the Saga Prefectural Senior High School of Engineering. His was a generation of potters from different ceramic centers who began to investigate the origins and traditional styles of certain great wares of Japan—Shino, Bizen, Karatsu. In 1929, under the sponsorship of local families, he began the investigation of the Old Karatsu kilns of Hizen (Nagasaki and Saga prefectures). While such diggings were fairly crude affairs compared with the more scientific excavations of the postwar period, they resulted in scholars, potters and critics learning much and gave impetus to more scholarly research later. The old kiln remains and shards three centuries old inspired Tarōuemon XII to learn as much as possible about early Karatsu and to revive its style and techniques.

By 1931 Tarōuemon XII was exhibiting in Japan; in the postwar period he was shown in Europe, the United States, Latin America (including the 1953 biennale in São Paulo,

Brazil), and in Asian countries other than Japan. In 1969 he retired, leaving the family leadership to his oldest son, Tadao, who took the title Nakazato Tarōuemon XIII. Under the art name Muan, Tarōuemon XII remained an active potter. He also became an extern member of the Daitoku-ji temple in Kyoto, assuming still another name, Dō-ō Sōhaku. In 1984 he and Tarōuemon XIII had a joint exhibition, which was shown in seven Japanese cities. He died January 5, 1985, at the age of 89.

The life of Nakazato Tarōuemon XII spanned the period of new acceptance and knowledge of Karatsu. Karatsu regained its importance in Japan and was exhibited and collected internationally. Tarōuemon XII rose from the second son of a traditional potter to being a "Living National Treasure," an honor awarded to only a dozen or so potters. From a relatively diversified ceramic center, making sculptures as well as pottery, Ochawangama has become one of the most traditional and renowned kilns in Japan. Tarōuemon XII's delving into the past and successful efforts in reestablishing the style of Old Karatsu were not only artistic successes but were extremely rewarding financially as well. Modern tea ceramics, in particular, command prices that astonish foreigners, and, when the pieces are products of a family of potters who trace their lineage back for centuries, items can be and are priced in thousands of dollars. By any yardstick, Tarōuemon XII led a successful life—he had status within his country, he brought Old Karatsu and his own products to an international audience, he stimulated new interest in Old Karatsu and its history, reestablished the ancient style of Karatsu, and lived the contented life of a potter.

The ceramic center at Ochawangama continues to be a family operation, expanding without losing the small manufactory character so typical of Japan. Tarōuemon XIII continues making wares in the traditional style and is admired for the grace of his underglaze painted designs. He also keeps experimenting with other styles, glazes, and techniques. He produces handsome inlaid ware (Plate 55), which he exhibits alongside his traditional Karatsu. Like many a successful modern potter, he is torn from pottery production as the demands of national arts organizations increase, exhibitions at home and abroad require his presence, publications are prepared, and his own research into the origins and development of the *tataki* technique take him into Southeast Asia and Korea. In addition to the pottery studio at Ochawangama, the family maintains a small sales room and a gallery where items from the family collection are exhibited—Old Karatsu and shards as well as world ceramics, particularly those that have an affinity to the Karatsu style.

While the tradition of a small family ceramic center is being maintained, modern pressures and standards are disrupting it. The four living sons of Nakazato Tarōuemon XII reflect these changes and tensions. Tarōuemon XIII heads Ochawangama. Although more and more involved in business responsibilities and public demands, he is the only member of his generation still potting at Ochawangama. His brother, Ken'ichi, manages the museum and shop, a sales and shipping center. The two other brothers, Shigetoshi and Takashi, formerly worked at Ochawangama making both traditional Karatsu and pieces according to their individual styles. Each now operates his own kiln in the Karatsu area. Most Karatsu made to fill large orders from department stores, retailers, and organizations is produced by apprentices and members of the next generation of Nakazatos. One of Tarōuemon's daughters, Keiko, follows her father's penchant and concentrates on decorating; her husband, Robert Okasaki, and another daughter, Yumiko, throw. A son, Tadahiro, in his mid-twenties at the time of this writing, shows promise as a potter-sculptor. The kiln master, Matsumoto Toshimitsu, has been at Ochawangama for almost twenty years, and a number of women who assist in loading and cleaning pots also have long associations there.

Nakazato Shigetoshi (b. 1930) established his own pottery at Kōda, Karatsu city, in 1973. Even while at Ochawangama, he was evolving a personal style using large, simple forms for his work, which included architectural ceramics. He has won prizes in Japanese exhibitions and has been shown in Mexico, the United States, and Europe. His kiln, Sangen, was named after the jar that brought him his first distinguished award, the Hokuto Prize at the eighth Nitten exhibition. He is renowned for his expertise with kilns and the subtle beauty of his glazes and ceramic finishes (Plate 56).

The youngest brother, Nakazato Takashi, has the reputation of being the top ceramic thrower of Japan. He studied at the Kyoto City Ceramic Institute and the Saga Prefecture Ceramic Research Institute, and was apprenticed to various potters before joining the family at Ochawangama. He, too, made traditional Karatsu, developed his own style, and won prizes. In the late 1960s he spent a year and a half lecturing and giving pottery demonstrations in the United States, traveling to and studying at ceramic centers in Europe, the Middle East, Southeast Asia, and Korea. Then, in 1970 he left Ochawangama and established a ceramic center on Tanegashima, a tiny island south of Kyushu with an unusual ceramic tradition. There, near Nishinoomote city, he built an *anagama* type kiln, made unglazed pottery from local clays, and experimented with injecting water into the kiln while firing. The result was a new style of ceramics—Tanegashima. The ware is unglazed except for natural ash glaze or vitrification of the clay and is richly colored by the oxides the prolonged firing process forces to the surface (Plate 57). Returning to the Karatsu area, Takashi established a new kiln, Ryūtagama ("Dragon Kiln"), in 1976, where experiments in the Tanegashima and other styles continue.

The Tanegashima-type kiln and unglazed process now have a few replicas in Japan and abroad. Apprentices Terry Allen, who worked on Tanegashima island, and Richard Bresnahan, who worked at Ryūtagama, have taken the kiln type and processes to the United States. Steen Kepp, a Danish potter working in La Borne, France, has been to Karatsu several times and now operates a Tanegashima-type kiln in France. The influence of the traditional potters abroad appears to be more through their personal style than through traditional Karatsu. One apprentice of Tarōuemon XII from the United States, Malcolm Wright, worked at Ochawangama. At his Turnpike Road Pottery, Marlboro, Vermont, he operates a wood-burning kiln. His handsome stoneware has an affinity to Karatsu in spirit, and some is made in the Karatsu style.

New elements are now intruding into the history of Karatsu. It is not unusual for traditional Japanese craftsmen to develop new styles, but the extension of Karatsu beyond Japan is new. While the kilns remain family-sized, the audience for their products is becoming more sophisticated and international. The production of modern Karatsu and conscious linkage with the past peaked during the lifetime of Tarōuemon XII. The diversification of styles, establishment of independent kilns, preoccupation with exhibitions, and outreach into the international arena certainly have consequences for the future of traditional Karatsu production. As in the past, continued demand for Karatsu style ceramics depends heavily on its integration with the Japanese tea ceremony. As long as it continues to be a strong element of Japanese society, demands for Karatsu style ceramics can be expected to continue. Meanwhile, the family potters, all highly skilled artists with personal styles, meet demands for Karatsu style wares while establishing themselves as renowned potters in their own right.

Whatever the future of the potters in Karatsu city may be, the Karatsu style is an integral part of the Japanese ceramic vocabulary and is beginning to be employed by some non-Japanese potters as well. The enduring and universal appeal of the Karatsu style has reached generations and cultures beyond the imagination of Edo potters, merchants, and men of tea. Some Karatsu pieces are designated as "National Treasure" (Plate 69) and "Important Cultural Property" (Plates 127, 153, 154), some are prized museum pieces, still others continue to be used and admired as tea ceramics. Out-of-the-way shops in Japan are searched for undiscovered old pieces, and collectors and museums seek Old Karatsu as avidly as the ancient tea connoisseurs, who, charmed by the humble table ceramic, focused attention on this unique ware.

NOTES

1. For a comparative study of the interchange of motifs between Karatsu and Mino, see Toki City Mino Ceramic Research Center, 1983.

2. Becker 1974, pp. 183–217.

3. Ceramic lids are the exception for Karatsu, most being of wood or lacquer; for tea caddies, ivory lids were used.

4. Katō, Hajime, "Tōgi jō kara mita Karatsu," *Tōsetsu*, October 1954, p. 22.

5. "Influences of the Wares in Southeast Asia on Japanese Ceramics," *International Symposium* 1973, p. 175.

6. Gompertz 1968, p. 72.

7. Louise Cort, "Medieval Japanese Ceramics and the Tea Ceremony," *Keramos* Vol. 85, July 1979, pp. 56–57.

8. Faulkner and Impey 1981, pp. 33–37.

9. Toki City Mino Ceramic Research Center 1983.

10. Brochure: *Karatsu yaki.*

11. Brochure: *Karatsu Ware and Nakano Ceramics* and information supplied by Dr. John A. Pope.

12. Korean *punch'ŏng* pots dipped in (or swabbed with) white slip are called *kohiki* by the Japanese. *Kohiki* pieces are not as numerous as slip-brushed (*hakeme*) pots. The slip-dipping technique was not widely adopted by the Old Karatsu potters, but appears at some of the private kilns resulting from the Potters' War and has entered the repertoire of the modern Karatsu potters.

Notes to the Plates

1. Plain Karatsu tea caddy, rice-straw ash glaze. H. 4.9 cm., D. 7.0 cm. Ivory lid. Formerly in the collection of the Imperial Household Guard. Idemitsu Museum of Arts.

2. Plain Karatsu tea caddy, name: Tama Tsushima ("Beautiful Islet"). H. 8.9 cm., D. 6.6 cm. Two brocade bags. Idemitsu Museum of Arts. (See Plates 58, 59)

3. Plain Karatsu teabowl, *oku-Gōrai* shape, rice-straw ash glaze. H. 9.2 cm., D. 14.7 cm. Formerly in the collection of Lord Matsudaira Fumai. Tanakamaru Collection.

4. Plain Karatsu teabowl, name: Haku-ō ("White Seagull"), rice-straw ash glaze with streaks of blue, attributed to Hobashira kiln. H. 12.2 cm., D. 13.2 cm., D. foot 5.0 cm. Tanakamaru Collection.

5. Plain Karatsu teabowl, *oku-Gōrai* shape, name: Aki no Yo ("Autumn Night"). H. 9.0 cm., D. 15.4 cm. Listed in the Unshū Treasurehouse Register. Idemitsu Museum of Arts.

6. Plain Karatsu teabowl, *oku-Gōrai* shape, name: Sazare Ishi ("Pebble"), crawling of glaze on trimmed area above foot. H. 8.1 cm., D. 15.2 cm. Formerly in the Matsuura Household Collection. Idemitsu Museum of Arts.

7, 8. Plain Karatsu teabowl, traces of *nameko* blue in interior bottom, pinholes on the exterior, tea stains on the interior near lip. H. 18.2 cm., D. 14.1 cm., D. foot 5.9 cm. Idemitsu Museum of Arts.

9. Plain Karatsu teabowl, incised with bold diagonal crosshatched lines (*hori* Karatsu type). Shards of this type unearthed at both Upper and Lower Handōgame kiln sites, made originally as teabowl. H. 9.6 cm., D. 13.8 cm. Private collection, Japan.

10. Plain Karatsu teabowl, heavily crackled glaze. D. 12.6 cm. Formerly in the Kuroda Household Collection. Idemitsu Museum of Arts.

11. Plain Karatsu teabowl, shape and glaze (almost pure feldspar) called Seto Karatsu, glaze has crawled on trimmed area above foot, attributed to Shiinomine kiln. H. 6.7 cm., D. 14.6 cm. Idemitsu Museum of Arts.

12. Plain Karatsu teabowl, black glaze ground under a crawling white glaze (*jakatsu*—snakeskin—effect), indented at four places, lip has been rounded, attributed to the Shōkoya kiln. H. 7.7 cm., D. 11.9 cm. Idemitsu Museum of Arts.

13. Plain Karatsu spouted bowl, name: Hanare Goma ("Stray Horse"), household piece used as a teabowl. H. 7.0 cm., D. 13.0 cm. Tanakamaru Collection.

14. Plain Karatsu water jar, dark iron glaze, incised horizontal grooves, ceramic handle and lid. H. 20.8 cm. without handle, D. 19.6 cm. Tanakamaru Collection.

15. Korean Karatsu vase, opaque white glaze on body, lip dipped into dark iron glaze, lip began to vitrify and slumped into shape called "carp" mouth; excavated from the Fujinkawachi kiln. H. 20.3 cm., D. 9.3 cm. Tanakamaru Collection.

16. Korean Karatsu water jar, opaque white glaze, lip dipped into dark iron glaze and marked with heavy drippings of white glaze. D. 20.1 cm. Private collection, Japan.

17. Korean Karatsu water jar, name: Robaku ("Waterfall on Mt. Lu"), opaque white glaze on upper section forms a run over dark iron glaze on body, attributed to Fujinkawachi kiln. H. 17.1 cm. Fujita Art Museum.

18. Korean Karatsu tea caddy, name: Roku-ji ("Temple at the Foot of the Mountain"). H. 8.6 cm., D. 7.4 cm. Ivory lid. Formerly in the Matsuura Household Collection. Idemitsu Museum of Arts.

19. Korean Karatsu vase, glossy finely crackled white glaze over a speckled dark iron glaze, hexagonal shape, vertical slashes on body, two ears, two holes for hanging drilled in the lip rim. H. 23.6 cm., D. 12.4 cm. Formerly in the Koike Household Collection. Idemitsu Museum of Arts.

20. Korean Karatsu water jar, blue streaks occur where the rice-straw ash glaze runs into the dark glaze. H. 20.2 cm., D. mouth 9.7 cm., D. body 14.2 cm., D. base 9.6 cm. Lacquer lid (not shown). Formerly in the Imperial Household Guards Collection. Idemitsu Museum of Arts.

21. Korean Karatsu saké bottle, thick iron glaze on neck, thin rice-straw ash glaze on body, decoration on body sometimes identified as a peony. H. 20.2 cm., D. 10.8 cm. Tanakamaru Collection.

22. Korean Karatsu bottle, a household pot used in the tea ceremony as a vase. H. 20.5 cm. Idemitsu Museum of Arts.

23. Korean Karatsu water jar, dark iron glaze and white rice-straw ash glaze trailing on body, dipped into white glaze from lip to shoulder. H. 19.0 cm., D. mouth 8.4 cm. Tanakamaru Collection.

24. Korean Karatsu water jar, concave body with two small lugs, incised designs, unglazed lip, dark and light glazes trailed on body, attributed to Fujinkawachi kiln. H. 20.3 cm., D. 17.6 cm. Idemitsu Museum of Arts.

25. Korean Karatsu ewer, white rice-straw ash glaze shows slight traces of blue where it feathers into the thin, translucent iron glaze, attributed to Fujinkawachi kiln. H. 23.8 cm., D. 18.5 cm. Lacquer lid (not shown). Idemitsu Museum of Arts.

26. Korean Karatsu ewer, blue streaking formed by highly fluxed white rice-straw ash glaze running over most of the vessel. H. 20.6 cm., D. body 15.0 cm, D. base 12.0 cm. Idemitsu Museum of Arts.

27. Korean Karatsu ewer, twisted handle, dark iron glaze runs into the lower white glaze. H. 15.8 cm., D. 14.2 cm. Lacquer lid (not shown). Freer Gallery of Art.

28. Underglaze Decorated Karatsu tea caddy, pale feldspar glaze over underglaze iron decoration of wild grape spray, formerly used as a *mukōzuke* dish, attributed to Dōzono or Matsuura Kameyanotani kiln. H. 8.8 cm., D. 5.7 cm.

29. Underglaze Decorated Karatsu teabowl, name: Ayame ("Iris"). The straight sides indicate that this was fashioned as a teabowl. The two freely painted iris designs have exceptional vitality. Although several kilns of the Kishidake and Matsuura groups have been suggested as the provenance of this piece, the lack of comparable shards makes kiln attribution unclear. H. 9.2 cm., D. 12.0 cm. Tanakamaru Collection.

30. Cylindrical Underglaze Decorated Karatsu teabowl, horizontal combing on body, freely painted design of a shrine. The white glaze, straight sides, and design suggest influence from Shino ware. H. 8.4 cm., D. 9.0 cm. Idemitsu Museum of Arts.

31. Underglaze Decorated Karatsu finely potted teabowl, incised and impressed patterns filled with white slip (*mishima* technique), high foot rim. H. 7.5 cm., D. 13.7 cm.

32. Underglaze Decorated Karatsu teabowl, name: Suehiro ("Folding Fan"), *kawakujira* style (underglaze iron dipped) lip. H. 9.1 cm., D. 10.0 cm. Tanakamaru Collection.

33. Underglaze Decorated Karatsu teabowl, *tokusa* (stylized horsetail) design. H. 9.0 cm., D. 12.5 cm. Tanakamaru Collection. (See Plate 196)

34. Underglaze Decorated Karatsu teabowl, *kawakujira* style (underglaze iron) lip, spiral designs. Parts of the underglaze painting remain uncovered by glaze, evidence that the Karatsu potters painted underglaze iron on the green clay. H. 7.8 cm., D. 12.5 cm. Idemitsu Museum of Arts.

35. Underglaze Decorated Karatsu teabowl, *kawakujira* style (underglaze iron dipped) lip, two designs of cross within circle (on opposite sides of bowl). H. 9.0 cm., D. 14.3 cm. Idemitsu Museum of Arts.

36. Underglaze Decorated Karatsu water jar, "abacus bead" shape, crawling glaze on trimmed lower section, flowers and bamboo fence decoration on facing side, linked curling vines on opposite side. H. 16.1 cm., D. body 23.0 cm., D. mouth 16.6 cm., D. base 10.8 cm. Idemitsu Museum of Arts. (See Plate 129)

37. Underglaze Decorated Karatsu water jar, name: Tsu no Kuni ("Harbor Kingdom"), finely crackled rice-straw ash glaze, underglaze iron reed design, attributed to a kiln of the Kishidake group. H. 15.8 cm., D. body 19.3 cm. Idemitsu Museum of Arts.

38. Underglaze Decorated Karatsu water jar, "abacus bead" shape. Darkened blotches under the glaze caused by water seepage either during or after firing are called *amamori* ("leaking rain"). H. 13.0 cm., D. body 18.3 cm., D. mouth 11.0 cm., D. base 8.1 cm. Idemitsu Museum of Arts.

39. Underglaze Decorated Karatsu water jar, incised and impressed patterns filled with white slip (*mishima* technique), two lugs at the neck. H. 17.5 cm., D. 13.9 cm. Tanakamaru Collection.

40. Underglaze Decorated Karatsu water jar, roundels made by dipping jar into iron oxide. Area above foot is unglazed, while thick glaze has run down from shoulder, creating an interesting variety of effects. H. 17.1 cm., D. body 18.9 cm., D. mouth 12.8 cm.

41. Underglaze Decorated Karatsu tea jar, three ears, persimmon tree decoration, fruit painted by fingerstips dipped in iron oxide. H. 17.1 cm., D. body 17.5 cm. Lacquer lid (not shown). Idemitsu Museum of Arts.

42. Underglaze Decorated Karatsu *mukōzuke* dishes, wheel-thrown pieces squared at the lip by raised corners, which are accentuated by the underglaze iron painting, attributed to Dōzono or Kameyanotani kiln. H. 7.1 cm., D. body 9.9 cm.

43. Takeo style plate, brushed white slip, pine design in underglaze iron covered with a clear, glossy glaze and three spots of copper glaze, attributed to Kawagokamanotani kiln. The branching pine is a frequent motif on Takeo plates, bottles, and jars. H. 8.0 cm., D. 28.4 cm.

44. Underglaze Decorated Karatsu food dish, central floral motif, *kawakujira* style (underglaze iron painted) lip, attributed to Kameyanotani kiln. Pock marks in glaze at upper right resulted from condensed moisture in kiln dripping on the pot before the glaze matured. H. 5.7 cm., D. 7.5 cm. (See Plate 185)

45. Underglaze Decorated Karatsu platter, six-branched pine design. H. 8.1 cm., D. 36.3 cm., D. foot 10.7 cm. Idemitsu Museum of Arts. (Compare painting with Plate 212)

46. Underglaze Decorated Karatsu dish, five-branched pine design, attributed to Dōzono kiln. H. 3.8 cm., D. 18.0 cm. Tanakamaru Collection.

47. Underglaze Decorated Karatsu *mukōzuke* dish, lip bent up in four sections to suggest a square shape, design of pair of crossed arrows and the Japanese character for "bow" (弓), *kawakujira* style (underglaze iron painted) lip. Design painted without regard for physical or implied borders in pot shape. H. 4.8 cm., D. 15.6 cm.

48. Underglaze Decorated Karatsu plate, finely crackled glaze in varying thicknesses, underglaze iron paired crossed arrows principal motif, underglaze iron painted lip (the term *kawakujira* seems by custom not to be used for underglaze iron lips on plates), attributed to Kameyanotani kiln. D. 18.5 cm. Collections Baur, Geneva.

49. Underglaze Decorated Karatsu *mukōzuke* dish, wheel-thrown with indented corners, crackled glaze, underglaze iron decoration. H. 3.1 cm., D. 12.3 cm.

50. Underglaze Decorated Karatsu large bowl, two handles affixed with clay balls, design of birds flying over rushes (shown), a hilly landscape (opposite side), and flowering plants (interior), spotted decoration on rim. H. 13.2 cm., D. 26.5 cm. Mr. Sakamoto Gorō. (See Plates 163, 164)

51. Underglaze Decorated Karatsu saké cup, *kawakujira* style (underglaze iron dipped) lip, rim mended with gold lacquer ornamented with a delicate bee. H. 5.1 cm., D. 7.8 cm. Idemitsu Museum of Arts.

52. Underglaze Decorated Karatsu hemispherical water dripper, design of hilly landscape, attributed to Takeo Uchida kiln. H. 3.1 cm., D. 6.2 cm. Idemitsu Museum of Arts.

53. Unglazed Karatsu bottle, called Bizen Karatsu. Unglazed Karatsu is extremely rare; some pieces such as this have been found in the remains of the Fujinkawachi kiln. H. 24.0 cm., D. mouth 6.7 cm.

54. Contemporary Karatsu teabowl, name: Hanabi ("Fireworks"), by Nakazato Muan (Tarōuemon XII). Crackled opaque white glaze with patterned crawling over an iron-rich red clay. 1963. H. 8.5 cm.

55. Contemporary Karatsu water jar by Nakazato Tarōuemon XIII. Incised and impressed designs filled with white slip (*mishima* technique); characters for wind and flower are shown. H. 18.4 cm., D. mouth 14.1 cm.

56. Jar by Nakazato Shigetoshi. Unglazed, burnished surface with white clay rubbed into the body; *tataki* (paddling) technique, using three differently patterned paddles; fired in a sagger. 1975. H. 32 cm., D. 30.5 cm.

57. Jar by Nakazato Takashi. Unglazed Tanegashima style, all colors resulting from oxides within the clay or kiln atmosphere. 1970. H. 20.8 cm., D. widest section 20.2 cm. Author's collection. Photograph by Jim Eckberg.

58, 59. Plain Karatsu tea caddy, name: Tama Tsushima ("Beautiful Islet"), two incised lines below shoulder and one above foot. Unidentified incising on foot could be a kiln mark, rare among Karatsu products. H. 8.9 cm., D. 6.6 cm. Idemitsu Museum of Arts. (See Plate 2)

60. Plain Karatsu tea caddy, name: Omoigawa ("River of the Heart"; named by Kobori Enshū), deep amber glaze on upper portion trailing into light body glaze. H. 8.6 cm. Listed in Matsudaira Fumai's *Unshū meibutsuki*. Hatakeyama Collection.

61. Plain Karatsu tea caddy, name: Hiyoko ("Chick"), streaked thick black iron glaze. H. 6.0 cm., D. 6.9 cm., D. mouth 4.4 cm. Idemitsu Museum of Arts.

62. Plain Karatsu tea caddy, name: Kaku-daishi (" Priest Kaku"), runny iron glaze. H. 8.0 cm., D. 7.1 cm. Idemitsu Museum of Arts.

63. Plain Karatsu tea caddy, brown iron and white rice-straw ash glaze intermingled during firing. H. 11.5 cm. Gemeentelijk Museum het Princessehof, Leeuwarden.

64. Underglaze Decorated Karatsu tea caddy, evenly crackled light glaze and spots of iron underglaze. H. 4.0 cm., D. body 7.8 cm. Freer Gallery of Art, Washington, D.C.

65. Plain Karatsu teabowl, *oku-Gōrai* shape, crackled light glaze with irregular spotting, attributed to Handōgame kiln. H. 9.9 cm., D. 14.5 cm. Idemitsu Museum of Arts.

66. Plain Karatsu teabowl, name: Yamazato ("Mountain Village"), finely crackled opaque white glaze with irregular spotting (*amamori*), attributed to Hobashira kiln. H. 8.5 cm., D. 13.5 cm. Idemitsu Museum of Arts.

67. Plain Karatsu teabowl, *oku-Gōrai* shape, opaque light glaze with numerous pinholes, stain on lip attributed to tea. H. 8.2 cm., D. 14.7 cm. Idemitsu Museum of Arts.

68. Plain Karatsu teabowl, *oku-Gōrai* shape, name: Akebono ("Daybreak"), thin covering of a warm, opaque glaze. H. 7.7 cm., D. mouth 12.5 cm.

69. Plain Karatsu teabowl of the type known as *Zekan* Karatsu, name: Sambō ("Three Jewels"); designated National Treasure. D. mouth 15.5 cm., D. foot 6.6 cm. Kubosō Memorial Art Museum.

70. Plain Karatsu teabowl, name: Sanshō ("Mountain Happiness"), heavily crackled opaque white glaze of almost pure feldspar, attributed to Handōgame kiln. H. 9.6 cm., D. 11.5 cm. Idemitsu Museum of Arts.

71. Plain Karatsu teabowl, name: Haku-un ("White Cloud"), heavy opaque white glaze with crawling on the lower part of the piece (a characteristic of Seto Karatsu pieces), three interior spur marks. H. 6.8 cm., D. 13.6 cm. Idemitsu Museum of Arts.

72. Plain Karatsu teabowl, *oku-Gōrai* shape, thin, opaque light glaze with fine crackle and scattered pinholes. H. 7.9 cm., D. 15.2 cm. Formerly in the Suiko Household Collection. Idemitsu Museum of Arts.

73. Plain Karatsu teabowl, attributed to Matsuura Dōzono kiln. H. 8.2 cm., D. 12.7 cm. Idemitsu Museum of Arts.

74. Plain Karatsu teabowl, *oku-Gōrai* shape, slightly rolled lip, thin opaque glaze with drippings formed at time of glazing. H. 8.7 cm., D. 13.9 cm. Idemitsu Museum of Arts.

75, 76. Plain Karatsu shallow teabowl, name: Kiri-Hitoha ("Paulownia Leaf"), tea stains in interior below lip. H. 4.0 cm., D. 15.2 cm. Idemitsu Museum of Arts.

77. Plain Karatsu shallow teabowl, glazed to base, "bamboo node" foot rim, attributed to Kojirōkaja kiln. H. 4.6 cm., D. 17.4 cm. Idemitsu Museum of Arts.

78. Plain Karatsu teabowl, textured black iron glaze. Narrow foot rim, glaze, and indentation below lip show influence of the Chinese *temmoku* teabowl. H. 7.3 cm., D. mouth 11.2 cm.

79. Plain Karatsu teabowl, rolled lip and deformed (*kutsu*) shape, black glaze ground under a crawling white glaze (*jakatsu*—snakeskin—effect), attributed to Shōkoya kiln. H. 8.0 cm., D. 15.4 cm. Idemitsu Museum of Arts.

80. Plain Karatsu teabowl, rounded lip indented at three points, *jakatsu* effect (see preceding), pronounced crawling on upper half of piece and large pockmarks on lower half. H. 8.4 cm., D. 12.6 cm. Idemitsu Museum of Arts.

81. Large Plain Karatsu spouted bowl, squat deformed (*kutsu*) shape with rolled lip, thin coating of a translucent glaze. H. 11.3 cm., D. 25.5 cm. Idemitsu Museum of Arts.

82. Plain Karatsu water jar and ceramic lid, wheel-thrown piece with trimmed foot rim, soft rice-straw ash glaze, thrown lid shows cutting mark (*itokiri*) underneath. H. 11.4 cm., D. body 16.7 cm. Idemitsu Museum of Arts.

83. Plain Karatsu jar, "abacus bead" shape, feathery lines of blue just below lip, an example of the *namako genshō* (see Glossary). H. 11.5 cm., D. 14.0 cm. Honolulu Academy of Arts.

84. Plain Karatsu water container, attributed to Handōgame kiln. H. 15.9 cm., D. 17.3 cm. Lacquer lid (not shown). Idemitsu Museum of Arts.

85. Plain Karatsu water jar with two small loop handles, two horizontal grooves below broad lip, runny dark iron glaze, attributed to Shōkoya kiln. H. 18.2 cm., D. body 19.1 cm. Idemitsu Museum of Arts.

86. Plain Karatsu water jar with two handles and three added feet, *tataki* technique, mottled reduced iron glaze called *ao* Karatsu. H. 19.7 cm., D. body 22.6 cm. Idemitsu Museum of Arts.

87. Lidded Plain Karatsu water jar with two handles and three small feet, square body and round lip, *tataki* technique, horizontal incisions and vertical paddle marks. H. 19.1 cm., D. body 18.6 cm. The base has a relief design similar to one on a shard found at Kameyanotani kiln remains (see Plate 184). Furuta Oribe's tea ceremony diary of 1603 lists a Karatsu water jar with three feet and one with horizontal incisions possibly similar to this piece.

88. Plain Karatsu vase, bamboo stalk shape, incised horizontal line accentuates node and base, vertical gouges above base, poured black iron glaze. H. 27.8 cm., D. 13.1 cm. Idemitsu Museum of Arts.

89. Small Plain Karatsu bottle used as a shaker for sweets (*furidashi*) in tea ceremonies. H. 11.2 cm., D. 7.0 cm. Idemitsu Museum of Arts.

90. Tea storage jar dedicated to the Shōmo Shrine, bearing inscription of dedication dated Tenshō 20 (1592); shape, added neck, ash glaze, and folded lip rim characteristic of Pre-Karatsu wares. Attributed to a Karatsu kiln and relates to shards found at early Kishidake kiln sites. H. 21.8 cm., D. base 10.9 cm. Shōmo Jinja, Ikinoshima.

91. Plain Karatsu pedestalled dish, finely crackled opaque white glaze speckled with pinholes and patches of crawling. H. 8.4 cm., D 18.7 cm. Idemitsu Museum of Arts.

92. Plain Karatsu saké cup, rice-straw ash glaze, scattered pinholes. H. 5.0 cm., D. 5.8 cm. Idemitsu Museum of Arts.

93. Plain Karatsu incense box, "precious Buddhist jewel" shape, attached foot. H. 4.5 cm., W. 5.4 cm. Idemitsu Museum of Arts.

94. Korean Karatsu water jar, horizontal incisions, streaks of opaque white glaze cascading over highly fluxed, translucent brown iron glaze. H. 16.0 cm., D. body 15.7 cm. Idemitsu Museum of Arts.

95. Korean Karatsu vase, bulbous ridged lip and two loop handles at narrow neck, body paddled into slightly hexagonal shape, attributed to Fujinkawachi kiln. H. 24.8 cm., D. 11.9 cm. Idemitsu Museum of Arts.

96. Korean Karatsu vase, name: Saru ("Monkey"), bulbous lip with slight flare, opaque white rice-straw ash glaze showing strong traces of blue, dark iron glaze trailed over body. H. 21.7 cm., D. 10.9 cm. Idemitsu Museum of Arts.

97. Korean Karatsu vase, undulating body contour and two twisted handles, horizontal incisions below neck, vertical combing above base, lip dipped in white rice-straw ash glaze over iron glaze, white and iron glaze tailed on body. H. 21.7 cm., D. 10.1 cm. Idemitsu Museum of Arts.

98. Korean Karatsu vase with two loop handles, ridges at bulbous neck, flared, irregular lip rim, heavy dark iron glaze with irregular speckels on matte surface, trailed white rice-straw ash glaze on body. H. 22.1 cm., D. 11.9 cm. Freer Gallery of Art, Washington, D.C.

99. Korean Karatsu vase with two handles, two horizontal gouges at bulbous lip, trailings

of iron and rice-straw ash glaze on body, attributed to Fujinkawachi kiln. H. 18.5 cm., D. 12.5 cm. Idemitsu Museum of Arts.

100. Small Korean Karatsu bottle, name: Yomogigashima ("Island of Sagebrush"), utilitarian piece used as a shaker for sweets (*furidashi*) in the tea ceremony, attributed to Fujinkawachi kiln. H. 21.3 cm., D. 10.8 cm. Idemitsu Museum of Arts.

101. Korean Karatsu bottle, dipped in white rice-straw ash glaze to shoulder ridge, body dipped in black iron glaze, wiped off on bottom section. H. 22.2 cm., D. 11.9 cm. Idemitsu Museum of Arts.

102. Underglaze Decorated Karatsu tea caddy, opaque rice-straw ash glaze crawling in large patches. H. 3.4 cm., D. 6.0 cm. Formerly used as an incense burner. Idemitsu Museum of Arts.

103. Underglaze Decorated Karatsu tea caddy, name: Yakiyama ("Burning Mountain"), metallic patches where underglaze iron painting has bled into the white glaze, dense crackle in opaque body glaze, throwing marks, diagonal gouges near base. H. 10.3 cm. Idemitsu Museum of Arts.

104. Underglaze Decorated Karatsu shallow teabowl, stamped and incised designs filled with white slip (*mishima* technique), stenciled central medallion of white slip with characters from Japanese chess (*shōgi*) counters reversed due to placing the stencil upside down. Comparable to shards unearthed at Kawagokamanotani kiln. H. 5.0 cm., D. 18.5 cm.

105. Underglaze Decorated Karatsu shallow teabowl, stamped and combed designs filled with white slip (*mishima* technique), milky glaze. D. 15.24 cm. Museum of Fine Arts, Boston; Morse Collection.

106. Underglaze Decorated Karatsu teabowl, simple underglaze iron decoration under a translucent rice-straw ash glaze, slight indentation below lip. D. mouth 13.4 cm. Tanakamaru Collection.

107. Underglaze Decorated Karatsu teabowl, spiral design, attributed to Matsuura Dōzono kiln. H. 8.3 cm., D. 11.9 cm.

108, 109. Underglaze Decorated Karatsu teabowl, straight sides and central bulge, folded lip pulled into a broad shape, double foot rim similar to that found on *hori* Karatsu teabowls, dark iron glaze in interior, opaque white rice-straw ash glaze on exterior. Shape, foot rim, and special glazing of interior indicate that this was made as a teabowl. H. 9.7 cm., D. 10.4 cm., D. foot rim 7.6 cm. Idemitsu Museum of Arts.

110. Cylindrical Underglaze Decorated Karatsu teabowl, *kawakujira* style (underglaze iron dipped) lip, horizontal combing on lower half, fisherman motif. H. 9.5 cm., D. 7.5 cm. Idemitsu Museum of Arts.

111. Underglaze Decorated Karatsu teabowl, random decoration of underglaze iron beneath an evenly crackled rice-straw ash glaze. H. 7.2 cm., D. 10.4 cm. Idemitsu Museum of Arts.

112. *Hori* (carved) Karatsu teabowl with underglaze decoration, opaque white rice-straw ash glaze with crawling on the entire exterior but most pronounced in the carved areas. D. 12.3 cm.

113. Underglaze Decorated Karatsu teabowl, *temmoku* shape, thin glaze, playful underglaze iron painting. H. 8.5 cm., D. 13.5 cm. Idemitsu Museum of Arts.

114, 115. Underglaze Decorated Karatsu teabowl, *temmoku* shape, "bamboo node" foot rim, painted design of paired arrows and an arrow striking the bull's eye, a thick, opaque rice-straw ash glaze. H. 6.2 cm., D. 11.9 cm. Idemitsu Museum of Arts.

116–118. Underglaze Decorated Karatsu teabowl, heavy lip and squat, irregular (*kutsu*) shape, underglaze iron wash on interior and drippings on exterior, white rice-straw ash glaze, double foot rim. H. 8.2 cm., D. 11.6 cm. Idemitsu Museum of Arts.

119. Underglaze Decorated Karatsu teabowl, wheel-thrown pot with heavy folded lip and distorted into a squat, irregular (*kutsu*) shape. H. 7.8 cm., D. 15.6 cm. Idemitsu Museum of Arts.

120. Underglaze Decorated Karatsu shallow teabowl, lotus leaf design. Identical to shards excavated from Taku Kōraidani kiln. H. 5.5 cm., D. mouth 16.2 cm., D. foot 4.3 cm.

121. Underglaze Decorated Karatsu spouted bowl, radiating lines in underglaze iron below lip, characteristic of Old Karatsu from Michinayatani kiln. A utilitarian piece now used as a tea utensil. H. 13.1 cm., D. 20.9 cm. Gold lacquer mend on lip. Idemitsu Museum of Arts.

122, 123. Underglaze Decorated Karatsu spouted bowl, "C" motif on each side, rice-straw ash glaze alternating between crackling and crawling. H. 10.7 cm., D. 25.2 cm. Gold lacquer mends on lip and spout. Idemitsu Museum of Arts.

124–126 Underglaze Decorated Karatsu spouted bowl, sides and tip of spout dipped into iron oxide, pronounced crawling of rice-straw ash glaze over areas of underglaze iron and trimmed area above foot. Details reveal spout-making technique: a clay slab is bent over a finger, its edges joined onto the vessel, and reinforced by small balls of clay. A hole is cut into the wall, leaving the lip rim intact. H. 9.9 cm., D. 22.5 cm., D. foot 8.3 cm. Idemitsu Museum of Arts.

127. Underglaze Decorated Karatsu water jar, six splashes of underglaze iron at shoulder and touches of underglaze iron on lip, matte rice-straw ash glaze with crawling on trimmed lower area, registered Important Cultural Property. H. 17.3 cm., D. mouth 9.4 cm., D. body 12.9 cm. Private collection, Japan.

128. Underglaze Decorated Karatsu water jar, underglaze painted decoration of reeds, milky glaze speckled by iron content of clay, formed by *tataki* technique, rolled lip. Utilitarian piece used as a tea vessel. H. 17.0 cm., D. 17.5 cm. Lacquered lid (not shown). Asian Art Museum of San Francisco, The Avery Brundage Collection.

129. Underglaze Decorated Karatsu water jar (top view of Plate 36), showing the curling vines motif and gilt lacquer lip mends decorated with wave patterns on exterior, finger marks made when throwing the pot and central crawling of glaze in the interior. H. 16.1 cm., D. body 23.0 cm., D. mouth 16.6 cm. Idemitsu Museum of Arts.

130. Underglaze Decorated Karatsu water jar, "abacus bead" shape, underglaze iron painting of reeds, crawling of glaze in trimmed area above foot. H. 14.7 cm., D. body 22.1 cm. Idemitsu Museum of Arts.

131. Underglaze Decorated Karatsu water jar, thick rice-straw ash glaze, underglaze iron on lip (*kawakujira* style) running in streaks over upper body, attributed to Hobashira kiln. H. 13.8 cm., D. 9.0 cm. Idemitsu Museum of Arts.

132. Underglaze Decorated Karatsu water jar, modified "abacus bead" shape, crisp underglaze iron painting on body and shoulder softened by milky glaze, ridged upper section accentuates the undulating contour seen on many Karatsu jars with narrow lips. H. 15.7 cm., D. body 20.2 cm. Idemitsu Museum of Arts.

133. Underglaze Decorated Karatsu flower vase, underglaze iron painting of rushes and two bands on neck, matte rice-straw ash glaze; attributed to Uchida kiln group. H. 41 cm. Nezu Art Museum.

134. Takeo style bottle, brushed white slip, underglaze iron painting of a pine tree with accents of green copper glaze covered with clear glaze. H. 30.1 cm. Saga Prefectural Museum.

135, 136. Underglaze Decorated Karatsu vase with two loop handles near foot and two holes drilled in the sides for hanging, underglaze iron painting ignores shifts in contour of the body, squared shape, thick lip has slumped during firing, beaten indentation above foot, undeciphered carved characters on fold inside lip (detail), attributed to Fujinkawachi kiln. H. 24.0 cm., D. 17.7 cm. Idemitsu Museum of Arts.

137. Underglaze Decorated Karatsu *mukōzuke* dish, shape and design influenced by Shino ware of Mino, thick, matte rice-straw ash glaze. Tanakamaru Collection.

138. Underglaze Decorated Karatsu *mukōzuke* dishes, (from a set of five) cylindrical bodies with flared lips shaped into outline of Japanese folding fan, *kawakujira* style (underglaze iron) lips and diagonal striped border below, trailing grapevine design. Shapes of lips and flowing painting relates these to the decorative Oribe ware style of Mino. Painting so similar to shards found at Taku Kōraidani that attribution has altered. H. 8.2 cm., D. 11.4 cm. Idemitsu Museum of Arts.

139. Underglaze Decorated Karatsu *mukōzuke* dishes (set of five) with flared lips pinched into a square. H. 7.5 cm., D. 11.0 cm. Idemitsu Museum of Arts.

140. Underglaze Decorated Karatsu lobed *mukōzuke* dishes (from a set of five), finely thrown and reshaped, *kawakujira* style (underglaze iron) lips and trailing vine designs. Painting influenced by Oribe ware style; note variations in painting of leaf motif. H. 8.0 cm., D. 9.6 cm. Idemitsu Museum of Arts.

141. Underglaze Decorated Karatsu fluted *mukōzuke* dish, underglaze iron decoration forming scallops linking the flutes, attributed to Takeo Oyamaji kiln. H. 9.2 cm., D. 9.6 cm. Idemitsu Museum of Arts.

142. Underglaze Decorated Karatsu tall and square *mukōzuke* dish, each side painted with a flowering plant, thick rice-straw ash glaze. H. 11.4 cm., D. 8.1 cm. Dr. and Mrs. Roger Gerry Collection, Long Island, New York. Photograph by Eric Pollitzer.

143. Underglaze Decorated Karatsu tall *mukōzuke* dish, *kawakujira* style (underglaze iron) lip, heavy pattern of pinholes in glaze, incised horizontal groove in upper part and indentation above foot. H. 9.9 cm., D. 7.7 cm. Freer Gallery of Art, Washington, D.C.

144. Underglaze Decorated Karatsu tall square *mukōzuke* dish, *kawakujira* style (underglaze iron) lip, underglaze iron painting of wild grass, shallow horizontal grooves below lip, attributed to Dōzono kiln. H. 10.4 cm. Idemitsu Museum of Arts.

145, 146. Underglaze Decorated Karatsu beaker used as a *mukōzuke* dish, *kawakujira* style (underglaze iron) lip, motif of fisherman on one side. The three pines on the other side show influence from Oribe ware designs. Tanakamaru Collection.

147. Underglaze Decorated Karatsu deep *mukōzuke* dish, design of circle, crosses, and lines, opaque glaze. H. 9.3 cm., D. mouth 9.1 cm., D. foot 4.5 cm. Idemitsu Museum of Arts.

148. Takeo style platter, combed patterns filled with white slip (*mishima* technique), painted underglaze iron vine tendrils, shiny amber and runny copper green glazes. D. 41.9 cm. Objects in this style have been unearthed in Thailand and at Japanese trading ports. Museum of Fine Arts, Boston; Morse Collection.

149. Takeo style large dish, combed white slip, transparent glaze with trailed copper green glaze; unearthed at Ayutthaya, Thailand. H. 10.0 cm., D. 28.8 cm.

150. Takeo style large bowl, combed and tooled patterns in white slip, scattered areas at rim and center not covered by slip, transparent glaze. H. 16.0 cm., D. 52.2 cm. Idemitsu Museum of Arts.

151. Underglaze Decorated Karatsu plate, slip-painted stencil patterns, brushmarked (*hakeme*) background. H. 3.7 cm., D. mouth 14.8 cm., D. foot 5.0 cm. Dark lacquer mends.

152. Underglaze Decorated Karatsu dish, stamped designs filled with white slip (*mishima* technique), transparent glaze over dark brown clay. The decoration shows the careful and slick mode associated with Presentation Karatsu. H. 6.0 cm., D. 25.4 cm. Idemitsu Museum of Arts.

153, 154. Underglaze Decorated Karatsu large dish with fluted rim, underglaze iron painting of pine tree, painted border band with two clusters of tapered lines, milky translucent glaze, attributed to Kameyanotani kiln; registered Important Cultural Property. H. 13.5 cm., D. 43.5 cm., D. foot 13.5 cm. Umezawa Memorial Museum.

155. Underglaze Decorated Karatsu shallow dish, rolled lip, underglaze iron painting of millet stalk flanked by paired diagonal lines, slight crawling of glaze with scattered pinholes, spur marks in center. D. 33.1 cm. Seattle Art Museum, Eugene Fuller Memorial Collection.

156, 157. Underglaze Decorated Karatsu large dish, underglaze iron painting of pine tree, finely crackled glaze with scattered pinholes, glaze starting to crawl in center. H. 8.1 cm., D. 36.3 cm. Idemitsu Museum of Arts. (See Plate 44; c.f. Plate 212)

158, 159, 160. Three examples of the same painted underglaze iron motif: 158 is painted in the most crisp, deliberate manner, 159 is characteristic of much Karatsu underglaze painting, and 160 is unusually light and delicate.

158. Underglaze Decorated Karatsu dish, painted underglaze iron rim and plant design. H. 4.1 cm., D. 18.0 cm. Idemitsu Museum of Arts.

159. Underglaze Decorated Karatsu dish, painted underglaze iron rim and plant design. H. 4.3 cm., D. 18.5 cm. Idemitsu Museum of Arts.

160. Underglaze Decorated Karatsu large dish, painted underglaze iron plant design, thinly potted. H. 11.7 cm., D. 37.2 cm., D. foot 10.9 cm. Idemitsu Museum of Arts.

161. Underglaze Decorated Karatsu dish, metallic sheen in areas of heaviest underglaze iron, design of plants and birds in center and repetitive linear and floral motifs on rim influenced by Mino ceramics. H. 5.4 cm., D. 17.5 cm. Idemitsu Museum of Arts.

162. Underglaze Decorated Karatsu square dish with cut rim, wheel-thrown pot trimmed to a square shape with angled corners, underglaze iron painting of flowering stems, stylized horsetails at corners, broad strokes at edge; shape and decoration influenced by Oribe ware. H. 5.7 cm., W. 16.5 cm. Idemitsu Museum of Arts.

163, 164. Underglaze Decorated Karatsu large bowl with two handles, delicately painted thin underglaze iron design of plants. The precisely trimmed foot rim harmonizes with the careful fashioning of the entire piece, suggesting that, in spite of its scale and shape, it was not made for daily household use. H. 13.2 cm., D. mouth 26.5 cm. Mr. Sakamoto Gorō. (See Plate 50)

165, 166. Underglaze Decorated Karatsu square dish, wheel-thrown pot with rim folded to create a square shape, underglaze iron painting of mountains and trees in interior, stripes on folded rim appear to have been painted directly across. H. 8.6 cm., W. 26.6 cm., D. foot 7.8 cm. Idemitsu Museum of Arts.

167. Underglaze Decorated Karatsu triangular dish, wheel-thrown pot with rim inverted to form triangle, painted underglaze iron plant design, spur marks in interior, attributed to Dō-zono kiln. H. 9.3 cm., W. 17.2 cm. Idemitsu Museum of Arts.

168. Underglaze Decorated Karatsu conical lobed dish with slightly squared shape, painted underglaze iron design of fishnets, a basket, and two small fish. H. 7.4 cm., D. 20.3 cm. Idemitsu Museum of Arts. (See Plates 169, 177)

169. Underglaze Decorated Karatsu square dish, three indented corners and one unindented corner to accomodate decoration, painted underglaze iron design of basket and two sets of stylized horsetails, simple bowl-shaped contour with slight bulge above foot rim. H. 8.4 cm., D. 17.8 cm. Idemitsu Museum of Arts. (See Plates 168, 177)

170. Underglaze Decorated Karatsu large shallow dish with broad rim, painted underglaze iron design of iris and reeds, small areas of glaze crawling, swirls of glaze at bottom and upper left resulting from rapid dipping green pot in glaze, four spur marks in the center. H. 11.2 cm., D. 41.2 cm. Idemitsu Museum of Arts.

171. Underglaze Decorated Karatsu stemmed bowl with attached thrown stem, painted underglaze iron simple spiral design, except for smudges and drippings, the stem is unglazed, attributed to Michinayatani kiln. H. 11.9 cm., D. 15.5 cm. Idemitsu Museum of Arts.

172. Underglaze Decorated Karatsu saké cup, deep dip of underglaze iron at lip (*kawakujira* style), attributed to the Matsuura group kilns. H. 3.8 cm., D. 6.6 cm. Idemitsu Museum of Arts.

173. Underglaze Decorated Karatsu saké cup, painted underglaze iron design of wild grass, finely crackled glaze. H. 5.0 cm., D. 7.1 cm. Idemitsu Museum of Arts.

174. Underglaze Decorated Karatsu saké cup, painted underglaze iron design of paired mirror-image plants. Fingerprints of glaze-dipper visible at base. H. 7.4 cm., D. 7.9 cm. Idemitsu Museum of Arts.

175. Underglaze Decorated Karatsu saké cup, painted underglaze iron character for "big" (大) shown and character for "small" (小) on opposite side. H. 5.1 cm., D. 6.9 cm. Idemitsu Museum of Arts.

176. Underglaze Decorated Karatsu saké cup for use while riding a horse, underglaze iron painting of plant. H. 8.0 cm., D. 6.4 cm. Idemitsu Museum of Arts.

177. Underglaze Decorated Karatsu stemmed saké cup stand (interior), three corners indented and one corner unindented, *kawakujira* style (underglaze iron) lip, underglaze iron painting of basket and stylized horsetails. H. 8.3 cm., D. 20.5 cm. Idemitsu Museum of Arts. (See Plates 168, 169)

178. Small Underglaze Decorated Karatsu fire container in the shape of fish basket, underglaze iron painting of a cormorant. H. 5.5 cm., D. 4.4 cm. Tanakamaru Collection.

179. Underglaze Decorated Karatsu square fire container, wheel-thrown pot paddled into a square shape, opaque white glaze with crackling, overlappings, and dripping, scattered large pinholes, crawling just above base, underglaze iron design, shape and glaze show influence of Shino ware of Mino region. H. 9.2 cm., D. 9.10 cm. Idemitsu Museum of Arts.

180. Underglaze Decorated Karatsu incense burner (Presentation Karatsu), carefully potted cylinder with three attached feet, painted underglaze iron design of reeds and wheels, two herons and a scroll on opposite side. H. 8.5 cm., D. 8.9 cm. Idemitsu Museum of Arts.

181. Underglaze Decorated Karatsu incense burner, hexagonal at the lip rim, three added feet, slight bulge at lip and just above base, painted underglaze iron design of crossed rice stalks. H. 9.0 cm., D. 8.6 cm. Tanakamaru Collection

182. Plain Karatsu shard excavated from lower Handōgame kiln; *hori* (carved) Karatsu type, fashioned to be a teabowl. This verifies that the early Karatsu potters working at the Kishidake kiln group produced at least some pots meant for the tea ceremony (See Plates 9, 112)

183. Underglaze Decorated Karatsu shard excavated from the Takeo Kawagokamanotani kiln bearing the painted underglaze iron inscription *Genna yonnen, ni gatsu, jūhachi nichi* (2nd month, 18th day, 1618). Inscriptions of characters are unusual in Karatsu; dating is even rarer.

184. Base of a paddled Plain Karatsu water jar (such as in Plate 87), three balls added as feet, unearthed from Kameyanotani kiln remains. The "J" or reversed "L" mark in relief resulted from a carving in the wheelhead. The purpose of these markings is undetermined, although it is suggested that they could identify pieces destined for specific dealers.

185. Shard of Underglaze Decorated ware showing the erosion of glaze caused by condensed moisture dripping within the kiln in the early stages of the firing. (See Plate 44)

186. Shard showing marks of seashells (placed face down) used as spurs. Although this is not a Karatsu shard, this practice was found at Karatsu kilns.

187. Shard from Fujinkawachi kiln showing the marks of shells used as spurs.

188. Shard from Dōzono kiln remains; foot of *tataki* (paddled) jar showing mixture of two clay bodies; bloating and porosity of Karatsu clay is evident.

189. Shard from Yamasaki Omedate kiln remains showing the typical bloating of Karatsu clay.

190. Shard from the Matsuura Kameyanotani kiln remains; interior of *tataki* (paddled) bottle showing pattern of overlapping arcs resulting from the use of an "anvil" inside the pot. The smooth interior of the neck is the result of throwing this part of the pot. Dark iron glaze, used on the exterior, is splashed on the upper part of the inner neck.

191. Shard from the Takeo Shōkoya kiln remains; interior of *tataki* (paddled) jar clearly reveals pattern of overlapping arcs left by "anvil" used inside the pot.

192. Underglaze Decorated shard from Kōraidani kiln remains in the Taku group. The shard section shows that the underglaze iron bled slightly into the unfired clay, which can happen only if it is applied before the glaze, verifying that the Karatsu technique was to paint iron oxide under rather than on the glaze.

193. Lip rims excavated from Handōgame kiln, showing the technique of folding over clay to produce a thick rim. This technique was used for large objects of the style preceding Karatsu and is not seen in Karatsu wares.

194. Evidence of porcelain and Karatsu ware being fired together; fused shards of Karatsu stoneware and porcelain (top) found at Mukaie no Hara kiln site, Arita, by Dr. Oliver Impey. H. 7.7 cm. Department of Eastern Art, Ashmolean Museum, Oxford.

195. Shard excavated from Shiinomine kiln remains; underglaze decoration in white slip applied through a stencil; eight spur marks.

196. Shard of Underglaze Decorated teabowl, *oku-Gorai* shape, stylized horsetail (*tokusa*) decoration. (See Plate 33)

197. Shard of plate with painted underglaze iron grass design.

198. Karatsu shard with underglaze painting of a rabbit; other than birds, animals are rare decorations on Karatsu ware and are seen primarily on shards. Examples of rabbits, shrimp, fish, and horses are known.

199. Shard from Takeo Kameyanotani kiln remains; flying birds painted in the manner seen on wares produced at the Mino kilns.

200, 201. Two views of shards fused together during firing; underglaze decoration shows influence from Mino wares; excavated from Takeo Kameyanotani kiln remains.

202. Page from the diary of Kiheiji written as a partial defense during the government investigation of the Shiinomine kilns (1697–1703); now in possession of the Nakazato family, Karatsu city.

203–205. Illustrations of ceramic techniques from the colored handscroll *Yakimono taigai* of *Matsuura bussan zukō* ("General Introduction to Pottery" of the "Illustrated Study of Matsuura Products"). Saga Prefectural Museum.

203. (right) Clay being pulverized. Water is added to the powder, and the clay wedged by foot. (left) Method of lifting large, unfired pieces with ropes (not a Karatsu technique).

204. Details of kiln construction, from right to left: the fire mouth with the initial fire; the interior of a kiln chamber showing interior brickwork; a cross-section of the vents leading from chamber to chamber, indicating how the low position of the vents provides for an updraft fire in each chamber. (See Plates 225, 226)

205. (right) The beehive type *noborigama*; linked chambers of the beehive kiln are each domed. Bricks used to seal the portals lie on the ground in front. Two men are stoking the rear chambers, while a third is about to open a porthole to investigate the condition of the firing wares. (left) A bundle of chopped wood is being delivered for fuel.

206, 207. Large blue-and-white porcelain plate depicting the preparation of clay and steps involved in the fabrication, decoration, and firing of ceramic ware. The rectangular central medallion of the ceramic studio shows merchants purchasing finished wares on the far right and craftsmen painting decoration on pots on the upper left. Although this is a porcelain workshop, the lower left depicts potters using techniques employed for Karatsu ware manufacture: (left to right) wedging large amounts of clay using the "chrysanthemum" wedging technique; throwing a bowl off the hump, using the *hera* tool; centering a large amount of clay on the wheelhead. Registered Saga Prefectural Cultural Property. Arita Ceramic Museum.

208. Oribe bottle showing Karatsu influence in Mino area. Light, crackled opaque glaze, Karatsu inspired underglaze iron design, upper section dipped in copper green glaze, attributed to Otani kiln. H. 17.7 cm. Collection of Dr. and Mrs. Roger Gerry. Photograph by Eric Pollitzer.

209. Korean Ido teabowl, Yi dynasty, name: Nara, glazed foot rim; designated Important Art Object. H. 7.1 cm., D. mouth 5.5 cm. This type of Korean bowl was highly prized as a teabowl by the Japanese at the time Karatsu was first being produced and probably inspired some Karatsu pieces. Idemitsu Art Museum.

210, 211. Korean rice bowl, Yi dynasty, glazed foot rim. H. 8.8 cm., D. 14.4 cm. Close resemblance between pieces such as these and Karatsu pieces in the *oku-Gōrai* shape once made the latter to be regarded as of Korean origin. Korean pieces have glazed foot rims. National Museum of Korea, Seoul.

212. Korean celadon oil jar, Koryŏ dynasty, showing underglaze painted design comparable in style to painting seen on Karatsu ware. This shape is not found among Karatsu pieces. H. 9.5 cm., D. 7.6 cm. Honolulu Academy of Arts. (See Plate 45)

213. Chinese rice bowl, Yue (Yueh) ware, Song dynasty, stoneware with greenish reduced feldspathic glaze. The simple shape, trimmed, unglazed foot rim, and dipped glaze give Karatsu an affinity to everyday ceramics like this, although there was no direct influence from such Chinese wares. National Palace Museum, Taipei.

214. Spotted Longchuan (Lung-Ch'uan) celadon spouted bowl, Yuan dynasty, shape influenced by metal prototypes, bowl lip behind spout left intact. National Palace Museum, Taipei.

215–219. *Tataki* (paddling) technique demonstrated by Nakazato Muan (Tarōuemon XII). 215. Ash is sprinkled on wheelhead to allow the pot to be easily removed. 216. Clay for the base is pounded onto wheelhead; the clay beyond circle of ash holds the piece to the wheel. 217. Vessel sides formed by joining coils of clay. 218. Coiled wall is paddled on outside while wooden "anvil" held against inside, and walls become thin and dense; overlapping arcs made by "anvil" can be seen; wheel turns clockwise as a result of the paddling strokes. 219. Pot given final shape and exterior texture, and lip is thrown.

220. View of a *noborigama* chamber showing the loading of the kiln with greenware that has been decorated and glazed. Area directly in front of portal is left free of ware since this is where the wood fuel is thrown when firing each chamber. Ochawangama, Karatsu city.

221. Handmade tools used to make Karatsu ware. (left to right) Above: three paddles used on pot exterior (*tataki* technique); fourth paddle used for pounding flat pot base on wheelhead; cutting cord. Below: three "anvils" for pot interior (*tataki* technique); wiping cloth; two tools for shaping, smoothing, and cutting. Ochawangama, Karatsu city.

222. Underglaze iron being painted on greenware by Nakazato Tarōuemon XIII. Before firing, each piece will be dipped in glaze. Ochawangama, Karatsu city.

223. Lightweight, fast-turning kick wheel used for throwing Karatsu ware; the small flywheel is kicked clockwise; potter's seat can be seen in the left corner; trimming, decorating, and measuring tools are on the counter; the *hera*, always kept wet, is in the bowl of water. Ochawangama, Karatsu city.

224. Remains of the Ochawangama kiln opened in 1831; located on the premises of the present Ochawangama studio and kiln, these remains have been dedicated as a sacred Shintō site.

225. Remains of the Handōgame kiln; the fire mouth is in the distance under an added shelter; the stepped ascending levels of the kiln floor are still evident beneath the overgrowth; each level was a separate kiln chamber; no superstructure of the kiln remains. (See Plate 205)

226. Fire mouth of Handōgame kiln remains; the low fire ports and their supports remain.

227. View of Karatsu city from Karatsu Castle. The Matsuura River is in the foreground; Ochawangama is in front of foothills left of the central canyon.

228. Pottery studio, Nakazato home and gallery, Ochawangama, Karatsu city. The Nakazato home is the first large building beyond the long train platform in the center of the picture; the potter's studios and kiln are clustered to the left of the home; the gallery is among the group of buildings to the right of the home.

229. Karatsu Castle now functions as a historic museum.

230. The ramparts of Karatsu Castle.

231. Roof tiles of Karatsu Castle, showing the clan crest of overlapping diamonds.

232, 233. Torii and stone lantern designating a sacred site for Korean potters. 232. Beyond the torii are remains of an ancient kiln; Korean potters are reputed to have assembled here for festivals in the past. 233. Ceramic plaque inscribed "Korean deity."

234. Shards from the Yamase kiln imbedded in the wall of the Nakano ceramic shop in Karatsu city, evidence both of the abundance of Karatsu remains in the area and of the nonsystematic early excavations of the Karatsu kilns.

Karatsu Kilns and Kiln Groups

The 119 Karatsu kiln sites are found in a remarkably small area—the majority occupy a triangle with angles at Karatsu city, Arita, and Hizen Yamaguchi, with sides roughly 23 miles (37 km) and base 20 miles (32 km) long. Going south from Karatsu city, the kilns are to the west of the Matsuura River, becoming more dense to the south, with some of the Takeo group kilns spilling beyond the base of the triangle (map, page 194). With the exception of Shirosakayama at Nagoya Castle and some of the official clans kilns, the kilns are grouped roughly according to regions defined by mountain ranges, time of development, and feudal domains. Similarities in styles of products and historic evolution of the kilns make it convenient to use this group designation.

Some of the official kilns of the Karatsu fief, not part of any group, were the only ones in the vicinity of Karatsu city. The oldest kilns, which were nestled around Kishidake Castle—the Kishidake kilns—are generally distinguished from those developing somewhat later within the broader surrounding territory, the Kishidake group kilns. Except for the relatively isolated Kojirō-kaja and Yamase sites, twelve Kishidake and Kishidake group kilns are located south of Karatsu city, followed by the twenty-five kilns of the Matsuura group. These were all within the Karatsu fief; the majority of the remaining kilns were within Nabeshima fief territory. The southern-most Karatsu kilns included the twenty-three Hirado, forty-seven Takeo, three Taku, and four Saga kilns. A line drawn east from Imari city to Taku provides a general dividing line between the Karatsu and Nabeshima fiefs. In the southwestern sector of the Karatsu kiln area are the Hirado kiln sites; the south-central area is occupied by Takeo kilns; Saga kilns are southeast of Imari city; and Taku kilns are in the eastern region. The Takeo group had the largest number of kilns, longest period of activity, and greatest quantity of products.

Kojirōkaja and Yamase, Kishidake group kilns, are traditionally thought to have been founded by displaced potters after the 1560 fall of Kishidake Castle. After the 1594 fall of the same castle, the remaining Kishidake group kilns developed. This is a generally accepted assumption, although other than Kojirōkaja and Yamase, it is not clear which kilns were begun after each fall. The final fall of Kishidake Castle occurred after the first Korean campaign and the impor-tation of the first Korean potters.

The Matsuura kilns must have begun about the same time, since the opening of the official Karatsu kiln at Tashirotsutsue, one of the Matsuura group, is generally placed around 1597 (Keichō 2). Meanwhile, the hundreds of potters Lord Nabeshima brought back to his territory were opening kilns in his domain. Although firm dates of opening cannot be assigned to specific kilns, it appears that all of the kiln groups, with the exception of the early Kishidake sites, had kilns opened primarily by Korean potters during the last five years of the sixteenth century.

In general, kilns of the Karatsu fief seem to have had Japanese and Korean potters working together (see page 21). None of the Karatsu fief kilns converted to porcelain production, but the majority of those of the Nabeshima fief either became porcelain kilns or, as in the case of most Takeo kilns, eventually developed an entirely different style of stoneware. The Hirado and Saga kilns became producers of porcelain and today are considered porcelain sites. There seems to be no more reason to continue to list them as Karatsu kiln sites than there would be to include the kilns of Agano, Takatori, Satsuma, and other private kilns that produced Karatsu ware at first but soon developed a different style. Since all Japanese and Western sources treating Karatsu in any detail include the Hirado and Saga kilns, they are not ignored here, but their limited Karatsu period should be recognized.

In each of the groups additional kilns opened, for the most part during the first quarter of the seventeenth century. The official Karatsu kiln Ōkawabaru of the Kishidake group has a traditional opening date of 1604 (Keichō 8); in the Matsuura group, Yakiyama opened in 1608 (Keichō 12), Abondani in 1615 (Genna 1), two of the Shiinomine kilns in 1616, and Uchiumezaka after 1615.[1] Kilns of the Takeo group increased throughout the seventeenth century and continued to do so into the eighteenth century, by which time their principal production was Takeo style stoneware. This is especially true of the south Takeo kilns. An exception is Oyamaji, a tea utensil kiln that produced quantities of Underglaze Decorated Karatsu with designs and shapes influenced by Oribe ware.

Of the six groups of Karatsu kilns, the Kishidake kilns (early Kishidake and Kishidake group), Matsuura group, and Takeo group are the most important. They include three kilns that catered to the production of tea ceremony wares: Michinayatani of the Kishidake kilns, Fujinkawachi of Matsuura, and Oyamaji of Takeo. With the exception of the official Karatsu kiln Ochawangama at Karatsu city, kilns that continued to make Karatsu ceramics after the mid-Edo period fall into these three groups.

There were nine official Karatsu clan kilns, two of which carried this designation twice.

OFFICIAL KARATSU CLAN KILNS

Karabori in Nishinohama	c. 1594–95 (Bunroku 3–4)
Karafusa in Karatsu city area	
Hieda Saraya (Kishidake)	
Tashirotsutsue (Matsuura)	c. 1597 (Keichō 1)
Ōkawabaru (Kishidake)	1604 (Keichō 8)
Shiinomine (Matsuura)	1615 (Genna 1)
Hirayama (Matsuura)	c. 1649 (Keian 2)
Shiinomine (Matsuura)	post 1649 (Keian 2)
Ōkawabaru (Kishidake)	c. 1658 (Manji 1)
Bōzumachi Ochawangama	1707 (Hōei 3)
Tōjinmachi Ochawangama	1734 (Kyōhō 19)
new kiln	1919 (Taishō 8)

During the first year that an official kiln was established, about 1594–95, four different sites were used. Little other than the names of the first two—Karabori and Karafusa—is known.

Saraya, the third official kiln, was one of the early Kishidake kilns already in production at the time the Korean Fukumoto Yasaku came there to produce wares for the lord. The fourth site, Tashiro of Matsuura, remained an official kiln for nine years beginning in 1597. From 1707 on, official kilns were located in Karatsu city, separate from any kiln group: Bōzumachi Ochawangama, and Tōjinmachi Ochawangama. These were operated by the Nakazato and Ō-shima potters. The last site is still active in the production of Karatsu style ceramics today, no longer as an official kiln of a feudal fief, but managed by the Nakazato family. Most of the ceramics produced there today are in the traditional style, not because the tradition continued without interruption, but because the last two generations of Nakazatos have maintained a serious interest in ancient wares, have excavated and studied them carefully, and have been able to recapture much of the character of the Momoyama and early Edo pieces.

NOTES ON SELECTED KILNS

The names of Karatsu kilns are complicated and confusing. Almost half of the kilns are known by more than one name, several have more than one writing and/or pronunciation, and no official list has been developed. The kiln names and groups listed in *Sekai tōji zenshū*, Mizumachi, Nakajima, and Satō all differ in some respects. The list below includes the most frequently encountered variants. This text uses the name commonly employed by the Nakazato Karatsu potters or Japanese scholars, the form cited first in the list of Karatsu kilns.

At many sites, such as at Shiinomine and Tōjinmachi Ochawangama, more than one kiln was constructed, usually only a few yards apart. In some cases, such as Shiinomine, all the kilns at a single site were operative at the same time. Others, such as Tōjinmachi Ochawangama, are distinguished by one kiln supplanting another. Ordinarily the products from a single site are similar in clay, glazes, decoration, and shapes, especially when the time lapse between the construction of different kilns is not great.

Certain kilns, listed below according to kiln groups, had histories or distinctive products that make them worthy of special note.

Kishidake and Kishidake Group

There is disagreement about which kilns constituted the early cluster around Kishidake castle before its two falls. Handōgame, Hobashira, and Saraya are uncontested early sites. Most authorities consider the early Kishidake kilns to have been Handōgame, Hiramatsu, Hobashira, Michinayatani, Ōtani, and Saraya. Here they are grouped with the later Kishidake group kilns.

Handōgame. See pages 147ff.

Hobashira. Excavated in 1948 by Nakazato Tarōuemon XII and Katō Toshiaki. The opaque white rice-straw ash glaze appeared for the first time on Hobashira wares. Many of these, found on the lowest strata, parallel the North Korean Hoeryŏng wares, suggesting the presence of North Korean potters brought to Japan by the Matsuura *wakō* prior to Hideyoshi's campaigns.[2] Examples of *hori* ("carved") Karatsu teabowls are among the remains. Some of the products of this kiln are made of a light, fine-grained clay, which does not produce the *chirimen-jiwa* (see Glossary) when trimmed. This is one of three Kishidake sites where naive, primitive underglaze painted designs are common—simple abstract decorations, wavy lines, dots, curved strokes, short lines radiating from a center, etc.—generally painted in small, isolated areas. At Hobashira, the first examples of the underglaze iron painted (*kawakujira* style) lip are found.

Kojirōkaja. A kiln located northwest of the main group of Kishidake sites producing wares from an extremely fine local clay, light in color, with little iron content, and not producing the *chirimen-jiwa*. Shards indicate that clay spurs rather than shells were used exclusively in stacking.

OLD KARATSU KILN SITES

NAGOYA CASTLE
Shirosakiyama
Bōzumachi• KARATSU CITY
Kojirōkaja
Tōjinmachi
Ochawangama

Kishidake Group
•Yamase

KISHIDAKE CASTLE
Saraya•
Hobashira•
Hiramatsu•
Handōgame• Ōtani
•Michinayatani
SAGA PREFECTURE

Hazenotani•
Ōkawabaru•

Matsuura Group
Hirayama•

Abondani•
Shiinomine•
Dōzono•
Fujinkawachi•
Gobōdani•
Kanaishibaru•
Tashiro•
Sajirō•
•Kameyanotani
Yakiyama•
Taku Group

IMARI CITY
Kōraidani•

Saga Group
Ichinoseyama•
North Takeo Group
TAKU CITY
Tōjinkoba•
SAGA CITY

Sabitani•
•Kawagokamanotani
Kanakōnotsuji•
Kotōge•
Kuromutayama•
Ōkōchi•

Hirado Group
Yanbeta•
Komizoyama•
ARITA CITY
TAKEO CITY
HIZEN YAMAGUCHI

Seirokunotsuji•
•Shōkoya
Tenjinmori•
Yoshinomoto•
Komononari•
Yanaginomoto•
Kiharayama•
Hyakken•
South Takeo Group
Oyamaji•
Niwaki•
Uchida Saraya•

Ushiishi•
•Hata no Hara
Mikōchi•

NAGASAKI PREFECTURE
Yuminoyama•
Kotaji Shirokiharu
•Ōkusano
•Ureshino
Uchinoyama•

0 1 2 3 4 5 kmm

adapted from Mizumachi 1973, Vol. I, p. 209, and Nagatake, Takeshi,
Hizen kogama: Shiseki fuzu (Map of Hizen Old Kiln Sites), (Arita: Arita
Ceramic Museum, 1969, rev. 1983)

Michinayatani. This was one kiln of the Kishidake region that specialized in tea ceremony utensils. The large, Plain Karatsu teabowls called *oku-Gōrai*, many with rice-straw ash glaze, are plentiful among its products. Both a coarse, sandy clay and a fine, light-colored clay were used. The feldspathic dark iron glaze used on many of its products is considered by Nakajima to be the best Karatsu *temmoku*. Foot rims of Michinayatani products are frequently splayed, and some underglaze designs are primitive in style.

Ōkawabaru. The remains of this kiln contain early Karatsu fragments from its first period as an official Karatsu kiln, 1604–15, and stylized examples of Presentation Karatsu from its second opening in 1657 under Jin'uemon and Wahei. The first period produced painted underglaze iron wares with simple, primitive designs. One of the Karatsu pieces designated an Important Cultural Property, a large jar with splashes of underglaze iron decoration (Plate 127), was attributed to this site by Satō, who recommended it for that distinction.

Ōtani. A circle cleared of glaze on the upper surfaces of pots to allow stacking without the use of shells or spurs is unusual for Karatsu but is found on wares from Ōtani. Another Karatsu kiln using this was Yasushirō of the Taku group.

Yamase. Together with Kojirōkaja, Yamase is considered the oldest of the Kishidake group kilns. It was separated geographically from other Kishidake kilns, the only one east of the Matsuura River. Its products are characterized by a yellowish clay, fired with minimal reduction to prevent excessive darkening of the high iron content. A high percentage of alumina made it extremely sticky, causing deep-textured *chirimen-jiwa* in the trimmed foot rims.

Matsuura Group

Dōzono. This is one of the oldest, if not the oldest, of the Matsuura kilns, probably having been established between 1596 (Keichō 1) and 1600. The underglaze iron painting found here has a direct, simple style.

Fujinkawachi. Of all kilns in the Karatsu fief, Fujinkawachi developed the most distinctive style. It was the Matsuura group kiln catering to tea ceremony ware production. More than at any other site, the two-glazed Korean Karatsu was made here. Although Plain and Underglaze Decorated pieces were also produced, Fujinkawachi has become so identified with Korean Karatsu that examples of it are readily attributed to this kiln. While some pieces are similar to those found at Kishidake sites, Fujinkawachi wares display dramatic evolutions of shape, size, and carved and incised surface decorations. The dramatic wares from this kiln climax in the glaze-trailed water jars and vases, which have the most daring decorations of all Karatsu ceramics. Influences from other kilns producing tea ceremony wares (Iga, Bizen, Tamba, etc.) are apparent in Fujinkawachi products, although direct copies were not made. Unlike other Karatsu kilns, its products are predominantly larger, *tataki* pieces. They were deliberately dented, squeezed, warped, and gouged—the most self-conscious production of all Karatsu ware. Some unglazed objects and shards among kiln remains suggest that bisque firing, uncommon for Karatsu, occurred at Fujinkawachi.

Hirayama. This became the official Karatsu kiln in 1649 (Keian 2) and was known to have had potters imported from other Karatsu kiln groups outside the Karatsu fief. It was here that Wahei came to begin production with potters from Hirado.

Shiinomine. The three kilns of some twenty chambers each at Shiinomine are the largest Matsuura kilns. The first and earliest of these, Kamitatara, produced only household wares. They are unusual thrown pieces lacking a trimmed foot rim, simply cut flat at the base. The central and lower kilns, said to have opened in 1616, supplied the majority of Shiinomine ceramics. They produced a wide range of Underglaze Decorated Karatsu types—slip-decorated pieces with brushed decoration, inlaid and stenciled designs, and painted underglaze iron pieces with a transparent gray, lustrous glaze. Some slip-inlaid (*mishima*) pieces from Shiinomine have a rice-straw ash glaze over the designs.

Shiinomine was well located for materials needed for large-volume ceramic production. It continued making high-fired stoneware when other kilns began using lower temperatures, indicating an abundant availability of wood. The only material in short supply was feldspar, which the Shiinomine potters, according to old records, sought in Nabeshima territory on stealthy nocturnal excursions.[3] Legends say imported materials were used at Shiinomine—for the manufacture of *hi bakari* teabowls (Korean materials) and for some porcelain pieces made with Amakusa clay, a highly plastic kaolin used for Hirado porcelain. Excavated *oku-Gōrai* teabowls and traces of porcelain found at Shiinomine imply some basis for these tales.

This large kiln was renowned for the quality pieces it produced during its long history. At the time of its fall, its products were Presentation Karatsu, made of levigated clay, with a cream-colored, high-gloss glaze, and refined shapes often decorated with slip-inlay or stencil designs.

Sajirō. The products of this kiln, which opened in 1736 (Kyōhō 20), exemplifies late Karatsu wares.[5] The products are entirely household wares of characteristic Karatsu shapes and scale, and include large tea storage jars as much as three feet (90 centimeters) in height.

Tashiro. This was the first Karatsu official kiln at which the Fukumoto, Nakazato, and Ō-shima potters collaborated in the early Keichō period (1596–1614). Although it was an official kiln, the majority of its products are simple utilitarian pieces. The fluted rims found at Handō-game and the early Kishidake sites were produced here also, although, in general, they tended to disappear at later Kishidake and Matsuura kilns.

Yakiyama. The two kilns of Yakiyama, said to have opened around 1608 (Keichō 12),[4] have a few examples of unglazed, bisqued remains. Among the motifs on Underglaze Decorated examples are some that are indicative of an influence from the kilns of Mino—wisteria, fishing nets, and delicate renditions of grasses.

Taku Group

Kōraidani. Nakajima identifies Kōraidani with the Taku kiln of Tōjinkoba and claims that the site was known even earlier as Yamanoguchi.[6] Tradition cites Kōraidani as the first kiln of Ri Sampei. Descriptions of his early products are based on examples found there—Underglaze Decorated Karatsu using plant and floral motifs, *kutsu-gata chawan* (see Glossary), a predominance of household utensils, and slip decoration, particularly spiral *hakeme* (brush-marking).

Saga Group

Ichinoseyama. Although the Saga kilns are primarily identified with porcelain production, the quantity of Karatsu among Ichinoseyama remains suggests that it continued to fire Karatsu stoneware for some time after porcelain production commenced. A flowering reed (millet?) painted between paired diagonal grasses was frequently repeated on decorated plates here.

Ōkōchi (Ōkawachi). This began as a Karatsu kiln only to become most noted as a Nabeshima porcelain kiln specializing in refined blue-and-white and overglaze enameled wares.

Takeo Group

Kawagokamanotani. The painted underglaze iron shard dated 1618 (Genna 4) was unearthed here (Plate 183). The kiln's shards include unusual examples of stenciled *hakeme*.

Konakōnotsuji. The products here include examples of the rare *jakatsu* glaze effect (Plate 80).

Kotaji Shirokiharu. Among the few Takeo kilns not converting to porcelain production was Kotaji Shirokiharu, a source of household wares of the Takeo style.

Kotōge. Brush-marked (*hakeme*) decoration is common among Takeo Karatsu, but slip inlay (*mishima*) dominates only at Kotōge and Ōkusano; at Kotōge, decoration with white slip is prevalent. Rare shards show sgraffito, slip trailing, and unusually elaborate *mishima* inlays.

Kuromutayama. This site has one of the longest histories of activity of the Takeo kilns. It produced some blue-and-white porcelain but never abandoned the production of stoneware. Its wares were principally utilitarian pots, and there was a large production of Takeo style ceramics using *hakeme*. Nakajima reported in 1955 that four families of potters were still making every-day utensils there.[7]

Oyamaji. This kiln site, excavated in 1931, was probably the official kiln of the Gotō family. The influence of Mino ceramics, especially Oribe, it apparent in the painted underglaze iron designs and unusual shapes. The painting is elegant, with fine lines describing graceful patterns, which often duplicate Oribe motifs. Borders developed, and surfaces were painted with zones to contain motifs. While emulating the irregular shapes of Oribe ceramics, the Oyamaji potters continued throwing their pottery on the wheel, trimming the foot rim, then manipulating the shapes and carving or bending the rims until the shape appeared molded. Further evidence of Mino influence is the use of copper instead of an iron underglaze on some Oyamaji pieces. The prominence of Mino characteristics gives weight to the assumption that Katō Kagenobu of Mino came here to learn Karatsu kiln techniques. A full scope of tea ceremony utensils was produced at Oyamaji, but the potters were most daring in the creation of unusual shapes for *mukōzuke* dishes. Spur marks are lacking on Oyamaji products, an indication that the kiln was subsidized so well that neither time nor space for stacking was at a premium. Oyamaji, a Takeo group kiln with Mino influences, maintained production in the Karatsu style without converting to porcelain manufacture or to Takeo style stoneware.

Shōkoya (Shōkodani). Together with Konakōnotsuji, this was a kiln making tea ceremony wares with the *jakatsu* glaze effect (Plate 12).

Uchinoyama and *Yuminoyama.* Both are Takeo kilns not converting to porcelain, producing Takeo style stoneware into the mid-Edo period.

Hirado Group

Kiharayama. This kiln continued to produce stoneware after the general shift to porcelain among the Hirado kilns.

Mikōchi. The name of Mikōchi (Mikawachi) is generally associated with porcelain, but it began as a Karatsu kiln. Some believe that it was founded by potters from Kishidake. Koma no Ōna, mother of the Nakazatos associated with the Karatsu official kiln at Tashiro, migrated to Mikōchi with her son Mouemon in the early seventeenth century and remained there until her death in 1672.

Ushiishi. Excavated Karatsu wares from Ushiishi have a crude character in both shape and decoration. Ushiishi shards manifest the relatively undeveloped character of the utilitarian Karatsu products found among Hirado remains.

Yanaginomoto. The influence of underglaze cobalt painting on porcelain can be seen on the stoneware of Yanaginomoto.

NOTES

1. Nakajima 1955, pp. 20, 21, 28, 36, 81.   2. Nakazato 1973, p. 8.   3. Nakajima 1955, p. 34.
4. *op. cit.*, p. 31.   5. *op. cit.*, p. 30.   6. *op. cit.*, p. 86.   7. *op. cit.*, p. 128.

KARATSU KILN LIST

NAGOYA CASTLE　名護屋城
- Shirosakiyama　白崎山

KISHIDAKE KILNS AND GROUP　岸岳・岸岳系
- Handōgame　飯洞甕
  - Kami (Upper)　上
  - Shimo (Lower)　下
- Hazenotani　櫨の谷
- Hiramatsu　平松
- Hobashira　帆柱
- Kojirōkaja, (Kojirō)　小次郎冠者
  - Kojūkanja, (Kojūkusu)　小十冠者
- Michinayatani (Michinayanotani)　道納屋谷
- Mikawabayama　三河葉山
- Ōkawabaru　大川原
  - Mominokidani　樅の木谷
    - Higashi (East)　東
    - Nishi (West)　西
- Ōtani　大谷
- Hieda Saraya　稗田皿屋
- Tanaka　田中
- Yamase　山瀬
  - Kami (Upper)　上
  - Shimo (Lower)　下

MATSUURA GROUP　松浦系
- Abondani　阿房谷
  - Kami (Upper)　上
  - Shimo (Lower)　下
- Dōzono　道園
- Fujinkawachi (Fujinokōchi)　藤の川内
  - Chinotani　茅の谷
    - Higashi (East)　東
    - Nishi (West)　西
- Gobōdani　御坊谷
- Hatado　畑島
- Hirayama　平山
  - Kami (Upper)　上
  - Shimo (Lower)　下
- Ichiwakayashiki　市若屋敷
- Kachikyū (Katsukyū)　勝久
- Kameyanotani　甕屋の谷
- Kanaishibaru Hirotani　金石原広谷
- Katakusa　片草
- Myōsonji　明尊寺
  - Myōsonji-ura　明尊寺裏
- Mutanoharu　牟田の原
- Sajirō　佐次郎
- Shiinomine　椎の峯
  - Kami (Upper)　上
  - Shimo (Lower)　下
- Takeno　岳野
  - Takeno Hayashi　岳野林
- Tatsugawa　立川
  - Nishinokidani　西の木谷
- Tashiro　田代

- Tashirotsutsue　田代筒江
- Teranotani Kuratsubo　寺の谷鞍壺
- Teranotani Gokeda　寺の谷御家田
- Uchiumezaka　内梅坂
- Umenosaka　梅の坂
- Yakiyama　焼山
  - Kami (Upper)　上
  - Shimo (Lower)　下
- Yamaingakura (Yamainugakura)　狼ケ鞍

SAGA GROUP　佐賀系
- Ichinoseyama Kōraijin　市の瀬山高麗神
- Makinoyama Keyakitani　牧山欅谷
- Ōkōchi (Ōkawachi, Ōkawachiyama)　大川内
  - Gongendani　権現谷
  - etc.
- Shōrikibō-ura　正力坊裏

TAKU GROUP　多久系
- Hoshirō (Yasushirō)　保四郎
- Kōraidani (Komadani)　高麗谷
- Tōjinkoba　唐人古場

TAKEO GROUP　武雄系
(including Uchida*, Hirakoba+,
and Kuromutayama kilns)
- Akindoyama　商人山
- Arita Hiekoba　有田稗古場
  - Kami (Upper)　上
  - Shimo (Lower)　下
- Ashinotani*　葦の谷
- Chōkichitani　長吉谷
- (Uchidayama) Furuyashiki　（内田山）古屋敷
- Hakamanokameya　袴野甕屋
- Higuchinotani　火口谷
- Hiraiwa　平岩
  - Tsutsue Hiraiwa　筒江平岩
  - Kami (Upper)　上
- Hirakoba+　平古場
- Hyakken　百間
- Ichiinokiyama*　一位の樹山
- Ienomae　家の前
- Inokoba　猪古場
- Kanayamatani*　金山谷
- Kawagokamanotani　川古窯の谷
  - Shimo (Lower)　下
- Kōbira　幸平
- Konakōnotsuji+　古那甲の辻
- Kotaji Shirokiharu　古田志白木原
  - Kotaji　古田志
    - Ichi (One)　一
    - Ni (Two)　二
- Kotōge*　小峠
  - Mae (Front)　前
  - Oku (Back)　奥
  - Uchidayama-kotōge　内田山小峠
- Kuromutayama (Kuromuda)　黒牟田山

Kuromutayama Kōrai　黒牟田山高麗
Motobe Yamazaki　本部山崎
Mukaiya　向家
Nanamagari　七曲
Nagao　永尾
Niwagi　庭木
　　Niwagi Kamaya　庭木窯屋
　　Niwagi Kamedani　庭木甕谷
Ōkusano　大草野
Otaru　小樽
Oyamaji　小山路
　　Uchida Saraya　内田皿屋
(Hirakoba) Rishōkoba　平古場李祥古場
Sabitani　錆谷
Shōkoya (Shōkodani) +　祥古谷
(Uchida) Sugamuda　（内田）菅牟田
Suginomoto +　杉の元
Tatarō Antabaru　多々良安田原
Tatarō Nishidake　多々良西嶽
Tobettō　戸別当
Tsutsuetsuji　筒江辻
Ubagahara　姥ケ原
Uchidayama*　内田山
　　Takeuchi　武内
Uchinoyama　内野山
　　Kami (Upper)　上
　　Shimo (Lower)　下
Udonotani　宇土の谷
Ureshino　嬉野
Yamasaki Ogawachi　山崎小川内
Yamasaki Omedate　山崎御目立
(Hirakoba) Yamasaki Otachime　山崎御立目
Yuminoyama　弓野山
　　Kami (Upper)　上
　　Shimo (Lower)　下

KARATSU OFFICIAL KILNS NOT IN KILN GROUPS
唐津藩窯
　　Bōzumachi　坊主町
　　Karabori　唐堀
　　　Nishinohama　西の浜
　　Karafusa　唐房
　　Ochawangama　御茶碗窯
　　　Tōjinmachi Ochawangama　唐人町御茶碗窯

HIRADO GROUP　平戸系
Shimomukainoharu Kōraijin　下向原高麗神
Genjabayashi　源左衛門林
Hara-ake (Hari-ake)　原明
Hata no Hara　畑の原
Hirado Saraya　平戸皿屋
　　Nakano　中野
Hiroseyama Komoridani　広瀬山小森谷
Hiroseyama Gongendani　広瀬山権現谷
Hiroseyama Mukaiya　広瀬山向家
Kaminangawara Temmoku　上南川原天目
Kiharayama　木原山
　　Kiharayama Jizōdaira　木原山地蔵平
　　Kiharayama Annomae　木原山庵の前
　　(Kihara Annomae)
Komizoyama　小溝山
　　Kami (Upper)　上
　　Naka (Middle)　中
　　Shimo (Lower)　下
Kuromuta Yanbeta　黒牟田山辺田
　　Ichi (One)　一
　　Ni (Two)　二
Mikōchi (Mikawachi)　三川内
　　Nagahayama　長葉山
　　Hayama　葉山
　　Nakazato　中里
Muraki　村木
　　Murakiyama Tanitsutsumi　村木山谷堤
Muraki Fudōsa　村木不動作
　　Kami (Upper)　上
　　Shimo (Lower)　下
Seirokunotsuji　清六の辻
　　Ichi (One)　一
　　Ni (Two)　二
　　San (Three)　三
Tenjinmori　天神森
　　Kami (Upper)　上
　　Shimo (Lower)　下
Temmoku　天目
Ushiishi　牛石
Yanaginomoto　柳の元
Yoshinomoto　葭の元
Yunada Torigoe　湯無田鳥越

Glossary

Agano (上野). Ware from a private kiln established by Hosokawa Tadaoki after the Korean campaigns of Hideyoshi; main Korean potter, Chon Hae; related to Takatori wares.

amamori (雨漏り). "Leaking rain;" the appearance of spots in a clay body under the glaze.

ame gusuri (飴釉). Amber-colored iron glaze, named after a hard, golden brown Japanese candy; also, *taiyū*.

anagama (穴窯). A simple kiln consisting of a single chamber carved into a hillside without interior baffles; used in Japan before the introduction of the climbing kiln.

ao Karatsu (青唐津). "Green or blue" Karatsu; Karatsu glazed with a reduced iron glaze, usually a translucent or transparent dark olive green.

Arita (有田). City in modern Saga Prefecture that became the center around which the rapid and extensive development of porcelain production evolved in the first quarter of the seventeenth century.

Bizen (備前). An ancient ceramic production site still active today; known for dense, unglazed ware; produces tea utensils as well as common ware; also called Imbe ware.

budō (武道). "The way of the warrior;" Japanese martial or chivalric code of conduct.

bunrin cha ire (文林茶入). A small ceramic container for powdered tea in the shape of an apple; obsolete word for apple.

chadō (茶道). "The way of tea:" the tea ceremony and its philosophy conceived as a way of life; also: *sadō*.

cha ire (茶入) Powdered tea caddy; one of the smallest and most honored of the tea utensils.

chajin (茶人). Devotee of the tea ceremony; tea masters and their followers.

chaki (茶器). Ceramics used in the tea ceremony, its setting, and for the accompanying meal.

cha no yu (茶の湯). The tea ceremony; its philosophy and aesthetics.

chatsubo (茶壺). Jar for the storage of leaf tea.

chawan (茶碗). Teabowl used in the tea ceremony; the most numerous type of pot among remaining examples of Karatsu ceramics.

Chien, *see* Jian.

chirimen-jiwa (縮緬皺). Fine crinkles on a raw clay surface produced by trimming; frequently apparent on Karatsu foot rims.

choku or *choko* (猪口). Common small saké cup.

Chon Hae (尊楷). One of the Koreans brought back to produce ceramics in Japan; traditionally linked with the origin of Agano and Yatsushiro style stonewares; also known as Sonkai and Ueno Kizō.

chōnin (町人). "Townsman"; particularly the urbane, wealthy merchants of the Edo period, some of whom patronized the ceramic industries because of their involvement in the tea ceremony.

chōseki (長石). Feldspar; a critical ingredient in the high-fired Karatsu glazes.

Chōsen (朝鮮). Korea.

Chōsen Karatsu (-Garatsu) (朝鮮唐津). Type of Karatsu usually characterized by the combined use of a dark brown or black iron glaze and an opaque white rice-straw ash glaze, large sizes, and bold shapes; the boldest type of Karatsu.

Doi (土井). Family of Karatsu fief lords (1691–1762).

doki (土器). Unglazed earthenware; earthenware.

donburi (丼). Ceramic bowl for rice dishes; usually a flaring shape with a wide mouth.

e-Karatsu (-Garatsu) (絵唐津). Underglaze Decorated Karatsu; characterized by underglaze iron painted directly on the green clay, covered with a single glaze, and completed in a single firing; the most numerous of the Karatsu types.

Enshū, *see* Kobori Enshū.

fuchi-naburi zara (縁なぶり皿). Dish with a pinched or fluted rim.

fude (筆). Writing or painting brush; used for painting underglaze iron designs on Karatsu ware.

Fukaumi Shintarō, *see* Sōden.

furidashi (振出). "Shake out"; small ceramic bottles or other shapes with narrow openings used in the tea ceremony to shake out special sweets.

Furuta Oribe (古田織部; 1544–1615). Tea master of great influence during the period of Karatsu's greatest production; a pupil of Sen no Rikyū who served Oda Nobunaga, Toyotomi Hideyoshi, and Tokugawa Ieyasu; renowned for his bold and original designs reflected in Oribe ceramics of the Mino area.

futa (蓋). Cover or lid.

getemono (げてもの). Low-class, everyday ware.

goyō gama (御用窯). Official kiln of a clan or lord.

guinomi (ぐいのみ). Large saké cup.

Gyokusen-ji (玉泉寺). Temple that originally owned the inscribed, Pre-Karatsu jar now in the possession of Mr. Hiwatari of Kyushu; the inscription date is ambiguous, but the style of the jar relates to the Tenshō 20 tea jar (q.v.).

hachi (鉢). Bowl.

Hagi (萩). Ceramic ware developed at the kiln of Lord Mōri Terumoto by the seventeenth century immigrant Koreans Yi Kyong and Yi Pyo-kwang; together with Karatsu and Raku, one the three preferred tea ceremony wares; still produced today.

hai (盃). Saké cup; alternate reading for the character commonly read as *sakazuki* (q.v.).

hai-gusuri or *haiyū* (灰釉). In general, a glaze made with wood ash; one of three major Karatsu glazes—a milky translucent to transparent glaze ranging from yellowish brown when oxidized to greenish tints when reduced.

Hakata (博多). Port city in northwest Kyushu, part of the modern city of Fukuoka; castle town of the Kuroda clan; flourishing trade center during the Muromachi, Momoyama, and Edo periods.

hakeme (刷毛目). "Brush-marked"; white slip applied with a stiff, coarse brush so that the texture of the brushstrokes remains visible.

hakogaki (箱書). The inscription by the maker or a known authority on a box housing a work of craft or art; this serves, in part, as its credential.

hana ike (花生), *hana ire* (花入). Flower vase.

Hankyū (範丘). Korean potter brought to Nagoya Castle in Kyushu to serve Hideyoshi's pottery needs.

hanyō (藩窯). "Clan kiln"; synonymous with *goyō gama* (q.v.).

Hata (波多) family. Branch of the Matsuura clan, lords of Kishidake from late seventh century to 1594; lords under whom the Karatsu style wares developed.

Hata Mikawa no Kami Chikashi (波多三河守親). Last lord of Kishidake; deposed by Hideyoshi at the close of the first Korean campaign in 1594.

hera (箆). General term for any elongated, broad wooden or bamboo tool; spatula; the long, broad, wooden tool used at Karatsu that has a curved, upturned, tapering end and is used to form the interior of a piece thrown off the hump.

hi bakari (火計). "Fire only"; ceramic wares traditionally said to have been made by Korean potters in Japan from imported materials, so that in their manufacture only the kiln fire was Japanese.

hi ire (火入). Fire container; ceramic vessel used to hold live coals and ash.

hikidashi guro (引出黒). A glossy jet black glaze obtained by removing pots from the kiln before they are completely cooled, thus arresting the oxidation process and leaving a rich black color.

himo tsukuri (紐作). The coiling technique of forming pots.

hira (平). Teabowls of a broad, low shape with sides flared at a wide angle.

Hirado (平戸). Important international Kyushu port during the late fifteenth and sixteenth centuries; an island off the coast of Kyushu; a group of early Karatsu kilns, most of which converted to porcelain manufacture; *see* map, page 194.

Hirotaka wa mono no shōya (広高は物庄屋). "Administrative Policies of Hirotaka"; document dated 11th day, 8th month, 1637, giving policies of Terasawa Hirotaka, first lord of Karatsu.

Hizen (肥前). Formerly a province of northwest Kyushu, where Karatsu ceramics originated and developed; modern Saga Prefecture and Higashi Sonoki-gun of Nagasaki Prefecture.

horidashi Karatsu (堀出唐津). Excavated Karatsu ware.

hori Karatsu (-Garatsu) (彫唐津). "Carved" Karatsu; a type of straight-sided teabowl having a large crosshatched pattern incised rather deeply into the body.

hori no te (堀の手). Excavated wares.

Hyakubasen (百婆仙; d. 1657). Widow of Sōden (q.v.); Korean renowned for leading a large migration of potters from Takeo to Arita in search of kaolin early in the second quarter of the seventeenth century.

ibitsu (いびつ). Warped and deformed pots.

Ienaga Hikosaburō Masachika (家永彦三郎方親). Japanese potter at Shirosakiyama kiln attached to Hideyoshi's Nagoya Castle; declared chief potter (*Iki no Kami*) by Hideyoshi; went to Korea with Lord Nabeshima in search of potters and in 1596 brought Hankyū to Nagoya.

Igarashi Jizaemon (五十嵐次左衛門). *Rōnin* of the Terasawa clan who became a potter for Lord Kuroda Tadayuki in 1628.

Iga ware (伊賀). Style of tea ceremony ceramics flourishing in Iga Province (modern Mie Prefecture) during the late Momoyama period; characterized by coarse clay and warped, distorted shapes.

Ikinoshima (壱岐島). Island off the coast of north Kyushu; location of Shōmo Jinja, owner of the Tenshō 20 dated Pre-Karatsu jar.

Imamura Sannojō (今村三之丞). Korean immigrant potter credited with the origin of Hirado style wares at Mikōchi, the official kiln of Lord Matsuura Sadanobu; son of Ko Kwan (q.v.).

Imari (伊万里). Thriving international port during the early Edo period, located southwest of Karatsu; export center for porcelains produced in the Arita region.

ishihaze (石はぜ). "Stone explosion"; small craters or cracks in a pot's surface resulting from stones or impurities in the clay body that, when they retain moisture, cause eruptions during the firing process.

itokiri zoko (糸切底). The shell-like pattern on the flat base of a ceramic piece resulting from the twisted thread used to cut the piece free from the wheelhead.

Iwaibe *doki* (祝部土器). Obsolete name for Sue ware; originally referred to ceremonial vessels (*iwai*) made by a potters' guild (*be*) during the Tumulus period; also known as Itsube ware.

jakatsu (蛇蝎). "Snakeskin" effect (splotched white on dark ground) found on some Karatsu and Satsuma wares; produced by applying dark iron glaze over a white glaze.

janome hage (蛇の目禿). A double ring, resembling a bull's eye, scraped clean of glaze on the upper surface of a pot to prevent sticking of stacked pots in a kiln.

Jian (建). Teabowls manufactured in Fukien Province, China, during the Song dynasty; used by monks at the monastery of Tianmu shan (天目山; Japanese: Temmoku-san), from whence they were, according to tradition, introduced into Japan by the Priest Dōgen in the first quarter of the thirteenth century; known in Japan as *temmoku*.

jiki (磁器). Porcelain.

Jikirinoura (地切りの浦). Early name for Karatsu port.

Jōmon (縄文) period (ca. 10,000–250 B.C.). Neolithic culture of Japan, characterized by earthenware vessels having mat- and rope-marked decoration.

Jū Jikan (従次貫). Potter from Yūsen, in the south of Korea, believed to have been brought to Japan by Lord Matsuura Shizunobu for Hideyoshi; potter at Shirosakiyama kiln attached to Nagoya Castle.

kaigara zumi (貝殻積). Shells used as kiln spurs.

kaime (貝目). "Shell mark"; marks left on the feet of pots resulting from shells used as kiln spurs.

kairagi (かいらぎ). Crawling; textural effect caused by shrinking of the glaze in the kiln so that it separates into small bumps; glaze effect common in Karatsu ware on trimmed areas of the body, probably resulting from a greater amount of moisture and exposed silica granules present in that area at the time of glazing.

kaiseki (懐石). "Bosom stone"; reference to the heated stone used by Zen monks to warm their empty stomachs; the meal served to guests at a tea ceremony; also *kaiseki ryōri*.

Kaitō shokokuki (海東諸国記). "Documents of Various Countries in the Eastern Sea," undated record probably written in the Edo period.

kakera (欠片). Fragment; shard.

kaki otoshi (搔落し). Sgraffito; decoration incised through a covering of slip.

kakō (火向). Warping of a pot resulting from vitrification of the clay body during firing.

kakuhimo tsukuri (角紐作). Type of *tataki* technique (q.v.) using clay slabs to form a pot.

kama (窯). Ceramic kiln; the same character is read *yō*.

kame (瓶, 甕). Jar, urn.

Kamiya Sōtan (神屋宗湛). Prominent merchant of Hakata; tea devotee acquainted with Hideyoshi and Sen no Rikyū; author of *Sōtan nikki*, a tea ceremony record book mentioning the use of Karatsu in the early part of the seventeenth century.

kandokuri (燗徳利). Bottle used for warming saké.

Kanegae Sambei, *see* Ri Sampei.

kangen (還元). Reduction; firing a kiln with a dearth of oxygen, thus producing a carbon-rich atmosphere.

kan'nyū (貫入). Crackle or crazing; the network of cracks in a glaze resulting from different shrinking rates of glaze and clay body while cooling.

karamono itokiri (唐物糸切). The right-leaning shell-like pattern (the usual Japanese pattern is left-leaning) on the base of a clay vessel created by the cord used to cut it free of the wheelhead; peculiar to Korea and Kyushu, where potter's wheels are revolved in a clockwise direction.

Kara Tsuchi no Fune (唐土の船). "Boats with Chinese clay [products]"; one of the suggested origins of the place name Karatsu.

karatsumono (唐津物) or *karatsu*. Term commonly used in areas of western Japan for household ceramics.

katakuchi (片口). Bowl with a pouring spout.

Katō Kagenobu (加藤景延). Potter of the Mino area regarded as the first in that region to use the climbing kiln.

kawakujira (皮鯨). "Whale skin"; lip of a pot painted with or dipped in underglaze iron; term based on the contrast of the blackish thin skin of the whale and the thick, white blubber underneath.

Kawasaki Seizō, *see* Sōkan.

kenjō Karatsu (献上唐津). "Presentation" Karatsu; Karatsu pieces used for official clan gifts; refined pots appearing first in the mid-eighteenth century and characterized by the use of levigated clay, glossy glaze, thin potting, and the frequent use of inlaid slip decoration (*mishima*).

kerokuro (蹴轆轤). Potter's wheel turned by a kicking action.

Kiheiji, *see* Nakazato Kiheiji.

ki Karatsu (黄唐津). Yellow Karatsu; type of Karatsu with an iron glaze fired to a yellowish color under oxidizing conditions.

kiku momi (菊揉). "Chrysanthemum wedging"; method of wedging clay that produces a flowerlike, spiral form then a cone-shaped lump; wedging process derived from Korea.

Kim Hae (金海). Korean immigrant potter who, together with his son and others, developed Satsuma style ceramics at the kiln of Lord Shimazu Yoshihiro in Kagoshima.

Kim Hwa (金和). Son of Kim Hae.

kiri ito (切糸). The cutting cord used to cut pots from the wheelhead.

ki Seto (黄瀬戸). Yellow Seto; Momoyama period ware made at the Mino kilns.

Kishidake (岸岳). Site of the castle of the Hata clan until its destruction in 1594; the earliest known group of Karatsu kilns, antedating the Korean campaigns of Hideyoshi; *see* map, page 194.

Kobori Enshū (小堀遠州; 1579–1647). Leading tea master, pupil and successor of Furuta Oribe.

kōdai (高台). Foot rim of a ceramic piece.

kōgō (香盒). Incense container or box, the smallest tea ceremony ceramic; also *kōbako*.

kohiki (粉引). Yi dynasty slip-dipped ware; a type of *punch'ŏng*.

ko Karatsu (-Garatsu) (古唐津). "Old" or "Early" Karatsu; Karatsu ware produced prior to the mid-Edo period.

kōki Karatsu (後期唐津). Folk wares deriving from Karatsu, produced in the latter part of the seventeenth century in north Kyushu.

Ko Kwan (巨関). Korean immigrant potter who opened the Nakano kiln on Hirado Island for Lord Matsuura Chinshin; father of Imamura Sannojō.

Koma, *see* Kōrai.

Koma no Ōna (高麗嫗). Wife of the Korean potter Nakazato Mouemon; she arrived in Japan about 1593 or 1595 with her family and that of Ōshima Hikoemon; *see* Genealogies of Official Karatsu Potters, page 28.

Komatsu Gennojō (小松源之允). *Rōnin* who became a potter about 1700, settling in Shiinomine, where the family continued as potters until the closing of the kiln.

Komatsu keifu (小松系譜). "Genealogy of the Komatsu Family," 1815, recopied 1818.

Kōrai (高麗). Japanese name for the Koryŏ dynasty of Korea (918–1392); Japanese generic term for Korea; formerly pronounced Koma.

kōro (香炉). Incense burner, censer.

ko Seto (古瀬戸). Early wares from the Seto kilns (q.v.).

kote (鏝). Fettling knife, used to trim the foot rim and body of a pot.

kuro Karatsu (黒唐津). Black Karatsu; Karatsu pots with a *hikidashi* black (q.v.) glaze and those having a very dark, opaque iron glaze.

kusuri (釉). Glaze; alternate reading of same character is *yū*; also *uwa gusuri*.

kutsu-gata (沓形). Teabowls, bowls, and dishes displaying a squat, irregular form and a thick lip rim.

kutsuwagata (轡形). Crest or design having a Greek cross within a circle.

Li Sampei, *see* Ri Sampei.

madara genshō, see *namako genshō*.

madara Karatsu (斑唐津). "Spotted," "speckled," or "mottled" Karatsu; type of Karatsu characterized by a glaze made from rice-straw ash and feldspar, which ranges from an opaque white through a stage displaying bluish streaks to a transparent form.

Matsudaira (松平). Karatsu fief lords from 1678 to 1690; related to the Tokugawa clan and famous as tea connoisseurs.

Matsuura (松浦). Powerful Kyushu clan with a domain including ancient Hizen and the Kishidake region, where Karatsu ceramics originated; clan operating one of the largest and most active *wakō* fleets; one of the groups of Karatsu kilns; *see* map, page 194.

Matsuura Karatsu ki. (松浦唐津記). "The Matsuura Record," 1637.

Matsuura ki shūsei (松浦記集成). "Collection of Matsuura Documents," undated, Edo period.

Matsuura koki (松浦古記). "Ancient Documents of Matsuura," 1789–1801.

Matsuura mukashi kagami (松浦昔鑑). "Ancient Records of Matsuura," 1704–11.

me (目). Small balls of unfired clay used as kiln spurs to separate ceramic pieces during firing.

mikazuki kōdai (三ケ月高台). Crescent-shaped foot rims resulting from trimming the inner and outer wall of the foot rim slightly off-center.

mimi (耳). "Ears"; small pottery loops or lugs placed high on the body of a jar or vase.

mingei (民芸). "Folk art"; specifically the folk art movement begun in Japan during the early part of this century.

Mino (美濃). Area of modern Gifu Prefecture adjacent to Seto; site of the kilns making Yellow Seto, Oribe, and Shino wares in the sixteenth and seventeenth centuries; "Mino ware" is used to designate these wares as a group.

mishima Karatsu (三島唐津). Karatsu ware decorated with stamped or incised designs inlaid with white slip.

mizu koboshi (水こぼし). Ceramic receptacle for waste water used in the tea room; pail.

Mizuno (水野). Karatsu lords (1763–1816) ruling during the time of the Shiinomine downfall and the move of the Nakazato, Ōshima, and Fukumoto potters to Karatsu city.

mizusashi (水指). Water jar; a tea ceremony vessel used to contain water.

mizutsugi (水注). Ewer.

Mori Zen'emon (森善右衛門). *Rōnin* of Kishidake or Karatsu; potter associated with revealing the principles of the climbing kiln to the potters of the Mino district.

muji Karatsu (無地唐津). Plain Karatsu; Karatsu type characterized by a single glaze without underglaze decoration.

mukōzuke (向付). Small dishes displaying a wide variety of shapes—from shallow to tall and cylindrical, round to square to irregular—used for serving food during the meal that is part of the tea ceremony; also a course of this meal.

Nabeshima (鍋島). The fief southwest of Karatsu fief; powerful lords in Kyushu; a precise and exquisite style of porcelain made at the official kiln of the Nabeshima fief for the exclusive use of the lords.

Nakano (中野). Ceramic ware developed by Korean potters under Ko Kwan on Hirado Island.

Nakao (中尾). Type of *oku-Gōrai* teabowl having a slightly flaring rim; its name is thought to come from that of an early tea master.

Nakazato, *see* Genealogies of Official Karatsu Potters, page 28.

Nakazatoke kyūki (中里家旧記). "Old Documents of the Nakazato Family," by Nakazato Kihei-ji, dated 1721.

Nakazato Kiheiji (中里喜平次; d. 1757). Fifth-generation Nakazato potter; potter at Shiinomine and Ochawangama, Karatsu city; author of two historic records concerning the early Korean immigrant potters.

Nakazato kiroku (中里記録). "Nakazato Documents," by Nakazato Kiheiji, dated 1721 and 1724.

Nakazato Matashichi (中里又七). Son of Koma no Ōna; the first Nakazato potter from Korea to make Karatsu ceramics.

namako (海鼠). "Sea cucumber"; Karatsu potters' term for their rice-straw ash glaze (also called *madara* glaze); glaze name found throughout Japan for glaze(s) causing blue streaking as a kiln effect when applied over dark iron glaze(s); *see* following entry.

namako genshō (海鼠現象). "*Namako* phenomenon"; streaks or spots of bright blue that appear when the Karatsu rice-straw ash glaze is used with an iron glaze; similar effects may occur when the rice-straw ash glaze (used alone) picks up iron from the clay body or from some other source in the kiln; one of the more spectacular kiln effects, and one that occurs with other glazes at other kilns.

neji momi (捩揉), see *kiku momi*.

nenuki (根抜). Type of *oku-Gōrai* teabowl; nineteenth century term meaning "very old"; also used for *ko* Seto wares.

ni-sai Karatsu (二彩唐津). "Two-color" Karatsu; term of recent origin for products of the Takeo kilns with brown and green glaze decoration over white slip.

noborigama (登窯). Climbing kiln; different periods and areas have different types of climbing kiln; general evolution is from a long half-tube built on a hillside with rudimentary baffle walls to domed, linked chambers, each built on a terrace and connected by flues through a baffle wall.

Ochawangama (御茶碗窯). "Kiln of the [Tea]bowl"; one of several Karatsu kilns so named; *see* Karatsu Kiln List, page 198.

Ogasawara (小笠原). Last feudal lords of Karatsu fief (1817–72).

oke (桶). Pail, bucket; tub.

Okinoshima (沖ノ島). Small island off the north coast of Kyushu in the Genkai Sea whose total land mass comprises one of the three ancient Munakata Shintō shrines; site of rich excavated finds of both Japanese and Chinese origin dating back as far as the Han dynasty.

Ōkubo (大久保). Karatsu lords (1649–77).

oku-Gōrai (奥高麗). *Oku* means "inner," *Kōrai* means "Korea," but it is unclear how the word *oku* should be interpreted in this compound term; a class of tea ceramics, primarily teabowls, of refined manufacture, previously believed to be of Korean origin, but, as the result of excavations in 1931 or 1932, now identified as Karatsu ware; a type of teabowl, usually hemispherical in shape, having a plain glaze fired in a predominantly oxidizing atmosphere.

oniwa-gama (御庭窯). Very small kiln in the precincts of a castle or manor, producing tea ceremony wares generally for the private use of a daimyo or chief retainer; such wares are called *oniwayaki* (c.f. *goyō gama).*

Oribe, *see* Furuta Oribe.

Ōshima, *see* Genealogies of Official Karatsu Potters, page 28.

Pal San (八山). Korean immigrant potter, founder of Takatori ware in Fukuoka Prefecture under Lord Kuroda Nagamasa; also known as Hassen.

Presentation Karatsu, see *kenjō* Karatsu.

punch'ŏng. Early Yi dynasty (1392–1597) Korean stoneware; gray body with white slip and clear glaze; production ceased after Hideyoshi's invasion of Korea in the 1590s.

raku (楽). Lightweight, porous, earthenware that is fired until the (lead) glaze flows and then, while still incandescent, is removed from the kiln (sometimes plunged into water); together with Karatsu and Hagi wares, one of the three most preferred tea ceremony wares.

Richō (李朝). Japanese term for the Yi dynasty of Korea (1392–1910).

rinkaen (輪花縁). Foliate lip rim of a pot.

Ri Sampei (李参平); Kanegae Sambei (金ヶ江参平). Korean immigrant potter who returned with Lord Nabeshima, produced Karatsu style ceramics, and traditionally is credited with the discovery of kaolin in Japan around 1616, thus launching the development of porcelain; also, Li Sampei, Yi Sam-p'yong.

rokuro (轆轤). Potter's wheel; see *kerokuro, terokuro.*

rōnin (浪人). Samurai without vassalage to a feudal lord either because of dissolution of a fief or reallocation of lands; masterless warrior; vagrant.

sadō, see *chadō.*

Saga (佐賀). One of the groups of Karatsu kilns located southeast of Arita; *see* map, page 194.

sakazuki (盃). Generic term for saké cup.

sakétsugi (酒注). Vessel used to pour saké; saké bottle.

sanka (酸化). Oxidizing; a kiln condition during firing characterized by a strong draft of air passing through the kiln, providing ample oxygen for the fire.

sara (皿). Plate, dish.

Satsuma (薩摩). Powerful fief in southernmost Kyushu ruled by the Shimazu clan; ceramic ware developed by immigrant Korean potters.

senbei (煎餅). Japanese cracker; hence, small squashed pads used to separate pots from kiln shelves during firing.

senkei (扇形). Fan shaped.

Sen no Rikyū (千利久). Founder of the *wabi* (q.v.) school of tea ceremony; tea master to Oda Nobunaga and Toyotomi Hideyoshi, who ordered Rikyū's suicide.

Seto (瀬戸). Pottery town in modern Aichi Prefecture; considered the oldest ceramic center in Japan.

Seto Karatsu (瀬戸唐津). Type of Karatsu teabowl resembling various Mino ware bowls, having flared sides, light clay, and a strong crackle in the cream-colored glaze.

shifuku (仕服). Cloth bag, often of precious brocade, cut to fit tea ceremony ceramics, especially the tea caddy, tying with silk cords at the top.

Shigaraki (信楽). One of the most famous medieval kilns; located in modern Shiga Prefecture; still active today.

Shiinomineyama kuzure (椎の峰山崩れ). The downfall and destruction of Shiinomine kiln, from the 6th month of 1697 to the 10th month of 1703.

Shimazu (島津). Powerful clan ruling the Satsuma fief in south Kyushu.

Shino (志野). Tea ware produced in the Mino area characterized by a light clay body and thick white glaze.

Shōmo Jinja (聖母神社). Shintō shrine at Katsumoto on Ikinoshima, owner of the Pre-Karatsu tea jar dated Tenshō 20.

soba (俑). Old Karatsu teabowl with such close resemblance to Korean bowls that when placed next to them (*soba ni*), the Japanese pot is difficult to distinguish from the Korean.

Sōden (宗伝); Fukaumi Shintarō (深海新太郎). Korean potter who came to Takeo with Lord Ienobu; husband of Hyakubasen; d. 1619.

Sōkan (宗歓); Kawasaki Seizō (川崎清蔵). Korean collaborator, spy, and guide for Lord Nabeshima; brought to Saga area, where he managed a kiln and perhaps was a potter himself; reputed to have secured thirteen potters from Korea for Nabeshima.

Sonkai, *see* Chon Hae.

soroban dama (算盤玉). ''Abacus bead''; jars whose contours resemble the shape of abacus counters—a daimondlike form.

Sōtan nikki (宗湛日記). ''Diary of Kamiya Sōtan,'' containing accounts of the early use of Karatsu in the tea ceremony.

Sue ware (須恵器). High-fired, dark gray pottery originating in the Tumulus period (ca. 250–ca. 600) and showing a close relationship to Korean Silla ware; originally was used mainly for funerary ware, hence the name (from *sueru*, ''to offer''); also Iwaibe, Itsube ware.

suiteki (水滴). Waterdropper; small ceramic or metal vessels with tiny openings used to drop water onto the inkstone when ink is being ground.

suribachi (擂鉢). Japanese grinding bowl or mortar.

Takatori (高取). Japanese ceramic ware originated by Korean immigrants under Pal San for Lord Kuroda of Hakata.

take no fushi kōdai (竹の節高台). ''Bamboo node foot''; foot rim having a central ridge resembling the node of a bamboo stalk.

Takeno Jōō (武野紹鷗; 1502–55). Influential tea master under the Ashikaga shoguns.

Takeo (武雄). Center of Karatsu production from the end of the sixteenth century; located south of Kishidake and Matsuura in the Nabeshima fief; style of stoneware developed at kilns that originally produced Karatsu; one of the groups of Karatsu kilns; *see* map, page 194.

Taku (多久). One of the groups of Karatsu kilns; *see* map, page 194.

tataki (叩き). Technique of joining clay coils or slabs and forming a pot by beating the outer surface with a wooden paddle and the inner surface with a wooden block (the ''anvil'') simultaneously; technique introduced from Korea; also *tataki de*.

tataki me (叩き目). Pattern of intersecting arcs on the inside of a pot formed by the ''anvil'' used in the *tataki* technique; also *uchinami*.

temmoku (天目). Saturated iron glaze; one of the three major types of Karatsu glaze, dark brown when oxidized and a blue-black when reduced; teabowl shape with flared sides, small foot, and slight indentation below the lip, deriving from Chinese Song dynasty Jian ware (q.v.).

Tenshō 20 tea jar (天正二十年茶壺). Stoneware tea storage jar inscribed with the date Tenshō 20

(1592); considered the earliest dated example of Karatsu, but actually Pre-Karatsu in style; in the possession of Shōmo Jinja, Ikinoshima.

Terasawa (寺沢). Lords of Karatsu fief from 1594 to 1647, during the period when the finest Karatsu ceramics were produced.

Terasawa Hirotaka (寺沢広高); Shimanokami (志摩守); Shishūkō (志州公). First lord of Karatsu fief (from 1594).

terokuro (手轆轤). Hand-turned potter's wheel.

tōchin (陶枕). Kiln furniture.

tōhen (陶片). Shard.

tōji (陶磁). Ceramics.

Tōjinmachi (唐人町). "Chinaman's town"; communities set apart for Korean immigrants.

toke (トケ). Block of wood ("anvil") tapped against interior of pot while outside is paddled in the *tataki* technique.

tōki (陶器). Stoneware.

tokuri (徳利). Bottle; usually refers to saké bottle.

tombe (とんべ). Soft, brittle, clay bricks used as the core of kiln walls in Kyushu; granite slabs customarily serve this function in Korea.

tōzansha (陶山社). Potters' shrine.

tsubo (壺). Jar.

Tsukushi (筑紫). "Where the land ends"; ancient name for Kyushu.

Tsuruta Echizen no Kami (鶴田越前守). Lord who conquered Kishidake Castle in 1560, thus bringing about the first closing of Kishidake kilns.

tsutsu (筒). Tube or cylinder.

uchinami, see *tataki me*.

uwa gusuri (釉薬). Glaze; overglaze; same characters also read *yūyaku*.

wabi (侘). Austere beauty associated with somber and colorless things having a quiet, simple, refined quality.

wakō (倭寇). Japanese pirates active from the thirteenth through seventeenth centuries along the Korean, Chinese, and Southeast Asian coasts.

waridake noborigama (割竹登窯). "Split-bamboo climbing kiln"; vaulted, link-chambered climbing kiln whose semicircular shape and walls dividing chambers suggest a bamboo stalk split in half.

Wungch'on (熊川; Japanese: Komogai or Yūsen). Site west of Pusan believed to have been the origin of some of the immigrant Korean potters after Hideyoshi's campaigns; Korean pottery site producing a ceramic ware with similarities to Karatsu.

yakimono (焼物). Pottery, ceramics.

Yakimono taigai (焼物大概). "General Introduction to Pottery," a section of the *Matsuura bussan zukō* ("Illustrated Study of Matsuura Products"), Edo period.

yakishime (焼締). Unglazed stoneware; Bizen ware is the most famous example.

yatsume (八目). Small balls of clay used as kiln spurs during firing.

Yayoi period (弥生; ca. 250 B.C.–A.D. 250). Early culture of Japan during which Korean ceramic techniques were first brought to Kyushu.

yone hakari (米量). Rice measuring bowls; ancient Karatsu product that became popular as teabowls; style of *oku-Gōrai.*

zakki (雑器). Household pots, common ware.

Zekan (是閑). An *okū-Gōrai* style teabowl with a flaring rim and glazed foot, named after a tea master.

zōgan (象嵌). Inlay.

Bibliography

Asakawa, Takumi (浅川功). *Chōsen tōji meikō* (朝鮮陶磁名考) [Special Studies in Korean Ceramics]. Tokyo: Kōseikai Shuppanbu, 1931.

Audsley, George Ashdown and Bowes, James Lord. *Keramic Art of Japan*. London: Henry Sotheran and Co., 1875.

Becker, S. Johanna. "Der Karatsu Stil und koreanische Einflüsse," *Keramos*, Heft 85 (Juli 1979), 59–76.

——. *The Karatsu Ceramics of Japan: Origins, Fabrication, and Types*. Vol. I, II. Ann Arbor, Mich.: University Microfilms, 1974.

Bowes, James L. *Japanese Pottery*. Liverpool: Edward Howell, 1890.

Brinkley, Captain F. *Japan, Its History Arts and Literature*. Vol. VIII: *Keramic Art*. Boston: J. B. Millet Company, 1901.

Ceramic Art of Japan: One Hundred Masterpieces from Japanese Collections. Seattle: Seattle Art Museum, 1972.

Cort, Louise Allison. "Korean Influences in Japanese Ceramics," *Orientations*, Vol. 15, No. 5 (May 1984), 18–29.

Dai Karatsu-ten (大唐津展) [The Grand Karatsu Exhibition]. Tokyo: Yomiuri Shimbunsha, 1978.

"E-Garatsu mimi-tsuki mizusashi" (絵唐津耳付水指) [Karatsu Water Jars with Underglaze Decoration and Small Handles], *Tōsetsu* (陶説) [Ceramics Explained, Journal of the Japan Ceramic Society], No. 156 (March, 1966), 3.

Faulkner, R. F. J. and Impey, O. R. *Shino and Oribe Kiln Sites*. Oxford: Robert G. Sawyers, Publ., 1981.

Fontein, J. "Japanese Porcelain and Pottery in Holland," *Tōsetsu*, No. 75 (June, 1959), 11–25.

Fujioka, Ryōichi (藤岡了一) (ed.). "Shino to Oribe" (志野と織部) [Shino and Oribe Wares], *Nihon no bijutsu* (日本の美術) [Japanese Art], No. 51 (August, 1970).

Fukui, Kikusaburō. *Human Elements in Ceramic Art*. Tokyo: Kokusai Bunka Shinkōkai, 1934.

Fukukita, Yasunosuke. *Cha-no-yu: Tea Cult of Japan*. Tokyo: The Hokuseidō Press, 1938.

Gompertz, G. St. G. M. *Korean Pottery and Porcelain of the Yi Period*. New edition. London: Faber and Faber, 1968.

Gorham, Hazel M. *Japanese and Oriental Ceramics*. Tokyo: Tuttle, 1971. (reprint of *Japanese and Oriental Pottery*, 1952)

Griffing, Robert P. (ed.) *The Art of the Korean Potter: Silla, Koryŏ, Yi*. New York: Asia Society, 1967.

Harada, Tomohiko (原田伴彦) and Nakazato, Tarōuemon (中里太郎右衛門). *Nihon no yakimono*: III, Karatsu, Takatori (日本のやきもの3 唐津・高取) [Japanese Pottery: III, Karatsu and Takatori Wares]. Kyoto: Tankōshinsha, 1969.

Hayashiya, Seizō (林屋晴三) (ed.). "Chawan" (茶碗) [Teabowls], *Nihon no bijutsu*, No. 14 (June, 1967).

Hazard, Benjamin H. "The Formative Years of the Wakō, 1223–63," *Monumenta Nipponica*, Vol. XXII, Nos. 3–4 (1967a), 260–77.

———. *Japanese Marauding in Medieval Korea: The Wakō Impact on Late Koryo*. Doctoral Dissertation. Berkeley: University of California, 1967b.

Hiwatari, Masaharu (樋渡政治). "Tenshō nijūnen mei Karatsu chatsubo ni tsuite" (天正二十年銘唐津茶壺に就いて) [About the Famous Tenshō 20 Karatsu Tea Jar], *Tōsetsu*, No. 24 (March, 1955), 15–20.

Honey, W. B. "Corean Wares of the Yi Dynasty," *Oriental Ceramic Society Transactions*, (London), Vol. XX, 1944–45.

Impey, O.R. "Ceramic Wares of Hasami," *Oriental Art*, XXI, No. 4, 1975, 344–355.

International Symposium on Japanese Ceramics. Seattle: Seattle Art Museum, 1973.

Japanese Ceramics from the Collection of Captain and Mrs. Roger Gerry. Brooklyn: The Brooklyn Museum, 1961.

Jenyns, Soame. *Japanese Pottery*. London: Faber and Faber, 1971.

Kanahara, Kyōichi (金原京一). *E-Garatsu kanshō zuroku* (繪唐津鑑賞圖録) [A Pictorial Collection of Painted Karatsu]. Tokyo: Gakugei Shoin Kan, 1940.

Karatsu (唐津). Nihon no tōji (日本の陶磁) [Japanese Ceramics], No. 5. Tokyo: Chūō Kōronsha, 1974.

Karatsu (唐津). Nippon tōji zenshū (日本陶磁全集) [A Pageant of Japanese Ceramics], No. 17. Tokyo: Chūō Kōronsha, 1976.

Karatsu (唐津). Osaka: Asahi Shimbunsha, 1973.

"Karatsu ayame e-bachi" (唐津あやめ絵鉢) [The Karatsu Bowl with Underglaze Iris Design], *Tōsetsu*, No. 189 (December, 1968), 62.

"Karatsu gama to Oribe gama" (唐津竈と織部竈) [Karatsu and Oribe Kilns], *Tōsetsu*, No. 5 (August, 1953), 74–78.

"Karatsu shio-zutsu chaji" (唐津塩筒茶磁) [Karatsu Tea Utensils: Salt Canisters], *Tōsetsu*, No. 194 (May, 1969), 5–8.

Katō, Hajime (加藤土師萌) "Tōgi jō kara mita Karatsu" (陶技上から見た唐津) [A Technical Analysis of Karatsu Pottery], *Tōsetsu*, No. 19 (October, 1954), 20–24.

Kawahara, Masahiko (河原正彦), ed. *Karatsu* (唐津), Nihon no bijutsu (日本の美術) [Japanese Art], No. 136 (Sept. 15, 1977). Tokyo: Shibundō, 1977.

Kim, Chewon and Gompertz, G. St. G. M. *Korean Arts*. Vol. II, *Ceramics*. Korea: Ministry of Foreign Affairs, Republic of Korea, 1961.

Ko-Karatsu, Nakazato Muan, to Nakazato Tarōuemon ten (古唐津・中里無庵と中里太郎右衛門展) [Early Karatsu, Nakazato Muan and Nakazato Tarōuemon Exhibition]. Tokyo: Yomiuri Shimbunsha, 1984.

Koyama, Fujio (小山冨士夫) (ed.). *Chaji* (茶磁) [Tea Ceremony Ceramics]. Vol. IV, *Nihon I* (日本 I) [Japan I]. Tokyo: Heibonsha, 1966.

———— (ed.). *Ko-Karatsu* (古唐津) [Early Karatsu]. Tokyo: Idemitsu Kōsan Kabushiki Kaisha, 1969a.

————. *Nihon tōji no dentō* (日本陶磁の伝統) [Japanese Ceramic Traditions]. Tokyo: Tankōshinsha, 1967b.

———— (ed.). *Nihon tōji sōran* (日本陶磁総覧) [Tea Management of Japanese Ceramics]. Tokyo: Tankōsha, 1969b.

———— and Mitsuoka, Tadanari (満岡忠成) (eds.). *Tōki zuroku* (陶器図録) [An Illustrated Handbook of Ceramics]. Vol. VI, *Kyūshū* (九州) [Kyushu Wares]. Vol. IX, *Chōsen* (朝鮮) [Korean Wares]. Vols. XI-XII, *Chaki* (茶器) [Tea Utensils]. Tokyo: Yūzan-kaku, 1938–39.

Kurahashi, Tōjirō (倉橋藤治郎) (ed.). *Ko-Karatsu* (古唐津) [Early Karatsu]. ("Tōki zuroku") Tokyo: Kōseikai Shuppanbu, 1933.

Kyūshū kotō kenkyūkai (九州古陶研究会) [Ancient Ceramics of Kyushu Research Society], *Kyūshū no kotō* (九州の古陶) [Old Kyushu Ceramics], No. 1 (1937).

Matsufuji, Shōhei (松藤庄平). "Yakimono Karatsu kaidō," (やきもの唐津街道) [Ceramics of the Karatsu Highway], *Geijutsu Shinchō*, Vol. 33, no. 3 (Mar. 1, 1982), 92–102.

McCune, Evelyn. *The Arts of Korea: An Illustrated History*. Rutland: Charles E. Tuttle Company, 1962.

Mikami, Tsugio (三上次男). "Yūsen Kinkoku no koyō" (熊川金谷の古窯) [Ancient Kilns of Wungch'ŏn and Keumkok, Korea], *Idemitsu Bijutsukan kampō* (出光美術館館報) [Idemitsu Art Gallery Journal], No. 9 (April 21, 1971), 1–8.

Miller, Roy Andrew. *Japanese Ceramics*. After the Japanese text by Seiichi Okuda, Fujio Koyama, Seizō Hayashiya, and others. Tokyo: Tōtō Shuppan, 1960.

Mino kotō (美濃古陶) [Old Wares of Mino]. Osaka: Osaka Shiritsu Bijutsukan, Tokugawa Bijutsukan, Nezu Bijutsukan, 1971.

Mizumachi, Wasaburō (水町和三郎), "Futatabi Karatsu no kigen ni tsuite" (再び唐津の起源に就て) [More about the Origins of Karatsu Wares], *Tōsetsu*, No. 42 (Setember, 1956), 13–19.

————. and Nabeshima, Naotsugu (鍋島直紹). *Karatsu* (唐津) [Karatsu Wares]. English summary by Harry Packard. Tokyo: Hakuōsha, 1963.

————. "Karatsu kigen kō" (唐津起原考) [Research into the Origins of Karatsu Wares], *Tōsetsu*, No. 24 (March, 1955), 3–14.

————. *Ko-Karatsu* (古唐津) [Early Karatsu]. Vol. I, II. (Idemitsu Art Gallery Publication, No.6). Tokyo: Heibonsha, 1973.

Moeran, Brian. "A Survey of Modern Japanese Pottery," *Ceramics Monthly*, Vol. 30, No. 9 (November, 1982), 44–46; No. 10 (December, 1982), 32–34.

Morse, Edward S. *Catalogue of the Morse Collection of Japanese Pottery, Museum of Fine Arts, Boston*. Cambridge: Riverside Press, 1901.

Munakata Taisha hōmotsukan (宗像大社宝物館) [Munakata Shrine Art Treasury]. Fukuoka: Munakata Taisha Shūmu Honkyoku, 1963.

Murayama, Takeshi (村山武). "Chōsen Garatsu mimi-tsuki hana-ike" (朝鮮唐津耳付花生) [Korean Karatsu Style Vases with Small Handles], *Tōsetsu*, No. 159 (June, 1966), 1.

Nagatake, Takeshi (永竹威). "Chatō Karatsu" (茶陶唐津) [Karatsu Tea Ceremony Wares], *Tōsetsu*, No. 131 (February, 1964), 66–67.

————. *Japanese Ceramics from the Tanakamaru Collection*. New York: The Metropolitan Museum of Art, 1980.

————. *Kyūshū ko tōji* (九州古陶磁) [Ancient Ceramics of Kyushu]. English summary by Haruo Igaki. Tokyo: Toko Shoin, 1963.

————. *Tōki Kōza: III Nippon III: Edo zenki* (陶器講座 日本III 江戸前期) [Lecture on Ceramics, No. III, Japan III, Early Edo]. Tokyo: Yūzankaku, 1971.

Nakajima, Kōki (中島浩気) (ed.) *Hizen tōji shi* (肥前陶磁史) [A History of Hizen Ceramics]. Kyū-shū: Hizen Tōji Shi Kankōkai, 1955.

Nakamura, Ken'ichi (中村研一). "Tanakamaru tei ni te" (田中丸邸にて) [At the Tanakamaru Household], *Tōsetsu*, No. 91 (October, 1960), 59–61.

Nakazato, Tarōuemon XIII. *Karatsu-yaki*. Translated by Robert K. Okasaki. (no city) Karatsu-yaki Society for the Preservation of Ochawangama, 1979.

Nakazato, Tarōuemon (中里太郎右衛門). *Karatsu* (唐津). Nihon no yakimono (日本のやきもの) [Japanese Ceramics], No. 14. Tokyo: Kodansha, 1976.

———— and Minematsu, Chūji (峰松忠二). *Karatsu* (唐津). Nihon no yakimono (日本のやきもの) [Japanese Ceramics] no. 4. Kyoto: Tankōsha, 1974.

————. *Karatsu.* Famous Ceramics of Japan 9. Translated by Shigetaka Kaneko and Lynne E. Riggs. Tokyo: Kodansha International, 1983.

Nihon Tōji Kyōkai (日本陶磁協会) [Japan Ceramic Society]. *Karatsu* (唐津) [Karatsu Ware]. (Tōji Sōsho, Vol. 2) Tokyo.

Nogata Shi Kyōiku Iinkai (直方市教育委員会). [Nogata City Board of Education]. *Uchigaisoyōseki: Nogata shi bunkazai chōsa hōkokusho* (内ヶ磯窯跡：直方市文化財調査報告書) [Private Domain Kiln Ruins: Nogata City Cultural Assets Research Report], Vol. 4. Nogata: Kyōiku Iinkai, 1982.

Okada, Sōei (岡田宗淑). "Karatsu matsu-e ō-kame" (唐津松絵大甕) [The Large Karatsu Jar with Pine Tree Design], *Tōsetsu*, No. 200 (November, 1969), 64.

Okuhara, Shin'ichi (奥原信一). "Dōzono nikki" (道園日記) [Journal of the Dōzono Kiln Site], *Tōsetsu*, No. 17 (August, 1954), 12–17.

Sadler, A. L. *Cha-no-yu: The Japanese Tea Ceremony*. J. O. Thompson and Co. Ltd., 1930.

Sansom, G. B., *A History of Japan: 1334–1615*. Stanford: Stanford University Press, 1961.

————. *A History of Japan: 1615–1867*. Stanford: University Press, 1969.

Satō, Masahiko (佐藤雅彦). "Tanakamaru shi no korekutaashippu" (田中丸氏のコレクターシップ) [Characteristics of the Tanakamaru Collection], *Tōsetsu*, No. 91 (October, 1960), 62–65.

Satō, Shinzō (佐藤信三). *Chatō Karatsu* (茶陶唐津) [Karatsu Tea Ceremony Wares]. Tokyo: Tokuma Shoten, 1963a.

————. *Hizen no Karatsu yaki* (肥前の唐津焼) [The Karatsu Wares of Hizen]. (Tōki zenshū, Vol. III) Tokyo: Heibonsha, 1961.

————. "Karatsu cha ire no kōsatsu" (唐津茶入の考察) [A Brief Study of Karatsu Tea Caddies], *Tōsetsu*, No. 6 (September, 1953), 16–18.

————. "Karatsu katatsuki cha ire" (唐津肩衝茶入) [Karatsu Tea Caddies with Pronounced Shoulders], *Tōsetsu*, No. 86 (May, 1960a), 9–12.

————. "Karatsu wari-zanshō mukōzuke wa Agano yaki de aru" (唐津割山椒向付は上野焼である) ["Split-Pod" Karatsu *Mukōzuke* Dishes Should Be Agano Ware], *Tōsetsu*, No. 144 (March, 1965), 11.

————. "Karatsu yaki no gainen" (唐津焼の概念) [Outline of Karatsu Pottery], *Tōsetsu*, No. 19 (October, 1954), 3–11.

————. "Karatsu yaki wa itsu goro hajimatta ka" (唐津焼はいつ頃始まったか) [When Did Karatsu Pottery Originate], *Tōsetsu*, No. 122 (May, 1963b), 57–72.

————. "Kishidake shutsudo no hori Garatsu" (岸嶽出土の彫唐津) [Carved Karatsu Excavated at the Kishidake Kiln Site], *Tōsetsu*, No. 48 (March, 1957b), 47–50.

————. "Ko-Karatsu" (古唐津) [Early Karatsu Wares], *Tōji* (陶瓷) [Oriental Ceramics], No. 6 (1955a). (The identical article and illustrations can be found in *Tōsetsu*, No. 25, April, 1955).

————. "Mizumachi shi no 'Futatabi Karatsu no kigen ni tsuite' o bakusu" (水町氏の「再び唐津の起源に就て」を駁す) [A Stand Against Mr. Mizumachi's "Origin of Karatsu Wares"], *Tōsetsu*, No. 46 (January, 1957c), 37–39.

————. "Oyamaji gama no seihin ni tsuite" (小山路窯の製品に就て) [About the Products of Oyamaji Kiln], *Tōsetsu*, No. 91 (October, 1960b), 39–46.

————. "Tenshō mei Karatsu chatsubo ni tsuite" (天正銘唐津茶壺に就て) [The Karatsu Tea Jar Inscribed "Tenshō"], *Tōsetsu*, No. 24 (March, 1955b), 21–24.

Satow, E. "The Korean Potters in Satsuma," *Transactions of the Asiatic Society of Japan*, Vol. VI, part II (February 23, 1887), 193–203.

Sekai Tōji Zenshū (世界陶磁全集) [Compendium of World Ceramics]. Vol. III. *Momoyama* (桃山) [Momoyama Period]. Vol. IV, *Edo Jō* (江戸 上) [Early Edo]. Vol. VII, *Chaki* (茶器) [Tea Ceremony Utensils]. Vol. XIII, *Chōsen Jōdai, Kōrai* (朝鮮・上代・高麗) [Korea: Antiquity to Koryŏ Dynasty]. Vol. IV, *Ri* (李朝) [Yi]. Tokyo: Zauhō Press and Kawade Shobō, 1955–58.

Shiba, Ryotarō. *The Heart Remembers Home*. Tokyo: Japan Echo, 1979.

Tanaka, Minoru (田中稔). "E-Garatsu no kakera" (絵唐津のかけら) [Shards of Painted Karatsu], *Tōsetsu*, No. 196 (July, 1969), 45–50 and No. 198 (August, 1969), 76–83.

————. "Ko Garatsu asari" (古唐津あさり) [Searching for Early Karatsu Wares], *Tōsetsu*, No. 185 (August, 1968), 28.

Toki Shi Mino Tōji Rekishikan (土岐市美濃陶磁歴史館) [Toki City Mino Ceramics History Research Center]. *Ko Garatsu: Mino to Karatsu no kōryū o tazunete* (古唐津：美濃と唐津の交流を訪ねて) [Old Karatsu: Examination of the Mino and Karatsu Cultural Exchange]. Toki City: Mino Tōji Rekishikan, 1983.

Watanabe, Terundo. (渡辺輝人) *Yakimono no seisaku jissai* (やきものの制作実際) [Facts about Pottery Production]. Kyoto: Rikō Gakusha, 1971.

Index

Agano, 24
Agano ware, 27, 170, 171, 200, 201
Allen, Terry, 175
anagama, 16, 26, 149, 175, 200
ao Karatsu, 161, 200
Arita, 20, 24, 25, 169, 200, 202, 208
Ashikaga shoguns, 16, 209
Ashikaga Yoshimasa, 41
Ayutthaya, 167

bags, brocade, 41
Bizen, 47, 145, 200
Bizen Karatsu, 166, 180; *Pl. 53*
Bizen ware, 41, 171, 173, 210
Black Karatsu, 163, 205
Black Seto ware, 171
bloating, 150, 187; *Pl. 189*
bottle(s), 162, 166, 182–184; *Pls. 22,
    53, 89, 100, 101*
bottle(s), saké, 178, 204, 208, 210; *Pl.
    21*
bowl(s), 25, 161–163, 166, 180, 185,
    186, 189, 201, 208; *Pls. 50, 150,
    163–164, 171, 210–211, 213*
bowl(s), rice,, 45, 146, 189, 211
bowl(s), spouted, 25, 51, 146, 153, 166,
    177, 181, 184, 204; *Pls. 13, 81,
    121–126, 214*
box(es), incense, 162, 166, 182, 205;
    Pl. 93
Bōzumachi kiln, 20, 31, 32
Brinkley, Captain F., 34, 41
budō, 16, 22, 200

"carved" Karatsu, see also *hori* Karatsu
celadon(s), 169, 171, 189; *Pls. 212, 214*
chadō, 16, 22, 200
cha ire, see also tea caddy
chajin, 22, 200
chaki, 38, 41, 42, 45, 50, 158, 162, 166,
    174, 200
Chikugo Province, 23
China, 14, 17, 18, 39, 48, 50, 150, 203
chirimen-jiwa, 146, 153, 201
Chon Hae, 24, 200, 201
Chōsen Karatsu, 161, 201
chuck, 153
chūkō meibutsu, 41
clay(s), 38, 40, 45, 51, 146, 147, 150,
    151, 152, 153, 162, 188, 204, 204
clay(s), levigated, 170

coiling, 51
cones, pyrometric, 159
container(s), fire, 187; *Pls. 178, 179*
crawling, glaze, 40, 203
cup(s), saké, 182, 187, 201, 208; *Pls.
    51, 92, 172–176*
cutting thread, 152

dish(es), 25, 164, 179, 180, 182, 185,
    186, 208; *Pls. 44, 46, 91, 149,
    152–162, 165–170*
Doi clan, 20, 31, 201
Dō-ō Sōhaku, 174

Edo period, 16, 40, 145, 165, 201
e-Karatsu, 161
enamel, overglaze, 29, 32
ewer(s), 153, 162, 178; *Pls. 25–27*

fire container(s), 162
foot rim, "bamboo," 163, 181, 183;
    Pls. 77, 114–115
foot rim(s), 39, 40, 50, 146, 147, 153,
    164, 201, 205, 206
Frasché, Dean, 167
fuchi-naburi zara, see lips, fluted
fude, 155, 201
Fujinkawachi kiln, 25, 147, 160, 166
Fukaumi Shintarō, see Sōden
Fukumoto family, 27, 206
Fukumoto Tazaemon, 27
Fukumoto Tōemon, 27
Fukumoto Yajiemon, 29
Fukumoto Yasaku, 27, 29
furidashi, 182, 183, 201; *Pls. 89, 100*
Furudate Kyūichi, 145
Furuta Oribe, 17, 38, 42–44, 155,
    167, 169, 172, 201, 205
Futagawa ware, 169

Ganka meibutsuki, 41
Genkai Sea, 11
glaze(s), 37–40, 45, 47–51, 146, 149,
    154–156, 159, 161–164, 167–170,
    200, 201–207
glaze(s), rice-straw ash, 45, 48, 146,
    149, 156, 169, 173
Gotō Ienobu, 24
goyōgama, 20, 201
Griffing, Robert, 48
guinomi, see saké cup

Hagi, 24
Hagi ware, 41, 170, 201, 208
Hakata, 15, 17, 202, 204, 209
hakeme, 25, 49, 50, 154, 166, 172, 185,
    202; *Pl. 151*
hakeme Karatsu, 161
handle(s), 153
Handōgame kiln, 39, 49–51, 145,
    146, 148, 149, 152, 156, 170, 190;
    Pls. 225, 226
Hankyū, 23, 26, 202, 203
Haruta Matazaemon, 43
Hassan, see Pal San
Hata clan, 11, 20, 35, 146, 202, 205
Hata Hisashige, 19
Hata Mikawa no Kami Chikashi, 19
Hazenotani kiln, 20
Heizaemon, 26
hera, 147, 151–153, 160, 189, 202; *Pl.
    223*
hi bakari, 31, 202
hidasuki, 47
Hideyoshi, see Toyotomi Hideyoshi
Hieda Saraya kiln, 27
Hiekoba, 26
Hiekoba Kannon Iwa, 26
Higo Province, 17
Hirado, 15, 22, 24, 29, 30, 33, 202,
    203, 205, 206
Hirayama kiln, 30, 32
Hisayoshi, 43
Hizen Province, 11, 17, 19, 22, 24, 26,
    27, 29, 50, 146, 169, 170, 173, 202
Hobashira kiln, 145, 149, 169
Hoeryong, 48, 160, 169
horidashi Karatsu, 40, 202
hori Karatsu, 39, 146, 153, 161, 177,
    187, 202; *Pls. 9, 112, 182*
Hosokawa Tadaoki, 24, 200
Hyakubasen, 26, 202, 209

Ichijōdani Castle, 169, 170
Idemitsu Sazō, 52
Ido teabowl, 19, 49, 189; *Pl. 209*
Ienaga Hikosaburō Masachika, 22, 23,
    26, 35, 203
Ienobu, Lord, 26, 209
Igarashi Jizaemon, 26, 203
Iga ware, 47, 171, 203
Ikinoshima, 203, 209
Imamura Sannojō, 24, 29, 203, 205

Imari, 11, 20, 27, 32, 203
Ina Masanori, 22
incense burner(s), 162, 187, 205; *Pls. 180, 181*
incising, 162, 166
Ishida Mitsunari, 17
ishihaze, 42, 150, 203
Iwao Matsuo, 145
Izumiyama, 25

jakatsu effect, 146, 161, 177, 181, 203; *Pls. 12, 79, 80*
jar(s), 25, 51, 146, 162, 163, 166–168, 177–179, 181, 182, 184, 204; *Pls. 14, 16, 17, 20, 23, 24, 36–40, 55–57, 82–87, 94, 127–132, 212*
jar(s), "abacus bead," 153, 164, 179, 182, 184, 209; *Pls. 36, 38, 83, 130, 132*
jar(s), oil, Korean, 189
jar(s), tea, 179, 182; *Pls. 41, 90*
Jian ware, 39, 160, 203
Jikirinoura, 14, 15, 203
Jin'emon, 31
Jōmon pottery, 15
Jouy, Pierre Louis, 151
Jū Jikan, 22, 203

Kagami, Mt., 172
Kagoshima, 24
kaigara zumi, 148, 203
kaiseki meal, 162, 204
Kamakura period, 145
Kamanokuchi kiln, 24
Kameyanotani kiln, 163
Kamiya Sōtan, 17, 43, 44, 204
Kanegae Sambei, *see* Ri Sampei
Kanō Mitsunobu, 17
Kanō Naizen, 17
kaolin, 23, 25, 26, 37, 202
Karabori kiln, 27
Karafusa kiln, 27
karamono itokiri, 152, 204
Karatsu Castle, 14, 190; *Pls. 229–231*
Kara Tsuchi no Fune, 204
katakuchi, *see* bowl(s), spouted
Katō Hajime, 164
Katō Kagenobu, 27, 204
Katō Kiyomasa, 17
Katō Mineo, 171
kawakujira, 38, 46, 146, 165, 179, 180, 183, 185, 204; *Pls. 32, 34, 35, 44, 47, 48, 51, 110, 138, 140, 143–146*
Kawanami Kōzō, 21
Kawarayashiki, 22
Kawasaki Seizō, *see* Sōkan
kenjō Karatsu, *see* Presentation Karatsu

Kenzan Karatsu, 161
Khmer ware, 167
kick wheel, *see* potter's wheel, kick
Kiharayama kiln, 32
Kiheiji, *see* Nakazato Kiheiji
ki Karatsu, 161, 204
kiku momi, 150, 205
kiln, fire box, 158
kiln atmosphere, 37
kiln chamber(s), official, 30
kiln construction, 188
kiln firing, 16, 37, 149, 154, 158
kiln firing, bisque, 155
kiln(s), 26, 30, 34, 45, 49, 145, 148, 149, 156, 158, 200, 202, 204, 207
kiln(s), climbing, see *noborigama*
kiln(s), electric bisque, 173
kilns, official Karatsu, 27, 32
Kimbara Koichi, 145
Kim Hae, 24, 205
Kim Hwa, 24, 205
Kishidake, 11, 14, 19, 20, 27, 35, 39, 49, 50, 145, 146, 148, 149, 152, 154, 156, 164–166, 168, 169, 173, 202, 205, 206, 209
Kishidake Castle, 19, 23, 26
Kitaōji Rosanjin, 171
Kobori Enshū, 44, 180, 205
kohiki, 173, 176, 205
Kojiki, 14
Kojirōkaja kiln, 11, 14, 20
ko-Karatsu, 14, 20, 205, *see also* Old Karatsu
Ko Kwan, 24, 29, 203, 205, 206
Koma no Ōna, 27, 29, 30, 34, 205, 207
Komatsu family, 26
Komatsu Gennojō, 29, 205
Kōraidani, 25
Korea, 11, 14, 15, 17–19, 21–23, 25–27, 31, 37, 39, 47–50, 150, 155, 170, 174, 201, 203, 205, 207–209
Korean ceramics, 48–50, 155, 189; *Pls. 209–212*
Korean Karatsu, 45–47, 50, 146, 149, 153, 155, 156, 161, 162, 166, 167, 172, 178, 182; *Pls. 15–27, 94–101*
Koshoku densho, 43, 52
Koshoku shōden Keichō otazunesho, 43, 52
Koshoku zensho, 43, 52
Kotaji kiln, 32, 167
Kotōge kiln, 167
Kōzuru Gen, 171
Kurahashi Tōjirō, 145
Kurate, 24
Kuroda Nagamasa, 24, 208
Kuroda Tadayuki, 26, 203
kuro Karatsu, 161, 205

Kuromuta kiln, 21, 24, 26, 32
kutsu-gata, 25, 152, 161, 181, 183, 205; *Pls. 79, 81, 116–119*
kutsuwagata, 39, 205
Kyoto, 16
Kyōzangama, 172

lid(s), 163, 176
lip(s), 146, 163–165, 188; *Pl. 193*
lip(s), fluted, 146, 152, 201
lip(s), foliate, 208
Longchuan celadon, 189
lug(s), 153

madara, *see* glaze(s), rice-straw ash
madara Karatsu, 161, 163, 205
Maeda Tōjiuemon, 31–33
Maeda Tokuzaemon, 29
Maeda Toshiie, 23
Matsudaira clan, 20, 31, 206
Matsudaira Fumai, 44
Matsudaira Norimura, 44
Matsumoto Toshimitsu, 175
Matsuura, 11, 14, 19, 20, 27, 147, 148, 155, 165, 169, 209
Matsuura bussan zukō, 188; *Pls. 203–205*
Matsuura clan, 17, 202, 206
Matsuura Karatsu ki, 34, 206
Matsuura mountains, 29
Matsuura River, 15, 167
Matsuura Sadanobu, 24, 203
Matsuura Shigenobu, 20, 22, 24, 203, 205
me, 148, 206
meibutsu, 41
Meiji period, 20, 34, 42
Meiji Restoration, 172
merchants, Edo, 42
Mian Xianjie, 43
Michinayatani kiln, 148, 159
Mikami Tsugio, 48
mikazuki kōdai, 206
Mikōchi kiln, 20, 24, 29, 34, 203
mimi, 153, 206
Ming dynasty, 15, 18
Mino, 20, 22, 26, 27, 39, 145, 149, 156, 161, 165, 166, 170, 188, 189, 201, 205, 206, 209
Mino Bizen ware, 171
Mino Iga ware, 171
Mino Karatsu ware, 171
Mino ware, 171, 188, 206, 208
mishima, 49, 50, 154, 155, 166, 183, 185, 204; *Pls. 104, 105, 148, 152, 195*
mishima Karatsu, 161, 206

Mizumachi Wasaburō, 172
Mizuno clan, 20, 34, 206
mizusashi, 43, 45, 206
Mizutani Ise no Kami, 29
Mominokidani kiln, 27
Momoyama period, 14, 16, 27, 40, 41,
    203, 205
Mōri clan, 16
Mōri Terumoto, 23, 24, 201
Mori Zen'emon, 26, 27, 206
Motoyashiki kiln, 27, 170, 171
muji Karatsu, 163, 206
Mukaie no Hara kiln, 188
mukōzuke dish(es), 50, 151, 152, 162,
    164–166, 179, 180, 184, 185, 206;
    Pls. 42, 47, 49, 137–147
Murata Gen, 171
Muromachi period, 16, 45

Nabeshima, Lord, 208, 209
Nabeshima clan, 17, 19, 22, 24, 25, 203
Nabeshima fief, 21, 206
Nabeshima Naoshige, 23, 24
Nagahayama kiln, 29
Nagasaki, 19
Nagoya Castle, 11, 17, 18, 22, 23, 43,
    202, 203, 203
Nagoya Hizen no Kami, 17
Nakajima Kōki, 31
Nakano, 24
Nakano Eirin, 172
Nakano family, 172
Nakano Tōji, 172
Nakazato family, 27, 29, 31, 33, 34,
    147, 172, 176, 190, 206
Nakazato Jin'emon, 30, 32
Nakazato Keitarō, 34
Nakazatoke kyūki, 28, 33, 189, 207
Nakazato Ken'ichi, 174
Nakazato Kiheiji, 14, 30–32, 34, 36,
    173, 188, 204, 207; *Pl. 202*
Nakazato kiroku, 29, 207
Nakazato Matashichi, 27, 29, 30, 207
Nakazato Mouemon, 27, 29, 34, 205
Nakazato Sakuhei, 32
Nakazato Shigeo, 34, 173
Nakazato Shigetoshi, 174, 175, 180
Nakazato Tadahiro, 175
Nakazato Tadao, 174
Nakazato Takashi, 156, 159, 174, 175,
    180
Nakazato Tarōuemon, 32
Nakazato Tarōuemon IV, 32
Nakazato Tarōuemon XII (Muan), 34,
    41, 48, 145, 173–175, 180, 189; *Pls
    54, 215–219*
Nakazato Tarōuemon XIII, 27, 31, 34,

146, 159, 174, 180, 189
Nakazato Ten'yū, 34, 173
Nakazato Tokio, 34
namako, see glaze(s), rice-straw ash
namako phenomenon, 156, 182, 205
Nambō Sōkei, 44
Nanbō roku, 42
Naosaki Chōemon, 22
Nara period, 14
Nihon shoki, 14
Nishikawa Ikkō, 172
Nishioka Satoru, 172
Nishiyama kiln, 32
Niwagi kiln, 167
Nōami, 41
noborigama, 146, 148, 170, 171, 173,
    188, 189, 207; *Pls. 204, 205, 220,
    224–226*
noborigama, waridake, 145, 156, 173
Nogata kiln, 170

Ochawangama kiln, 11, 27, 207; *Pl. 224*
Ochawangama kiln, Shiinomine, 32
Oda Nobunaga, 16, 41, 201, 208
ōgama, 149
Ogasawara clan, 20, 34, 207
Ogata Kenzan, 161, 165, 171
Ogawa Sōemon, 22
Okasaki, Robert, 175
Ōkawabaru kiln, 20, 27, 30, 31
Okinoshima, 14, 207
Ōkubo clan, 20, 30, 207
oku-Gōrai, 41, 48, 158, 161, 163, 177,
    181, 188, 206, 207; *Pls. 3, 5, 6, 65,
    67, 68, 72, 74*
Old Karatsu, 23, 29, 30, 35, 40, 41,
    52, 147, 150, 155, 161, 163, 167,
    170, 172–174, 176, 205, 209
Old Seto ware, 171
ō-meibutsu, 41
Onizuka, 167
Oribe, *see* Furuta Oribe
Oribe ware, 27, 152, 164, 165, 167,
    170, 171, 201, 206
Osaka Castle, 17, 22
Ōshima family, 27, 29, 31, 34, 206, 207
Ōshima Hikoemon, 27, 29, 205
Ōshima Kaheiji, 32
Ōshima kyūki, 28
Ōshima Mannosuke, 34
Ōshima Shichibei, 32
Ōshima Yajihei, 32
Ōshima Yakichi, 34
oxidation, 158, 208
Oyamaji kiln, 27, 155

Pal San, 24, 208, 209

Philippines, 15, 20
Plain Karatsu, 48, 50, 149, 162, 163,
    171, 177, 180–182, 187; *Pls. 1–14,
    58–63, 65–93*
plate(s), 51, 146, 162, 164, 179, 180,
    185, 208; *Pls. 43, 48, 151*
platter(s), 179; *Pls. 45, 148*
porcelain, 15, 18, 23–25, 29–31, 36,
    37, 149, 154, 165, 168, 169, 171,
    188; *Pls. 194, 206–207*
Portuguese, 15, 19
potters, official Karatsu, 27–29
Potters' War, 18, 25, 176
potter's wheel, 15, 16, 151–154, 173
potter's wheel, electric, 173
potter's wheel, hand, 151, 210
potter's wheel, kick, 37, 50, 147, 151,
    189, 204; *Pl. 223*
Pre-Karatsu, 51, 149, 168, 169, 170,
    201, 203, 210
Presentation Karatsu, 30, 32, 33, 170,
    171, 187, 204; *Pl. 180*
punch'ong ware, 49, 50, 155, 166, 176,
    205, 208
pyrometers, 173

Qin dynasty, 14

Raku ware, 41, 201, 208
reduction, 16, 149, 158, 204
Ri Sampei, 24–26, 204, 205, 208
Ryūtagama, 175
Ryūzōji clan, 19

Saga, 17, 22–25, 208, 209
saggers, 155
Saifuku-in, 43
Sakai, 169
Sakaida Kakiemon, 32
saké cup(s), 46, 162, 163, 166
Saraya kiln, 145
Satow, Ernest, 22
Satsuma fief, 15, 19, 21, 22, 24, 208,
    209
Satsuma ware, 170, 203, 205
sculpture, ceramic, 33, 34
Sen no Rikyū, 17, 18, 20, 38, 41, 42,
    167, 172, 201, 204, 208
Seto, 40, 145, 206, 208
Seto Karatsu, 161, 163, 177, 208; *Pl. 11*
Seto ware, 39
shards, 187
Shiinomine kiln, 20, 26, 27, 29, 30, 31,
    32, 35, 148, 173, 205, 206, 207
Shiinomineyama kuzure, 32, 208
Shimazu clan, 17, 19, 21, 208, 209
Shimazu Yoshihiro, 24, 205

Shino Oribe ware, 171
Shino ware, 39, 164, 165, 167, 170, 171, 173, 206
Shirosakiyama kiln, 22, 23, 26, 203
Shishibei, 31
Shōmo Shrine, 168, 169, 182, 203, 209
shuin-sen, 16
Silla dynasty, 48
slip, 25, 149, 152, 154, 162, 163, 166, 168, 173, 188, 202, 204
Sōami, 41, 44
soba teabowl(s), 163, 169
Sōden, 24, 26, 202, 209
Sōkan, 25, 204, 209
Song dynasty, 160, 167, 189, 203, 209
Song dynasty, Southern, 15, 16
Sonkai, *see* Chon Hae
soroban dama, 164, 209, *see also* jar(s), "abacus bead"
Sōtan, *see* Kamiya Sōtan
Sōtan nikki, 17, 35, 43, 204, 209
Southeast Asia, 15, 48, 167, 174
split-bamboo climbing kiln, see *noborigama, waridake*
spout(s), 153
sprigging, 162
spurs, kiln, 148, 206, 210
spurs, shell, 187, 203; *Pls. 186, 187*
stamping, 154
stand, saké cup, 187; *Pl. 177*
stenciling, 166, 188
stilts, kiln, 148
stoneware, 26, 41, 47, 149, 168, 209
Sue ware, 11, 15, 16, 48, 154, 203, 209
suiteki, 209
suribachi, 25, 45, 209

Taishō period, 27, 42
Takahashi Sōan, 44
Takatori, 24
Takatori ware, 27, 170, 171, 200, 208
Takeo, 14, 21, 24, 26, 29, 145, 149, 155, 165, 167, 169, 170, 171, 202
Takeo style ware, 184, 185, 207; *Pls. 134, 148-150*
Takeuchi kiln, 26
Taku, 14, 24, 25, 209
Tanakamaru Zenpachi, 52

Tanaka Yoshimasa, 23
Tanegashima, 19, 159, 175, 180; *Pl. 57*
Tarōkaja, 14
Tashiro kiln, 27
Tashirotsutsue kiln, 27
tataki technique, 15, 45, 51, 146, 147, 153, 154, 163, 164, 168, 173, 174, 182, 184, 187-189, 204, 209; *Pls. 86, 87, 128, 190, 215-219, 221*
Tatsugawa, 26
teabowl(s), 19, 30-34, 38-43, 45, 49, 51, 146, 153, 155, 158, 161-167, 177, 179, 181, 183, 184, 189, 200, 202, 203, 205-209; *Pls. 3-12, 29-35, 54, 65-80, 104, 120, 209*
teabowl(s), *soba*, 169
tea caddy(ies), 43-45, 51, 162, 177, 178, 180, 181, 183, 200; *Pls. 1, 2, 18, 28, 58-64, 102, 103*
tea ceramics, 18, 26, see also *chaki*
tea ceremony, 16-18, 20, 30, 38, 40-42, 146, 162, 176, 200, 204
temmoku, 39, 40, 156, 160, 163, 169, 183, 203, 209; *Pls. 113-115*
temmoku Karatsu, 161
Tengudani kiln, 24, 25
Tenshō 20 jar, 182, 203, 209; *Pl. 90*
Terasawa clan, 19, 20, 26, 29, 30, 203, 210
Terasawa Hirotaka, 20, 27, 202, 210
Thailand, 169
throwing, 50, 146, 151-154, 164
Tōbeikaja, 14
tōchin, 148, 210
Tōjinkoba kiln, 25
tōjinmachi, 22
Tōjinmachi kiln, 25, 32
Tokugawa clan, 20, 206
Tokugawa Ieyasu, 16, 23, 201
Tokugawa shoguns, 42
tools, 173, 189; *Pls. 221, 223*
Toyotomi Hideyoshi, 16-20, 22, 23, 26, 37, 41, 42, 47, 49, 50, 151, 172, 200-205, 208, 210
trimming, 39, 40, 50, 146, 147, 153, 163, 164
Tsuruta Echizen no Kami, 19, 210
Tsushima, 31

Tsushima Straits, 11
Tumulus period, 15, 209

Uchida kiln, 24, 26
Umemura Wahei, 29-33
Underglaze Decorated Karatsu, 48, 50, 149, 154, 155, 158, 161-166, 169, 171, 172, 178, 179-188, 201; *Pls. 28-53, 64, 102-147, 151-181*
underglaze decoration, 37, 49, 51, 146, 149, 155, 164, 165, 188, 189; *Pl. 222*
underglaze iron, 38, 40, 51, 146, 156, 167, 168, 188, 201; *Pl. 192*

Valignano, Alessandro, 41
vase(s), 162, 166, 167, 178, 182, 184; *Pls. 15, 19, 88, 95-99, 133, 135-136*

wabi, 18, 38, 46, 208, 210
Wahei, *see* Umemura Wahei
wakō, 15, 17, 35, 206, 210
water dropper, 180, 209; *Pl. 52*
wedging, 150, 189, 205
Wungch'on, 22, 36, 210

Yakimono taigai, 188, 210; *Pl. 203-205*
Yamanoguchi, *see* Kōraidani
Yamanouchi Hyōe, 29
Yamanoue Sōji, 44
Yamase kiln, 20, 159
Yatsushiro, 24
Yatsushiro ware, 201
Yayoi period, 15, 211
Yellow Karatsu, 204
Yellow Seto, 171, 206
Yi dynasty, 37, 47-50, 150, 151, 169, 189, 205, 208
Yijo silrok, 15
Yi Kyong, 24, 201
Yi Pyo-kwang, 24, 201
Yi Sun-sin, Admiral, 18
Yuan dynasty, 167, 189
Yue ware, 189
Yuminoyama kiln, 32

zakki, 38, 40, 45, 146, 162, 166, 211
Zekan Karatsu, 181; *Pl. 69*
Zen Buddhism, 16, 204

定価10,000円
in Japan